The Dalkey Archive Bibliography Series

III

RONALD FIRBANK

The Dalkey Archive Bibliography Series

1. Clifford Mead. *Thomas Pynchon: A Bibliography of Primary and Secondary Materials*

2. William McPheron. *Gilbert Sorrentino: A Descriptive Bibliography*

3. Steven Moore. *Ronald Firbank: An Annotated Bibliography of Secondary Materials*

Ronald Firbank

An Annotated Bibliography of Secondary Materials, 1905-1995

by

Steven Moore

Dalkey Archive Press

Library of Congress Cataloguing-in-Publication Data

Moore, Steven, 1951-
Ronald Firbank : an annotated bibliography of secondary materials,
1905-1995 / by Steven Moore.
p. cm. — (The Dalkey Archive bibliography series ; 3)
Includes bibliographical references and index.
1. Firbank, Ronald, 1886-1926—Bibliography. I. Title. II. Series.
Z8298.M66   [PR6011.I7]
016.823'912—dc20   1996   96-15667
ISBN 1-56478-133-X

Dalkey Archive Press
Illinois State University
Campus Box 4241
Normal, IL 61790-4241

Contents

Preface   vii

Acknowledgments   xi

1. Reviews of Firbank's Books   1

2. Books about Firbank (and their reviews)   33

3. Essays, Parts of Books, and Other Commentary   51

4. Creative Works   95

5. Dissertations and Theses   105

6. Foreign-language Materials   113

Index   143

Preface

There has never been a consensus on Ronald Firbank's status in modern literature: depending on the critic, he is above, beneath, or beyond criticism. As early as 1924, one reviewer warned that "To defend him, to apologize for him, to seek to prove that he is excellent would be ridiculous; one might as wisely attempt to defend an alligator pear." The same year, a young Harold Acton wrote that Firbank was too ahead of his time for intelligent commentary: "one has the melancholy feeling that, as in the case of Stendhal who foretold it of himself, Mr. Firbank will not be appreciated till the eighties of the present century." W. H. Auden went so far as to say Firbank had created a "private vision of Eden" and that his "earthly paradise is no place for literary critics." Compounding the problem is the often-forgotten fact—emphasized by Firbank fanciers Brigid Brophy and Colin MacInnes—that there isn't a consensus on what fiction itself is; depending on one's definition, Firbank is either a brilliant exemplar or a perverse aberration.

For these and other reasons, the history of the critical reception of Firbank's work is an erratic one. During his lifetime, there were the usual uncomprehending reviews that seem to be the inevitable lot of most innovative artists, and after that there have been occasional revivals of interest in his work: in 1929-30 upon publication of his collected works and Ifan Kyrie Fletcher's memoir (though, as the reviews of Fletcher's book indicate, there was something of a backlash as well); in 1949-50 with the publication of two omnibus volumes of his works; in 1961-63 with *The Complete Ronald Firbank, The New Rythum,* and Miriam Benkovitz's bibliography, and in 1969-73, in which four book-length studies on his work appeared. After the appearance in 1973 of Brigid Brophy's *Prancing Novelist,* which did indeed look like the final word on him, Firbank received only spotty attention: Lord Horder's fine volume of *Memoirs and Critiques* in 1977 and a revised edition of Benkovitz's bibliography in 1982 kept the flame flickering, but the pages of the annual *MLA Bibliography* were mute for some fifteen years.

Just as Acton predicted, however, the 1980s saw another revival of interest in Firbank, and one that looks to be longer-lasting than the earlier ones: in the late 1980s essays on him started appearing in scholarly journals more regularly, his collected stories were published in 1990, his plays a few years later, *Caprice* and *Santal* were reissued, and in 1994 a special session of the annual MLA Convention was devoted to him for the first time. He has even been sighted on the Internet, popping up on various pages of the World Wide Web. On the one hand, it would be rash to say that Firbank has now been canonized—despite Harold Bloom's wise decision to include Firbank's *Five Novels* among his twentieth-century candidates in *The Western Canon* (1994)—for his work has been revived largely by those interested in queer theory and camp; his works continue to be ignored in most books on modern British fiction, and he'll never be studied and taught as often as his more famous contemporaries. (A critic once commented: "The idea of a graduate seminar on Ronald Firbank would be Firbankian.") On the other hand, he does seem to have been rescued from oblivion, and the recent criticism on him is highly promising. This bibliography is a record of how Firbank has been ridiculed, praised, lost, and found again.

The bibliography is intended to be as comprehensive as possible, so literally everything that has been written about Firbank that I know of has been included: not only the usual essays, books, and reviews, but passing references to him in a wide variety of books and periodicals. They range from the first book review Firbank received in 1905 to material that appeared in late 1995. A separate section includes material on Firbank written in langauges other than English: Italian scholar Fabio Cleto expanded my original meager list by tracking down everything he could find in a half-dozen languages, giving a fascinating view of the foreign reception of Firbank's work—a more hospitable reception, Cleto points out, than it received in many British and American publications.

Several ways of organizing this material were possible. A chronological, year-by-year listing would have had the advantage of delineating the rise and fall of critical interest in Firbank over the years, but would make it difficult to see at a glance, for example, all the reviews a certain Firbank novel had received (because of reprints) or everything that a particular scholar had written on Firbank. A strict alphabetical listing of all materials would ignore the important generic distinctions between a book review, a critical essay, and a poem that mentions Firbank. I opted for organizing everything into six basic groups: part 1 is devoted to book reviews of Firbank's own works, both those published in his lifetime and those published posthumously. (Bibliographical details on the earliest reviews are sometimes sketchy or nonexistent, but they have been included for completeness' sake.) As extensive as this listing appears, there are probably any number of untraced reviews remaining: existing book review indexes are too selective to guarantee complete coverage in this area, and a person could spend a lifetime checking publishers' and newspapers' files (where they still exist) for every possible review. Part 2 lists book-length studies of Firbank's work and, for convenience, reviews of those books. Part 3, the largest section, includes essays on Firbank, chapters from books, conference papers, and briefer references to him in a variety of nonfiction sources. (Most encyclopedias and general reference books have been excluded; their entries on Firbank are of little value to the Firbank scholar; only those that have something distinctive to say have been included.)

Part 4, unusual for a bibliography such as this, includes creative works that either mention Firbank or seem to show his influence (or, at the very least, have strong affinities with his work). This section doesn't pretend to be complete; it includes merely those items that other Firbankians and I have noticed over the years. I have largely confined myself to the print medium: it is possible, perhaps, to find Firbankian elements in artists like Joseph Cornell and Andy Warhol (who illustrated the dust jacket of Firbank's *Three Novels*), playwrights like Charles Ludlam and Tony Kushner, filmmakers like Fellini and the Brothers Quay, photographers like Cecil Beaton and Robert Mapplethorpe, comedy troupes like Monty Python's Flying Circus, even rock bands like Army of Lovers and the Cocteau Twins and any number of fashion designers, but I suspect this would be stretching the adjective *Firbankian* too far—farther than the scope of this book, at any rate. Part 5 lists doctoral dissertations and theses written in English (even if submitted abroad); while comprehensive regarding U.S. dissertations, it is similarly incomplete with regard to dissertations and theses submitted to institutions outside the U.S., again due to the limitations of indexes.

Part 6, a section unto itself, lists foreign-language works on Firbank: it is organized along the same lines as the preceding English-language portion, with Firbank's novels (in translation) listed according to publication, followed by their reviews, book-length studies, then essays, creative works, and dissertations and theses. As stated earlier, this section is largely the work of Fabio Cleto; I have edited his annotations, but the précis are his. A comprehensive index of names concludes the volume and makes cross-referencing possible. Throughout the book, Ronald Firbank is raffishly abbreviated RF.

The distinction between book reviews and critical essays may seem unimportant, especially since many reviews are later reprinted in book form as essays. (In Ernest Jones's case, his review of Firbank's *Five Novels* was reprinted in expanded form as the introduction to *Three Novels*.) But their separation here stems from the circumstances under which such criticism is written: reviews are usually commissioned—sometimes assigned to reviewers indifferent, if not hostile, to the work under review—and written under a deadline, occasionally with mixed motives; essays, on the other hand, are usually the expression of personal interest and developed at leisure. This difference has little to do with quality—some reviews are far superior to some of the essays that have been written on Firbank—but this generic distinction seemed worth maintaining here. Works are listed according to their first appearance: a review that was later included in a writer's book is listed in part 1 with the reviews, not in part 3 with chapters from books. Introductions to Firbank's books are annotated in part 3 as though they were independent essays. In some cases, assigning a genre was difficult: Edmund Wilson's "Firbank and Beckford," for example, is simultaneously an obituary for Firbank, a review of *Cardinal Pirelli,* and, as the title indicates, a comparative analysis. This particular essay wound up in part 3, and there are a few other items that might have gone elsewhere.

The length of a précis depends largely on the length of the original work, but not always. Some longer works could be summarized briefly, some shorter works couldn't. Quotability has been a major factor, and I have given more space to those with insightful or witty or merely colorful remarks. Sometimes the obscurity or inaccessibility of a source has been a factor; I wanted to quote a few items for the record because other researchers may never have access to them. I have tried to keep my annotations fairly neutral, but admiration or scorn for certain entries were difficult to repress, nor did I think it remiss to steer readers toward some pieces and away from others. No one should ever have to read *all* of this material again.

I hope this book does its part in assisting, even inspiring, future Firbank scholars. Nothing would please me more than to see this book quickly go out of

Acknowledgments

This book began in the early 1980s when my friend and fellow Firbankian Maurice Cloud and I discussed the viability of collaborating on a bibliography of Firbank criticism. I began my part in earnest in the summer of 1983; Maurice later withdrew as co-author from the project, but not before supplying me with many materials and much advice. Other work prevented me from spending much time on the bibliography during the rest of that decade, aside from amassing notes and photocopies.

In early 1993 I began putting all this material on disk, and by May of that year I had a working manuscript to show to others, at which time I benefited from the advice of several Firbank scholars: Fabio Cleto sent me his just-published "An Updated Bibliography of Firbank Criticism," which contained about twenty items new to me (especially foreign criticism) and over the next three years he continued to supply me with a steady stream of new materials. His great enthusiasm for this project encouraged me to ask him to take over the foreign criticism section of the bibliography, with the splendid results now apparent in part 6.

Peter Parker, at work on a biography of Christopher Isherwood, took time to review the manuscript and he too made many valuable contributions, especially with regard to the "Creative Works" section.

Alan Hollinghurst was helpful in many ways: in the mid-1980s he supplied me with the names of most of the *Times Literary Supplement*'s anonymous reviewers of Firbank's books and over the years continued to express interest in the project.

Others who provided suggestions and leads include Robert Murray Davis, Ulla Dydo, and Bruce Kellner. The interlibrary loan staffs of three university libraries—University of Denver, Rutgers (New Brunswick campus), and Illinois State University—handled a huge number of requests with professional aplomb, and Christine Mason kindly unearthed for me Harold Acton's *Cherwell* essay from the Lower Reading Room of Oxford's Bodleian Library. Roseanne Reid and Richard Blankenship provided valuable editorial assistance at a late stage in the book's development, helping me to tie up many loose threads. Shirley Geever meticulously transformed my computer files into these printed pages. My thanks to one and all.

Part 1

Reviews of Firbank's Books

Odette d'Antrevernes and A Study in Temperament
London: Elkin Mathews, 1905

Times Literary Supplement, 9 June 1905, 187.
"Two pieces—one a pretty old world story, and the other, less successful, of modern society" [*in toto*].

Vainglory
London: Grant Richards, 1915
New York: Brentano's, 1925

Belfast Whig.
"Extraordinary [*sic*] clever."

"Delicate Travesty." *New York Times Book Review*, 18 October 1925, 8.
A knowledgeable, glowing review: "It has the characteristic orchestration of fashionable dialogue in which Mr. Firbank excels and which Oscar Wilde might well have envied. It is a consummate expression of an artificial temperament, flagrantly, frivolously, happily absorbed in itself." It concludes: "Mr. Firbank is at his blithe, debonair, brilliant best in 'Vainglory.' It has not the amusing negress of 'Valmouth,' the consistent satire of 'Caprice,' the rollicking drollery of 'Prancing Nigger,' the intricate, amiably grotesque buffoonery of 'The Flower Beneath the Foot.' It delicately travesties art movements, little theatres, esthetic graces and Mrs. Shamefoot. Above all, it is beautifully co-ordinated and superbly written entertainment."

Dial 80 (May 1926): 426.
A brief, unsigned note worth quoting in full: "Mr Firbank is the *Ariel de nos jours,* and determined optimists will be reassured by the discovery that even this age has one. His Vainglory is the most perfect flower of a fatigued society which having produced this masterpiece can now pass on confident of a 'niche,' to use one of the author's own words, in a history that knows how to value, say, a Lady Castlemaine, a Madame du Barry, an Horace Walpole, or the new Countess of Oxford."

New Witness.
"The author of this book has a gift for trenchant satire . . . one cannot help feeling that Mr Firbank must have gone straight to life for some of these people."

New York Post, 16 October 1925.

Observer, 4 July 1915.
"An incessant sparkle."

Pall Mall Gazette.
"A very clever book."

Publishers Weekly, 28 November 1925, 1818.
A brief announcement, stating that the U.S. edition was "rewritten by the author" ("moderately revised," as the *New York Times* said, is more accurate).

Times Literary Supplement, 22 April 1915, 138.
A brief and exasperated notice, setting the tone for most of *TLS*'s early reviews of RF's books: "He can be witty enough and gives a neat turn to his
sentences, but his endless flow of scintillating nonsense is most exhausting. . . .
Since this appears to be his first novel we trust that he is still young enough to
learn better, but we cannot hel[p] feeling a little afraid that he is too hopelessly
and impenitently clever."

Inclinations
London: Grant Richards, 1916

Freeman's Journal.
"Pleasant and clever, *Inclinations* is a book that won't tax the patience of any
reader."

Glasgow Herald.
"Mr Ronald Firbank's fiction bears a strong resemblance to the work of the
Futurists in painting."

Gould, Gerald. *New Statesman* 7 (22 July 1916): 378.
The novel is "amusing" and occasionally shows "the gem of true wit," but RF
"collapses into comparative coherence as seldom deviated into sense." Gould is
more baffled than irritated by the novel's incoherence.

Harrogate Herald.
"A quiet vein of humour."

Irish Times.
"Marked by a certain bizarre lightness of treatment."

New Witness.
"The scheme of his new book is novel."

Scotsman.
"The book is pleasant, vivacious and stimulating throughout."

Times Literary Supplement, 22 June 1916, 299.
"There is some humour, if one could get at it, underlying this tale. . . . But
as it is written almost entirely in snappy dialogue in which it is impossible to
make out who is speaking without close and prolonged calculations, and as the
characters have an inveterate habit of not finishing their sentences, we cannot
honestly say that the humour is worth the trouble. There is no time nowadays to
give to unnecessary puzzles."

Odette: A Fairy Tale for Weary People
London: Grant Richards, 1916

Glasgow Herald.
"The short story here published reveals a delicate descriptive power, a fine
perception of the value of color, and that restraint which is indispensable to the
making of a good short story."

Caprice
London: Grant Richards, 1917
New York: New Directions, 1993

American Institute of Discussion, Summer 1993, 11.
A brief notice of New Directions's "Bibelot" edition of *Caprice* and two others in the series.

[Dirda, Michael.] *Washington Post Book World,* 18 April 1993, 12.
A brief notice of the "Bibelot" edition. "Firbank is the master of campy humor, a major novelist in a minor mode."

Gould, Gerald. *New Statesman* 10 (29 December 1917): 310-11.
"If brevity is really the soul of wit, Mr. Firbank must be a wit indeed," Gould begins. "The sheer fantastic imbecility which made his *Vainglory* and his *Inclinations* so remarkable has here been curbed into something almost resembling a coherent plot," although at the expense of "that jocular air of absolute meaninglessness which gave the earlier books their peculiarity." Gould draws a parallel between RF's work and modern painting, and concludes: "occasionally through the nonsense gleams a comprehensible epigram, or a bit of characterisation deftly phrased."

Harrison, William H. *Studies in Short Fiction* 31.2 (Spring 1994): 267-68.
After a brief overview of the life and work, Harrison states: "*Caprice* is one of Firbank's lesser novellas and does not quite achieve the level of high camp so indicative of his style. However, what the book lacks in outrageousness, it makes up for in accessibility." A plot summary follows, concluding: "Sally is the Christian innocent consumed by the wildness of London-as-Sodom. But *Caprice* celebrates hedonism as a vivifying force."

Lambda Book Report 3 (July 1993): 44.

Moore, Steven. *Review of Contemporary Fiction* 13.2 (Summer 1993): 256.
A brief note on RF's stylistic affinities with other writers and on his own unique qualities; considers *Caprice* "a slim little treasure."

Publishers Weekly, 15 March 1993, 84.
A brief notice of New Directions's "Bibelot" edition.

Rogers, Michael. *Library Journal* 118 (1 May 1993): 115.
A brief notice of this and other "Bibelot" releases from New Directions.

Times Literary Supplement, 1 November 1917, 530.
"Out of Mr. Firbank's explosive style, his continuous barrage of crisp paragraphs and chippy talk, it is hard to get any continuity or sense of character and atmosphere. . . . He seems much more concerned to get out smart remarks than to tell the story, or even to let the reader know what is really going on (how did Sara [*sic*] die?), or in dialogue who is speaking."

Town Topics, 10 November 1917, 7.
Called it a "strange novel" and "intensely" amusing.

Valmouth
London: Grant Richards, 1919
London: Duckworth, 1956 (illustrated edition)
Valmouth | Prancing Nigger | Concerning the Eccentricities of Cardinal Pirelli.
London: Penguin, 1961
Valmouth and Other Novels. London/New York: Penguin, 1982, 1992

Daily News.
"Mr Firbank . . . can write really witty nonsense."

[Dirda, Michael.] *Washington Post Book World,* 27 September 1992, 12.
Notes that RF "is increasingly recognized as a serious artist whose witty novels are revolutionary in their technical achievement" and "have been a formative influence on modern British fiction."

[Huxley, Aldous.] *Athenæum,* 19 December 1919, 1386.
The future novelist wishes RF "would employ his in some way remarkable talents to better purpose. 'Valmouth' oscillates between the amusing and the tiresome. . . . But Mr. Firbank has talents—a gift of style, a capacity to write dialogue, an appreciation of the beautiful and the absurd. With such gifts he might produce a real comedy of manners. It is to be hoped that he will."

Irish Life.
"It is a weird medley of Beardsleyesque chatter."

Land and Water.
"This is the real decadence: Huysmans and his friends were muscular giants, playing at bizarre senility, compared with Mr Firbank."

Liverpool Post.
"Had Shelley written nothing but *Julian and Maddalo* and *The Cenci,* we might have called Mr Firbank a prose Shelley."

London Mercury 1 (February 1920): 473-74.
The reviewer finds a "superficial resemblance" between Dorothy Richardson's work and the *"fumisterie"* of RF's, but considers her novels genuine and his mere "stunts." It is clear (to this reviewer) "that his aim is to write nonsense rather than sense and perhaps to put forward under a film of absurdity a certain natural perversity which would not be welcomed if it were more lucidly expressed. He has a certain gift for inconsequence and highly etherealised frivolity; but this may be inextricably connected with his demerits, in which case it would be useless to ask him to change. If he does not, he will remain a curiosity, mildly amusing a few readers, deluding a few into a belief that they have found a super-genius and boring or displeasing the great majority."

Moore, Steven. *Review of Contemporary Fiction* 13.2 (Summer 1993): 256.
Briefly summarizes the contents of *Valmouth and Other Novels* in a review of the 1993 *Caprice.*

Philip, Neil. *British Book News,* July 1982, 399.
Notes Penguin's new edition of RF's "highly stylized and somewhat precious *Valmouth and Other Novels.*"

Powell, Anthony. "Firbank." *Punch,* 15 August 1956, 194.
A brief overview of RF's career—Powell mentions the part he played in the 1929 Rainbow Edition—and a measured appreciation of the novels: "The fact is there is nothing else quite like them. Deriving from the 'nineties, and stamped heavily with their own period, the 'twenties, they are little more than bursts of description and dialogue linked together. There is no shape, no story and only a vague suggestion of character. There are sudden crepitations of nervous wit, *double entendres*—sometimes extremely funny, sometimes less funny—fantastic ideas, and incredible situations. For the professional writer there are also all kinds of ingenious innovations in the manner of expressing how people look and talk; for the literary idler, the books can be opened at any page and closed again as soon as they have given sufficient entertainment. They make no demands whatever." Powell goes on to declare *Valmouth* "one of the best" and notes that "almost every satirical writer of to-day shows signs of Firbank influence, though perhaps not always necessarily acquired direct from Firbank himself." While Firbank didn't set out "to convey 'realism,'" he achieved "'realism' at another level."

Scotsman.
"There is no particular plot."

Times Literary Supplement, 27 November 1919, 697.
Complains that "the story consists of little more than a continuous clatter of snappy artificial talk, in which the chief object of the author—who is much more really *en évidence* than the talkers—seems to be to surprise and puzzle the reader. . . . The whole book is, in fact, a blinding medley of chattering eccentrics and posturers not always free from vulgarity, and not impeccable in matters either of spelling or punctuation."

The Princess Zoubaroff
London: Grant Richards, 1920
Staged versions in 1951, 1952, 1975

[Dalton, F. T.] *Times Literary Supplement,* 9 December 1920, 842.
A brief, lukewarm notice criticizing the lack of dramatic development, the inadequate plot, and RF's "curious adventures in spelling."

MacQuilland, Louis. *Daily Express.* Late Nov. or early Dec., 1920.
"Mr Firbank's endeavours to be wicked are almost pathetic. . . . Young men with side-whiskers and maids in Assyrian jumpers are raving about Mr Firbank's audacities" (quoted in Mayne's review of *The New Rythum*).

"Some New Plays." *Spectator* 126 (15 January 1921): 82.
"An exceedingly foppish satiric drama. There is something vaguely unpleasant in its *fin de siècle* attitude. Mr. Firbank has, however, an extraordinary knack of writing dialogue, and his entirely odious people move and breathe and are completely real. Perhaps some day Mr. Firbank will give us a comedy that is not all satire; when he does, it might prove an exceedingly brilliant acting play. The note of contempt is too much sustained in *The Princess Zoubaroff* to make it possible for acting except for a very special audience" [*in toto*].

Wardle, Irving. "Master of the Giggle." (London) *Times Saturday Review*, 12 April 1975, 9.

A review of a stage production at the Tower. After a brief comparison with Ivy Compton-Burnett's fiction, the reviewer pronounces *The Princess* "a remarkably robust piece of plotting" despite the fact that "Firbank overcomes construction problems by the simple device of ignoring them." Edgar Davies's semi-professional company nicely "reveal the thoroughbred high comic quality of the writing."

"Watergate Theatre: 'The Princess Zoubaroff' by Ronald Firbank." (London) *Times*, 9 June 1951, 8.

The anonymous reviewer finds the play "twice as amusing" to see than to read, though the label "play" is misleading: "There is no conflict, no plot, no themes even—only a picture of the 1920s as the 1920s delighted to be painted: scandalous, witty, perverse, secretly rejoicing in the existence of a 'lost generation.'" The reviewer admires the conversation immensely, and concludes: "With Miss Faith Owen as the most airily depraved of the ladies, and an amusing company, the piece is exactly what private theatres exist to give us."

The book was also reviewed by the *Tatler* and the London *Times* in December 1920 (Benkovitz's *Biography*, 193).

Santal
London: Grant Richards, 1921
New York: Bonacio & Saul/Grove, 1955
Los Angeles: Sun & Moon, 1995

[Dalton, F. T.] *Times Literary Supplement*, 15 September 1921, 598.

A brief but favorable review—the first one RF received from *TLS*. The entire review was quoted in Grant Richards's advertisement for the book in the 13 October 1921 issue of *TLS* (p. 659), which also quotes the favorable notice from the *Liverpool Post* (see below).

Dash, Robert Warren. *New Mexico Quarterly* 25 (Spring 1955): 108-10.

One might begin reading RF with *Santal* because most of his themes appear here in compressed form: "holiness, beauty both lasting and ephemeral, loneliness, sexual inversion." Dash reads the novella as a representation of "Firbank's discomforting sexual maladjustment."

Glasgow Evening News.

"Mr Firbank has acquired a reputation as a stylist which this work will enhance. Within its brief compass there is all the glamour, the colour, the heat, the smells, the vileness, the beauty, and the fervour of Islam. It is the sort of thing that Loti does on a grander scale, and, like Loti, Mr Firbank is an adept at the creation of atmosphere. He is guilty of a few affectations perhaps, but these are like precious flaws in a wondrous Turkish carpet—they are lost in the beauty of the design as a whole."

Kirkus Reviews, 15 November 1994, 1482.

RF creates "the tension between the sensual and the spiritual with uncharacteristic simplicity" and in "lapidary, luminous prose. . . . An exquisite miniature."

Liverpool Post.
"Mr Ronald Firbank has always had his own manner, and a very modish one. In *Santal* the elegance, almost dandyism, of his style has given just a faint hint of flippancy to a tale in itself very dignified, and full of an unexpected warmth and delicacy of feeling. It is a *nouvelle*—who could call a thing of such distinction a long short story?—with the vivid richly-colored background of the East. . . . Something there is, too, of irony and detachment, as though the Mr Firbank of *Valmouth* and of *The Princess Zoubaroff* were secretly smiling a little cynically at his unexpected tumble into sentiment."

Moore, Steven. *Review of Contemporary Fiction* 15.2 (Summer 1995): 235.
    A brief note on Sun & Moon's reissue.

Observer.
"Mr Firbank always had a sense of Style and a feeling for the mannered beauty of arranged words. . . . In *Santal* the passion for beautiful writing is still evident, but it is used with greater simplicity to achieve an effect such as a more reticent Pierre Loti might manage. . . . Mr Firbank has emotion rather than passion, and his East is viewed through a slight haze of sentiment; but it is a real country, and has its own spiritual excitements."

Southport Guardian.
"The incense of Santal pervades the book throughout. Mr Firbank is a discriminating artist; he has an exotic sense of words and of colour. Seldom have we met in so short a space so intense a characterisation of pilgrimage or so vivid a picture of the Algerian scene."

"Strange Bird." *Newsweek,* 21 March 1955, 109-10.
    Describes the book as "a tender Persian miniature" and "entirely musical. . . . If 'Santal' is only a footnote to a remarkable literary career, it certainly belongs with the rest." A brief account of RF's career follows, and *Santal* is summarized as a "Vivid footnote on faith."

Sullivan, John F. "The Wit of Dandyism." *Commonweal* 62 (22 April 1955): 84.
    After noting America's traditional hostility toward dandyism, Sullivan predicts most of RF's work will never be popular in the U.S. But because of *Santal's* "more obvious seriousness," it might prove an exception. "A study of vision and attainment," *Santal* concludes with what "will seem to some only a kind of existentialist self-realization; to others it may appear to be an ironic symbol of the folly of asceticism." The story "does not completely succeed"—largely because of its purple passages—but it succeeds well enough to prove memorable.

The Flower beneath the Foot
London: Grant Richards, 1923
New York: Brentano's, 1924 (with a preface by RF)
London/New York: Penguin, 1986 (introduction by John Mortimer)

"The Flower Beneath the Foot." *New Statesman* 20 (3 March 1923): 640.
    "A fantasy of fluttering, delicate, drooping creatures who have scarcely strength to finish their sentences or drop on to a convenient throne. . . . Unfortunately, the evocative quality with which Mr. Firbank's work is liberally

endowed is too mannered, too consciously focused upon a single aspect of life, to keep its freshness." The reviewer claims *Caprice* is a stronger work, and although *The Flower* "has grace and vividness and wit, and pathos, . . . all these ingredients, spiced as they are with innuendo and a dangerous-looking relish of foreign words, refuse to blend."

"Gifted but Distraught." *New York Times Book Review,* 9 November 1924, 8.
RF is unsuccessful at whatever he is attempting in this novel; after guessing at what that might be, the reviewer confesses "we do not 'get' Mr. Firbank."

Harwood, H. C. *The Outlook,* 3 February 1923, 118.
Although RF is "a master of innuendo" and can write dialogue of "sparkling clarity," he largely lacks wit and humor, and "his attitude towards all but the curiously erotic is puerile in its simplicity. The characters are barely distinguishable except by their names, and the construction is so loose as to suggest that the author invented as he went along without provision for what was to follow."

Lesserday, Lynton. "The Baroque Shirt-Lifter." *Punch,* 5 November 1986, 84.
Finds Mortimer's introduction more "commonsensical" than Powell's to *The Complete Ronald Firbank* and agrees that RF still influences comic writers, though "No other twentieth-century comic writer quite has that sad Firbankian longing." What fascinates the reviewer is not RF's plots but "his use of language," and he concludes: "Firbank can *not* be made into a film because it is writing meant to be read, not to have pictures made of it. It is not bogus realism or sham naturalism but *Comic Prose* written as carefully as poetry is written. That, for me at least, is the ticket and is where the way ahead lies for the English novel."

Moore, Steven. *Review of Contemporary Fiction* 9.1 (Spring 1989): 246.
Brief notice of Penguin's reprint, mentioned in conjunction with Alan Hollinghurst's novel *The Swimming-Pool Library.*

New York Post, 1 November 1924.

[Richmond, B.] *Times Literary Supplement,* 1 February 1923, 78.
"Mr Firbank continues to deny us the solid nourishment which our national character demands in its fiction as well as on the dinner-table. . . . Really it is superfluous to follow the plot, which is purposely disjointed, . . . [and] a style based too simply on grammatical, as the satire on sexual, inversions, very quickly becomes monotonous."

Van Vechten, Carl. "Ronald Firbank." *New York Tribune,* 24 June 1923, "Magazines and Books," 24.
Emphasizes RF's "light touch." Incorporated into his introduction to *Prancing Nigger* (see part 3).

Watson, Frederick. "Beyond Reproof." *Bookman* 64 (August 1923): 238.
"No one could be expected to review this book," Watson begins. "Even Mr. Firbank cannot enjoy more than an occasional elusive idea of what it is about." The reviewer disapproves of "the intemperance and blustering that has inflamed some reviewers" of RF's novel, but admits that reading it is "a graceful if conscienceless game" and that "the typically English vulgarity of his humour is only rescued at the last gasp by his immense agility of phrase." He concludes: "Like Mr. Norman Davey, Mr. Firbank seems to me to possess qualities of imagina-

tion and fantasy quite beyond his colleagues."

Wilson, Edmund. "Late Violets from the Nineties." *Dial* 75 (October 1923): 387-90. Rpt. in his *The Shores of Light* (New York: Farrar, Straus & Young, 1952), 68-72.
    A joint review of *The Flower* and Van Vechten's *The Blind Bow-Boy*—Wilson prefers Firbank—and their common source in fin-de-siècle literature.

According to a list in one of RF's notebooks, *The Flower* was also reviewed in the *Birmingham Gazette, Birmingham Post, Cambrian Leader, Daily Herald, Daily News, Manchester Guardian, Observer,* and the *Westminster Gazette* (Swann/Benkovitz catalogue, lot 246).

Prancing Nigger
New York: Brentano's, 1924 (introduction by Carl Van Vechten)
Sorrow in Sunlight. London: Brentano's, 1924
London: Duckworth, 1931

Bookman 68 (Spring Supplement, 1925): 86.
    The anonymous reviewer is disappointed: "His talent is not developing as at one time we hoped it might. He is still too preoccupied with ideas and phrases which might have shocked the public in the days of 'The Yellow Book.' . . . He is remarkable and still worth reading for the things he does to the English language—gay, inconsequential sentences, a kind of literary nonsense such as Beardsley might have written had he tried to compose Lewis Carroll's books."

Boston Evening Transcript, 4 June 1924, 4.
    "The author's style is brilliant. It is heady and exotic; it is airy and delicate; it is unreal and phantasmagorical. In this slight tale, however, it describes languorously and sensuously life and love on a decidedly low social plane."

Brickell, Herschel. "The Negro in Fiction" [rev. of *Prancing Nigger* and Jessie Redmon Fauset's *There Is Confusion*]. *Literary Review (New York Evening Post)* 4 (12 April 1924): 661.
    "*Prancing Nigger* is a highly sophisticated novel, the product of an experienced hand, and of a remarkable mind." Brickell compares it to "classical jazz" like Gershwin's, and concludes, "Beauty? Yes, and more than a little of mockery—a fling at civilization, humorous and high spirited."

Brooklyn Eagle.
    Dismissed the novel as "Silly. Bevo-naughtiness. Highly praised by Carl Van Vechten." RF later wrote Van Vechten: "I mean to send you my photograph as San Sebastian, all darts, & reading the Brooklyn *Eagle*" (both quotations from Benkovitz's *Biography,* 256, 266).

Dial 76 (June 1924): 559.
    "It is merely Mr. Firbank's latest and, for us, his most exquisite impropriety in prose. . . . But in Mr Firbank's pages the words 'sin' and 'goodness' would be anomalies because those pages are deliberately and delightfully unreal. The faintly sexual fooling, the bare suggestion of delicate depravity we find here, bear the same relation to reality as a rosy reflection in deep water bears to the body of a swimmer."

[Fausset, Hugh I'A.] *Bookman* 76 (July 1929): 229-30.

   Though unsigned, the sentiments and phrasing are similar to Fausset's review of the *Works* a year later in the *Bookman* (see below). Feels RF is "the kind of artist who appeals to a literary coterie by originating a new manner without having any really significant experience to express through it." But *Prancing Nigger* is his best work: "His exotic spirit found in the negroes a primitive quality wanting to Mayfair and Chelsea, which disciplined somewhat its extravagant caprice and lent it substance."

Franklin, John. "New Novels." *New Statesman* 24 (20 December 1924): 336.

   Groups RF with two other "exotic and highly spiced" novelists (Joseph Hergesheimer and James Stephens) and notes "the bold and dashing methods, the amazing technical gusto, with which such writers as these paint stage scenery to look like life, but more exciting." In support he quotes three paragraphs from *Sorrow in Sunlight*.

Gilmore, Louis. "A Dingy Lilac Blossom of Rarity Untold." *Double Dealer* 6 (April 1924): 132-33.

   Reminiscent of (but superior to) Beardsley's *Under the Hill*, *Prancing Nigger* constitutes "a world utterly fantastic yet real, since consistent and harmonious in itself." The bulk of the review consists of a plot synopsis, and concludes: "In creating the Mouth family, Mr. Firbank has created as delightful a family as any in literature, and in Cuna-Cuna . . . surely, the most delectable city!"

Krutch, Joseph Wood. "Two Sophisticates." *Nation* 118 (11 June 1924): 685.

   While granting RF "has indeed produced a little tale entirely *sui generis* and with a flavor undeniably intriguing if undoubtedly 'high,'" Krutch finds the novel lacking in the "moral earnestness" that characterizes truly great art.

Morning Post, 22 November 1924.

"A 'Prancing Nigger' Among the New Books of Fiction." *New York Times Book Review*, 23 March 1924, 8.

   The reviewer, long an admirer of RF's "innocently perverse provocativeness of ultimate sophistication," his "jewel-like insouciance," his "amazingly integrated dissociations," welcomes "this charming little book" as RF's first U.S. publication. "The very title, of course, is a triumph. It is impossible to conceive of a more insinuatingly hilarious invitation, as if to a glorious blackface minstrel show." The novel is "robustly tranquil, shimmeringly full-blooded, whole. . . . The story has a feeling at once aged and ageless. It is obliquely visual, as though it were witnessed in entirety from aloof yet discerningly selective eyes."

Publishers Weekly, 22 March 1924, 1059.
   A brief announcement.

Redman, Ben Ray. "A Ronald Firbank Comedy in the West Indies." *Literary Digest International Book Review* 2 (July 1924): 586, 588.
   The first half of the review traces RF's literary development to alert the new reader "what he need not look for in 'Prancing Nigger'": RF "is not given to significant study of vital problems. His qualities are purely literary, and one is entertained and delighted by them or one is not. To defend him, to apologize for him, to seek to prove that he is excellent would be ridiculous; one might as wisely attempt to defend an alligator pear." The novel is "highly civilized

entertainment" and represents RF "in his suavest and most amusing, tho not most indecorous, vein."

[Stace, H. W.] *Times Literary Supplement*, 18 December 1924, 873.
   A brief but positive notice, concluding: "The morals of these simple folk are no doubt reprehensible; but in this fantastic atmosphere, strangely blended of tropical passion and naive absurdity, nothing is to be taken more than half seriously."

Stagg, Hunter. "Decay and Disillusion." *Reviewer* 14 (April 1924): 236-47.
   The section of this group review entitled "A Diversion or Two" focuses on *Prancing Nigger* (243-45). Declaring RF "the most original author alive," Stagg quotes from Van Vechten's preface on this point, describes a number of his favorite scenes, and concludes that RF's books "are totally unlike anything else you have ever read before or are likely to read again."

Wilson, Edmund. "Mr. Firbank's Light Touch." *New Republic* 38 (21 May 1924): 342.
   Despite what Van Vechten in his introduction calls RF's "light touch," the novels "are in a sense very close to life . . . stitched together with great pains from the precious scraps of experience." Wilson praises *Prancing Nigger*'s vividness and argues that RF surpasses similar writers like Huxley and Beerbohm "through his superior artistic seriousness." Though he is a "first-rate artist," RF "is somehow unsatisfactory. . . . His chief themes are disappointed love and distressing humiliation; but when he illustrates these themes—along with his extravagant repertory of vices—with characters which are burlesque without taking actual body, the ugliness of the joke is likely to be the only thing that strikes us." RF seems to evade "reaching full artistic reality," and not, as Van Vechten suggests, "because bafflement is Mr. Firbank's aim." Rather, Wilson wonders if a "discordant melancholy" is responsible: "Mr. Firbank has been thinking and it has made him unhappy."

Concerning the Eccentricities of Cardinal Pirelli
London: Grant Richards, 1926

[Clarke, A.] *Times Literary Supplement*, 19 August 1926, 550.
   Although conceding "an apparently brilliant manner of impressionism, authenticated by a colloquial acquaintance with Spanish life," the reviewer feels the novel makes too many demands on "the unhappy reader" and, despite "an entirely individual sense of humour," RF appeals too often to "objectionable sources of mirth."

The Works of Ronald Firbank
Introduction by Arthur Waley, biographical memoir by Osbert Sitwell
London: Duckworth, 1929 (limited edition)
New York: Brentano's, 1929 (limited edition)
London: Duckworth, 1929-30 (the "Rainbow" edition)

Bennett, Arnold. "Three Modern Rebels." *Evening Standard*, 9 September 1929, 7. Rpt. in *Arnold Bennett: The "Evening Standard" Years*, ed. Andrew Mylett. London: Chatto & Windus, 1974, 305-7.

Bennett had refrained from reading RF for years because he suspected him of preciousness, but upon publication of the *Works* read *Caprice,* which he found "strange, odd, clever, queer, humorous, unlike anything else, and not appreciably precious. . . . The whole thing is lit with the refracting light that never was on sea or land. It is a lark, a joke, a satire, accomplished in a manner rather distinguished, mainly by dialogue and in brief paragraphs. It is brief, but it is homogeneous." But he suspects it isn't worth reading, and though he foresees a Firbank cult, Bennett won't join it. "And I should regard Firbank more seriously if he showed strong imaginative power. He does not show it. To me his is an elegant weakling."

Fausset, Hugh I'Anson. "Some Firbank Stories." *Bookman* 78 (April 1930): 41-42.

The reviewer doubts RF's novels will "appeal to more than a small audience, composed of those who are interested in an original literary technique. As a pioneer in a new method by which the logical continuity and circumlocutions of narrative were avoided, and as an executant, often brilliant, in the art of dialogue, Firbank is indeed worth study. But the more he is studied the more apparent becomes the vacuity behind his surface pyrotechnics." Fauset gives several examples of such vacuity, and concludes that RF's work is an unsatisfactory "combination of technical adroitness with adolescent silliness."

Forster, E. M. "Our Butterflies and Beetles." *New York Herald Tribune,* 5 May 1929, "Books," 1, 6. Rpt. as "Butterflies and Beetles" in *Life and Letters* 3 (July 1929): 1-9—a review of both the *Works* and David Garnett's *No Love*; rpt. (omitting most of the material on Garnett) as "Ronald Firbank" in his *Abinger Harvest* (London: Edward Arnold, 1936; New York: Harcourt, Brace, 1936), 115-21; rpt. in Lord Horder's *Memoirs and Critiques,* 180-84.

"To break a butterfly, or even a beetle, upon a wheel is a delicate task," for critics are reluctant to handle "literary fantasy," partly because "fantasts" reveal "the absence of a soul." RF has "nothing up-to-date in him. He is *fin de siècle,* as it used to be called; he belongs to the nineties and the *Yellow Book*; his mind inherits the furniture and his prose the cadences of Aubrey Beardsley's *Under the Hill.* To the historian he is an interesting example of literary conservatism." RF is affected but not self-conscious, healthy, nor particularly intelligent. He has genius "in his flit-about fashion. . . . What charms us in him in his taste, his choice of words, the rhythm both of his narrative and of his conversations, his wit, and—in his later work—an opulence as of gathered fruit and enamelled skies." Of his early books, Forster likes *Vainglory*: "It is frivolous stuff, and how rare, how precious is frivolity!" Of the later ones, *Prancing Nigger* shows an unexpected maturity. RF is "fundamentally unserious. This disconcerts the Anglo-Saxon reader," but not Forster himself, it seems. Waley's introduction to the *Works* is "masterly."

Rickword, Edgell. "Ronald Firbank." *Sunday Referee,* 1929; rpt. in his *Essays and Opinions: 1921-1931.* Ed. Alan Young. Cheadle Hulme: Carcanet, 1974. 267-68.

RF, "though not a 'serious novelist', was that much rarer thing, a serious writer." His technique may alienate the casual reader: "Everything that one expects in a novel seems to have been left out, except the conversation, and half of that probably seems missing, too. . . . He was a satirist, though with no axe to grind, and his aristocrats are not ludicrous because they are aristocrats but because they are vapid. . . . The sentimentalist may talk of his cynicism, but beneath the careful indifference of his style there is a hint of deeper feeling, of which *The Flower Beneath the Foot* is perhaps the aptest symbol." Rickword praises the design of the Rainbow edition and hopes it "will result in a wider admiration for Firbank's really genuine artistry."

"Ronald Firbank." *New Statesman* 33 (24 August 1929): 605.

RF "was a writer singularly apt at organizing and exploiting his capacities, even though it was his capacity for sheer silliness. . . . But, when he was really silly, his silliness was quintessential," and comparisons are made to *Tristram Shandy*. The review focuses on *Cardinal Pirelli:* "not one of Ronald Firbank's best books. . . . He knew what succeeded; he was beginning, we feel, to know the characteristics of his own wit, as it were from the outside." After praising RF's "genuine and unaffected" eccentricity, the reviewer concludes: "he was the possessor of that unmistakable something which cannot be gained by an intelligent reading of the classics. In a universe crowded with talent, uncomfortably overflowing with brilliance, his was not a gift which can be entirely ignored."

[West, Geoffrey (pseud. of Geoffrey Harry Wells).] "Ronald Firbank." *Times Literary Supplement,* 21 March 1929, 236.

RF's lack of "an adequate subject-matter" cancels out his gifts: "A golden tongue is worthless to the man who has nothing to say." The absence of "basic terms of human reference" makes his work pointless and often obscene. His books are all more or less alike, and "are all comedies less of manners or even of atmosphere than of remarks." Though his "technical mastery did increase greatly towards the end, he was by no means an impeccable craftsman" and continued to indulge in "certain repellant themes" (i.e., sexual perversion). "He was at his best an elegant and accomplished writer, but his attitude as a whole was fundamentally impossible, for just as far as it was not simply irrelevant to the essential elements in human nature it was cynical and corrupting. . . . His best work is to be found in the two short stories, 'Odette' and 'Santal,' and in 'Prancing Nigger'"—and the reviewer agrees with Waley that the latter deserves to be RF's best-known work. West concludes: "Firbank may live as a contemporary curiosity, but to uphold him as anything more serious seems to us to reveal neither taste nor critical balance."

Woolf, Leonard. "Butterflies." *Nation and Athenæum* 44 (14 January 1929): 495.

"Firbank was a writer of considerable talent, some originality, and a lively imagination, but he was essentially second-rate," as opposed to Max Beerbohm, a first-rate writer as "light, fantastical, and nonsensical" as RF. "Firbank's prose . . . is ostensibly well written. But it is terribly monotonous, always doing the same thing, and the monotony—so it seems to me—is the monotony of the fake." Woolf also condemns RF's subject matter because it is not weighted with "the solid and sordid seriousness of the real world," and when RF *is* serious, it is "the tiresome seriousness of the *poseur*." Possessing merely "the Yellow Book mind," RF "poses in his books, just as he posed when he went to a magnificent dinner and would eat only one green pea. That kind of pose cannot produce a masterpiece."

Apparently Woolf passed along his set of the *Works* to his wife Virginia: see part 3.

When asked by David Dougill in the late 1960s if he still considered RF a second-rate writer, Woolf replied that he "should now demote him to third-rate."

The Artificial Princess
Introduction by Sir Coleridge Kennard
London: Duckworth, 1934
London: Centaur, 1934 (limited, illustrated edition)

Armstrong, Martin. *Fortnightly Review* 136 (July 1934): 126.

RF "belongs to a class of writers which never produces great literature. Firbank, in fact, is an entertaining trifler—a cocktail, icy and exotic as a cocktail should be, but none the less a cocktail." He is identified with the 1890s, "but Firbank has the advantage of time." *The Artificial Princess* is flawed in its weak resolution, yet RF remains "a cocktail, and a good one."

"Firbank." *Life and Letters* 10 (July 1934): 501-3.

"Among the Dandies of literature, Firbank has a secure if inconspicuous place," a place even more secure than Wilde's. Ballet provides a perfect analogue to RF's writings and thus it is not surprising to learn he was a devotee of the Diaghilev Ballet. "Firbank is one of the very few writers on whom it would be impossible to improve. We cannot imagine another and greater Firbank rising in the future." *The Artificial Princess* "is certainly one of the most exquisite of Firbank's tales; . . . Foreground and background are one: how effortlessly Firbank has solved that difficulty of the novelist!" The reviewer continues and concludes with similar high praise.

Nicolson, Harold. 11 May 1934.

In *Author Hunting* Grant Richards quotes from this review (giving its date but not its source). "Firbank possessed a talent at the same time undulating and incisive. Being a shy man with acute instincts, he indulged in innuendo. It was not the demure innuendo of Samuel Butler, nor yet the hearty innuendo of Norman Douglas; it was a baroque type of innuendo. He dealt in porcelain hints. The timidity inseparable from such epicene giggling has discouraged me from becoming an admirer of Ronald Firbank. Yet, in his own medium, he was almost a supreme artist. . . . As a specimen of all that is most delicate and witty in Ronald Firbank this *Artificial Princess* could scarcely be surpassed. Yet would any serious reader, however fascinated he may momentarily be by the cachinnations of Ronald Firbank, contend that he is anything more than a literary curiosity? Had he lived longer he would certainly have written something of lasting value; his talent, however variable, was authentic and unexpectedly wise; yet he died while still in his experimental period; he achieved several brilliant improvisations on the theme of Beardsley in plus-fours; and brilliance is an evanescent quality."

Quennell, Peter. *New Statesman and Nation* 7 (23 June 1934): 958, 960.

Largely concerned with how difficult it is to convey RF's charm; though a born eccentric, "he was also a born writer, equipped with a delicate feeling for the beauty and mystery of words." Though "the machinery of *The Artificial Princess* is more haphazard" than that in RF's better novels, Quennell finds the posthumous novel enchanting and quotes two passages in demonstration.

Saturday Review (London) 157 (12 May 1934): 546.

[West, Geoffrey.] *Times Literary Supplement*, 10 May 1934, 340.

Borrowing from his review of the *Works*, West considers *The Artificial Princess* yet another "comedy less of events than of manners, and less of manners or even atmosphere than of remarks. . . . But it is as mature as 'Vainglory' or 'Valmouth' in its delicate use of an almost evanescent prose, in its grouping and shifting of quite incredible figures and in its exercise of a wit—if the word be applicable to so shadowy a thing—whose basis is incongruity."

Extravaganzas
The Artificial Princess and *Concerning the Eccentricities of Cardinal Pirelli*
New York: Coward-McCann, 1935

Benét, William Rose. *Saturday Review of Literature* 13 (23 November 1935): 16.

The Artificial Princess "is quite a charming device of spun sugar, with less innuendo than Firbank developed later. 'Cardinal Pirelli' has more, and is also by far the more difficult job. It distinctly impresses one with Firbank's ability as a writer. It seems a pity that he never developed out of the slyly salacious—but his salacity was of so delicate a type that it seldom becomes offensive. He had the ability to write with a style and beauty of language at his best, as well as with a subtle wit, that puts to shame many writers of our time."

Boston Evening Transcript, 23 November 1935, 5.

"These two stories may be Firbank of an experimental stage, but they are Firbank at his wittiest."

Kronenburger, Louis. "Hothouse Blooms." *New York Times Book Review,* 17 November 1935, 7, 24.

Notes that the Firbank "fad" passed quickly after his death, and predicts the "publication of the present two novelettes will not do much toward restoring Firbank's fame." These two "are not his best work" but are characteristic: "Firbank's was a world of pure fancy: it was the extreme of escapism," but closer to Lewis Carroll's escapism than that of Van Vechten or Cabell. "With Firbank we are well on our way toward Dada . . . he is at his best in disoriented moments of non-sequitur, in unfettered flights of madcap fancy, in amalgams of poetry with nonsense. He is at his best when he archly mingles absurdity with charm." But RF is not entertaining because he "is too much given to fuss and feathers. He is never spontaneous and never simple" and thus is tiresome, affected, over-refined.

Morris, Lloyd. *New York Herald Tribune,* 5 January 1936, "Books," 11.

All RF "succeeded in creating was an interior decorator's paradise, inhabited by parvenus," for "the robust qualities of satire and irony were beyond his range. . . . Yet, by virtue perhaps of its defects, Firbank's work is brilliantly evocative of the period which produced it. In it are to be found the sterility, the confusion, the cult of spurious elegance, the love for rococo decoration which the brief Edwardian reign bequeathed to an emancipated if untutored middle class."

Publishers Weekly, 9 November 1935, 1769.

A brief announcement.

Five Novels
Valmouth, The Flower beneath the Foot, Prancing Nigger,
Concerning the Eccentricities of Cardinal Pirelli, and *The Artificial Princess*
Introduction by Osbert Sitwell
London: Duckworth, 1949
Norfolk, CT/New York: New Directions, 1949, 1969, 1981

Auden, W. H. "Firbank Revisited." *New York Times Book Review,* 20 November 1949, 5.
　　RF's novels are "an absolute test. A person who dislikes them . . . may, for all I know, possess some admirable quality but I do not wish ever to see him again." The poet goes on to say the term "novel" is misleading in RF's case, for a novel suggests a plot, and "The Firbank plot is, clearly, simply a pretext, deliberately flimsy, for the existence of his characters." Likewise, setting is unimportant: "it is only a backdrop before which his characters behave. . . . Firbank's extraordinary achievement was to draw a picture, the finest, I believe, ever drawn by anyone, of the Earthly Paradise, not, of course, as it really is, but as, in our fallen state, we imagine it to be, as the place, that is, where, without having to change our desires and behavior in any way, we suffer neither frustration nor guilt." But RF didn't write "escape literature": "The fact that Firbank's novels are funny is proof that he never lets us forget the contradiction between life as it is and life as we should like it to be, for it is the impossibility of that contradiction which makes us laugh." Auden concludes by declaring that RF's "books have as permanent an importance as, say, 'Alice in Wonderland.'"

Bloomfield, Paul. *Manchester Guardian,* 9 December 1949, 4.
　　"A wonderful Christmas book for old and new readers of a short-lived, frail, and gilded young writer of genius who managed to condense enough travel and mixing into his thirty-nine years to be able to write infinitely subtle commentaries on nonsense almost everywhere but especially in exalted circles."

Bookseller, 3 December 1949.

Charques, R. D. *Spectator* 183 (23 December 1949): 900.
　　The reviewer has never really cared for RF, and this reissue has not changed his opinion of "a small talent all too seriously and assiduously inflated by a habit of preciosity."

[Dinnage, Paul.] "Wild, Pleasing Fables." *Times Literary Supplement,* 16 December 1949, 824.
　　Noting that "a generation has grown up which knows him only as a legend," Dinnage reviews RF's life, work, and influences. "The novels surely belong to the little-practised and elusive art of tragi-comedy, in which 'mirth to measure with sadness is annexed.' There are touches of satire, of comedy, of the lyricism that betrays a poet. But he is no more than an oblique satirist, having none of the bitterness that spurs on a Swift to break his vials on our heads." Dinnage comments on RF's many rhetorical achievements, then points the moral: "*Valmouth,* a 'romantic' novel, and *Prancing Nigger* have for their theme the seduction of innocence by experience, and this, at last, is the sad moral Firbank has always to relate to us in one or another form."

[Dirda, Michael.] *Washington Post Book World,* 19 April 1981, 12.
　　A brief recommendation of these "modern masterpieces of the rococo."

Farrelly, John. *New Republic* 122 (9 January 1950): 21.
  A mixed review: "this kind of writing is almost inevitably uneven, and Firbank at his incomparable best is too readily matched by Firbank at his arch and trivial worst."

Hodgart, Matthew (1969). See reviews of Benkovitz's *Biography* in part 2.

James, Jamie. *American Book Review* 4 (March-April 1982): 12.
  Condescending and rather obtuse, repeating sixty years later the same condescending and obtuse objections made against RF in the 1920s.

Jones, Ernest. "The World of Ronald Firbank." *Nation* 169 (26 November 1949): 520-21.
  A highly influential review and the basis for his introduction to *Three Novels*: see part 3.

Kirkus [*Bulletin from Virginia Kirkus' Bookshop Service*] 17 (15 October 1949): 589.
  Predicts that the novels' "esoteric qualities, the general effect of pointlessness will limit the appeal to today's audience but those with a taste for precious writing and sharp social comedy will have a pleasant discovery."

M., W. P. *Dublin Magazine* 25.2 (April-June 1950): 54-55.
  A brief but giddy appreciation of RF's achievement: "His art is mild and sweet and witty, and almost anything said about it must be dull. It is not satire, for it has knowledge of no possible state, social or moral, other than its own, and though one may think of Beardsley's *Venus and Tannhäuser*, it is only for a moment: the wings of his mischief are too fragile and too aimless for the gross weight of evil and his flowers of impropriety dance in too fresh an air to smell of sin." After commenting briefly on a few specific titles, the reviewer concludes: "In all of them wit breaks suddenly out of silliness and beauty out of eccentricity, while the irresponsible gaiety of a spectator uninvolved himself in the absurdity of life makes all a work of unimpassioned charm."

Martinetti, Ronald. "Cackle and Confusion." *Wall Street Journal,* 29 May 1969, 18.
  See under Benkovitz's *Biography* in part 2.

O'Hara, J. D. "Reflections on Recent Prose." *New England Review* 4 (Summer 1982): 615.
  At the end of this roundup review, O'Hara notes the new edition of *Five Novels* by "a sadly neglected author, a downright silly author and prolly gay to boot. . . . Once, during a class on *Flower,* a grown woman among my students began to read a passage out loud and laughed so hard that finally she staggered into the hall to get it over with."

"A Perfect Dear." *Time,* 21 November 1949, 114, 116.
  A generally favorable overview of RF's life and work.

Pritchett, V. S. *New Statesman and Nation,* 7 January 1950, 15-16. Rpt. as "Firbank" in his *Books in General.* London: Chatto & Windus, 1953. 229-34; and in *Complete Collected Essays.* London: Chatto & Windus, 1991; New York: Random House, 1991. 544-48.
  RF's works, full of sad folly rather than cheery fun, "are antics in a void left

by life, elegies on burst bubbles." Pritchett states "it is a simple fact that technically Firbank cleared dead wood out of the English novel, in one or two convul-
sive laughs." RF must be taken in small doses; fortunately, the economy of his
works saves them from becoming intolerable or wearisome. RF was sensitive "to
the transient in life. Time is his subject. He is a poet of the surface of life. . . .
The comedy is in the inconsequence; the poetry in the evanescence; the tragedy
in the chill of loneliness and desolation which will suddenly strike in a random
world. The element common to all these novels is melancholy. . . . His comic
genius rises from the fatality of rarely seeing life steadily and never seeing it
whole. It is in bits." Pritchett quotes several of RF's linguistic "bits"—"the
search for the *mot juste* disclosed to him the wild territories of the *mot injuste*"—
and praises his sensitivity to conversation. *Cardinal Pirelli* "has a cloying and
faded corruption and naughtiness"; Pritchett prefers *The Flower*. He concludes
that RF's "absolute originality, as well as his technical brilliance, seem to make
his survival as a minor treasure inevitable. . . . Of our contemporary satirists he
alone has the traditional quality of total artifice."

Publishers Weekly, 3 December 1949, 2337.
  Only lists contents.

Redman, Ben Ray. "Quintet from a Minor Dream Garden." *Saturday Review of
Literature* 33 (25 February 1950): 17.
  Though popular in the 1920s (Redman reviewed *Prancing Nigger* in 1924),
RF's "slender books, demure in nun's black, went discreetly underground" in
the 1930s. They are "fairy tales" in which RF could be at home in a way he
never could in the actual world. Though admittedly not for everyone, "it is
hardly possible that anyone interested in the art of words will find Ronald
Firbank's novels negligible. . . . But it would be a mistake to treat too solemnly
an author who was never solemn. It would do him no service to claim too much
for him, as some of his belated discoverers are now doing. He was, for all his art
and charm and cleverness, a minor artist who gracefully cultivated a minor
dream garden of his own creation. His little novels are as far from fiction of the
first order as a Charles Conder fan is from a masterpiece by Rembrandt."

Richardson, Maurice. Untraced review of English edition. Rpt. as "On Re-reading Firbank" in his *Fits and Starts*. London: Michael Joseph, 1979. 185-86.
  Happy to see that RF, despite a period of neglect, has survived, Richardson
praises the omnibus (except for *The Artificial Princess,* which "reads like a pastiche of one of several contributors to the Yellow Book"). RF's dialogue, "with
so much left unsaid, sometimes creates an extraordinary effect, as if Congreve,
Angela Brazil, and Douglas Byng had become alchemically fused. He is, in fact,
the oddest conglomeration of fantasy, satire, sentimentality, avant-gardism,
naughtiness, silliness, delicious wit and beauty."

Willis, Katherine Tappert. *Library Journal* 74 (1 November 1949): 1674.
  Praises both the Sitwell introduction and the novels themselves: "All are rap-
turously gay—inconsequential and bewildering. Henry Green, Aldous Huxley
and Ronald Firbank have much in common but Firbank is separated from them
all by sparkling audacity."

Wilson, Edmund. "A Revival of Ronald Firbank." *New Yorker,* 10 December
1949, 141-50. Rpt. in his *Classics and Commercials: A Literary Chronicle of the
Forties* (New York: Farrar, Straus, 1950), 486-502; and in Horder's *Memoirs
and Critiques,* 196-208.

Probably the most important and influential review written about RF's work. Wilson is convinced "that he was one of the finest English writers of his period and one of those most likely to become a classic." Wilson offers a brief biography (based on Fletcher's *Memoir*) and admits RF's books first looked like "foamy improvisations which could be skimmed up in rapid reading." Re-reading them, "one realizes that Ronald Firbank was one of the writers of his time who took most trouble over their work and who were most single-mindedly devoted to literature. . . . His books are not foolish trifles, scribbled down to get through the boredoms of a languid and luxurious life. They are extremely intellectual, and composed with the closest attention: dense textures of indirection that always disguise point. They have to be read with care, and they can be read again and again, because Firbank has loaded every rift with ore." Wilson places RF in the British school of comedy that includes Ben Jonson, Restoration dramatists, Peacock, Gilbert, and Aldous Huxley, and compares *The Princess Zoubaroff* with Congreve's plays. (*Zoubaroff* "is really an understatement of the same theme that D. H. Lawrence became violent and shrill about: the biologically sinister phenomenon of a slackening of the interest in mating on the part of the privileged classes of Europe.") RF's early novels catch certain aspects of English life and character, "particularly the English habit of pretending to disregard what is uppermost in people's minds and always talking about something else." Beginning with *Santal*, RF is concerned with the theme of "turning to religion from the life of the world," despite his apparently irreverent attitude. "Ronald Firbank was the poet of the *fou rire*. That is the key to the whole of his work. There is anguish behind it all—and the more ridiculous it is, the better he is expressing this anguish." This is best expressed in *Cardinal Pirelli*, which Wilson considers "his most preposterous book and the one that has most moral meaning; it combines his most perverse story with his purest and most beautiful writing."

Wind and the Rain 6.3 (Winter 1949-50): 211-16.

In this leisurely essay on both *Five Novels* and a *Yellow Book* anthology, the anonymous reviewer (perhaps editor Neville Braybrooke) first notes the continuity in outlook between *The Yellow Book*, RF, and early Huxley. The novels are difficult to describe: they are impressionistic, nearly plotless, religious, and carefully written. The reviewer finds signs of weakness in *Cardinal Pirelli* and argues RF "could not have written another novel in that same vein without one of two things happening: either overstepping the mark at which impiety becomes blasphemy and consequently bad taste, or else writing a completely different kind of book." Some stylistic analysis follows, the theatrical element in his writing is noted (though *The Princess Zoubaroff* is pronounced a failure), and some of his weaknesses are pointed out. The reviewer concludes: "towards the end of his life his situations became more and more absurd, more and more forced; and as the world in which he lived changed, so he had to fall back more and more on his own invention. In *Cardinal Pirelli* one begins to see that invention flagging. For he could only look back to the hey-day of the Café Royal with regret. . . . He wrote for patricians, not the proletariat. His century was the eighteenth century—the century of Horace Walpole and an architectural style in which alcoves abound. In one of those alcoves—sometimes sniggering, sometimes deadly serious—he found a niche for himself, kept it, and will continue to keep it."

Three Novels
Vainglory, Inclinations, and *Caprice*
Introduction by Ernest Jones
London: Duckworth, 1950
Norfolk, CT: New Directions, 1951
Three More Novels. New York: New Directions, 1986

Ash, John. "Considering the Eccentricities of Ronald Firbank." *Voice Literary Supplement,* November 1986, 10-11.

After noting the personas RF used in his work, Ash discusses the difficulty the novels present for some critics: "The problem seems to reside in the fact that Firbank joins radical technique to apparently frivolous content." RF learned from but surpasses Wilde in artistry ("Cardinal Pirelli . . . is a portrait of Oscar Wilde as Christ") and also learned from Jules Laforgue. RF made a "comprehensive reform of novelistic conventions. . . . After more than 70 years, the results still look remarkably avant-garde." Ash devotes most of his space to *Vainglory* but considers *Inclinations* and *Caprice* "essential reading" as well. He concludes: "Decorative and serene, Firbank's art will always be anathema to admirers of muscular effort in fiction, but for anyone prepared to approach them with an open and alert mind these novels are an inexhaustible source of pleasure."

Broadwater, Bowden. "A World of His Own." *New York Times Book Review,* 17 June 1951, 4.

RF's books "are rooted in the tradition of Restoration comedy, but also call to mind the quite personal styles forced upon painters like Henri Rousseau and Miro by the intensity of their private worlds." Broadwater suggests "Yearning is the theme of all Firbank's novels," and concludes: "His range was severely limited, but he found for it a perfect and unique form, playing on the black keys only."

[Brossard, Chandler.] *American Mercury* 72 (June 1951): 737.

Noted in the "Recommended" column: "Lovers of the baroque, the rococo, and the odd, this is your meat."

[Dinnage, Paul.] "Untarnished Finery." *Times Literary Supplement,* 29 December 1950, 825.

The early works "are formative and experimental," but "jewelled sentences, deft stabs of wit, are to be met with throughout these novels. But so are more sinister hints: Firbank's creatures, ruthless in their pursuit of what is scarcely worth while, delineate a terrible ennui; they make us aware of the transience of things; they show, however obliquely, a real concern with evil and transgression, with punishment and the Puritan conscience." Jones's introduction is "excellent and penetrating."

Fiedler, Leslie A. "The Relevance of Irrelevance." *Nation* 172 (21 April 1951): 381-82.

Although the novels in this collection are not as good as those in *Five Novels,* "'Caprice,' at least, is a wholly successful piece of sustained wit; and 'Vainglory' and 'Inclinations' provide instances of the cagy irrelevance and ironic pathos which characterize Firbank at his best. . . . We *need* all the Firbank we can get. We need the example of his splendid inconsequence—seen backward with special effect through the work of Henry Green—to deliver us from the dull consequence of plot. We can be stimulated by the strategies of his dialogue: the constant flow of talk, at once witty and silly, real and artificial, to which no one listens, and into which everything, action and introspection, is dissolved—even the author's comment becoming just another voice among drawing-room voices. The effect is that of extreme fenestration; his works are all window and no wall, every possible element of structure sacrificed for the sake of light." RF's work reminds us "that the truth of fiction is in inverse proportion to its resemblance to any superficial 'reality.' . . . His revival coincides with the resurrection of F. Scott Fitzgerald, and the two have a good deal in common," which Fiedler goes on to demonstrate. Yet "both writers suffer finally from the same flaw—an inability to disengage themselves sufficiently from the values of the milieu they portray."

M., W. P. *Dublin Magazine* 26.2 (April-June 1952): 59.
After chiding himself for being "ungracious enough to complain that *Vainglory* or *Caprice* had been omitted in favour of less essentially characteristic work" in his review of *Five Novels*, the reviewer applauds the new volume (and Jones's "subtle" introduction) and expands upon his observations from the earlier review. "Awareness of beauty and transience, a longing amid weariness for some goal, or glory, or affection—these are the constants which hold his mocking, perverse, occasionally obscene inconsequence together. These and a style laboriously perfected to its apparently carefree purposes preserve the true comedy and the satiric intention amidst the affectations and artificialities of his idle world."

New Yorker, 14 April 1951, 139.
"Briefly Noted" but favorably: "Dealing mostly with English life, [these three novels] are somewhat less exotic and fantastic than his better-known later ones, but they are almost equally brilliant."

Publishers Weekly, 31 March 1951, 1505.
Brief announcement.

Redman, Ben Ray. "Giddy and Gay." *Saturday Review of Literature* 34 (28 April 1951): 14.
Redman here repeats his qualified praise of RF from his review of *Five Novels* and again insists RF must not be taken too seriously: "One may even suspect that he was never happier than when he was saying nothing—or almost nothing—quite perfectly, while impishly conveying the impression that he must be saying much more." RF's novels, like Peacock's, "stand well apart from the broad highway of English fiction" but will always have their admirers.

Snow, C. P. "Books and Writers." *Spectator* 175 (19 January 1951): 82.
A joint review of reissues of the works of RF and Ada Leverson, between whom Snow finds some similarities. He considers RF "one of the pioneers of the moment-by-moment novel," which sacrifices mind and emotion for a succession of sensations. Snow finds such an approach artistically misguided, yet concedes RF "has several claims on our admiration—a genuine originality (when he began writing there was no one in the least like him), a remarkable eye, a kind of eldritch gaiety." Snow also finds RF "devoid of moral vanity; he was the least stuffed of men; he exposed the nerve of his perverse sexual temperament, with an abandon that few writers had done before him," and suggests this quality has had great impact, "especially on the young."

The Complete Ronald Firbank
Introduction by Anthony Powell
London: Duckworth, 1961
Norfolk, CT/New York: New Directions, 1961
The Complete Firbank. London: Duckworth, 1973
The Complete Firbank. London: Picador, 1988

Alvarez, A. "Prancing Aesthete." *New Statesman* 61 (12 May 1961): 753-54.
Rpt. in his *Beyond All This Fiddle: Essays 1955-1967.* London: Penguin, 1968.
202-7.
   "Firbank's novels have been done no good at all by the Firbank myth," but
fortunately the novels have outlived the myth and RF "emerges as a curiously
impressive writer—scarcely inspiring, perhaps, but of considerable subtlety and
originality. . . . In a way, all his work can be read as a kind of uneasy
acknowledgement of the tensions that run just below the level of social chatter."
RF's writing is usually economical and precise in its invocations; "Firbank's
lush, moody overwriting occurs extensively only in *Santal* and *Valmouth*—his
Brideshead Revisited, and equally disastrous. . . . In their bright way, Firbank's
novels have more in common with Eliot's 'A Game of Chess' than with the pure
purple of Lawrence Durrell or, as Mr Powell suggests, with Proust or Joyce."
But RF's characters are indistinguishable: "they all talk alike, think alike and
behave alike," and his plots are likewise "barely distinguishable." His fictional
events rarely lead anywhere, "Yet since all the works are, to use his own phrase,
'Studies in Temperament,' events are not really needed. He can achieve all his
effects through the pauses and flickering of polite talk." He thereby achieves "a
kind of verbal *pointillisme,* which, instead of defining the scene straight out,
makes it shine through the contrasting, often clashing details. . . . The persis-
tent, underlying theme in all his work is the total, heartless disconnection of one
person from another; everything is gossip and manoeuvering," but RF never
dealt with this theme seriously enough. James's *The Awkward Age* seems to have
been a stronger influence upon RF than the *Yellow Book,* but unlike James RF
could never get "far enough outside his characters to see them dispassionately
for what they were worth."

[Barber, Michael.] *Books,* February 1988, 9.
   Announces the forthcoming Picador edition of *The Complete Firbank* and
notes RF's influence on Waugh, Compton-Burnett, and perhaps Hemingway.

————. *Books,* April 1988, 9.
   Quotes Connolly on RF's class attitudes to explain "why Firbank is not
everybody's cup of tea. But his influence is apparent in writers as different as
Hemingway, Huxley and A. N. Wilson, which is why he's worth dipping into."

Hogan, William. *San Francisco Chronicle,* 22 December 1961, 29.
   The reviewer expresses wonder "that anyone would bother now to print such
a book by a talent that appears to be a carbon copy of so many other dazzling
talents of various nationalities with roots in the 19th Century." He allows that
"This collection stands a very good chance of becoming chic, if restricted in its
importance."

Jones, Alun R. "His Daydreams Were Works of Art." *New York Times Book
Review,* 5 November 1961, 1, 38.
   RF "is securely and agreeably lodged in literary history both as writer and

legend," and of his ten published novels "at least four are unique, if minor, works of art." All of them "chart the charming, absurd and narrow world of Firbank's imagination . . . a world in which daydream translates reality into fantasy; in which wit, feeling for exotic beauty and love of the theatrical have freedom to move with grace and style; in which a sense of life's comedy overcomes—though often only barely—a profound sense of life's pathos. Firbank's novels are, at one and the same time, both intensely personal and severely disciplined productions." Jones summarizes RF's life (drawing from Fletcher's *Memoir* and apparently Jocelyn Brooke's *Ronald Firbank*), singles out *Vainglory* as "perhaps his best novel," and praises RF's use of dialogue: "Notwithstanding certain irritating repetitions and mannerisms, Firbank's gift for reproducing the authentic tones and cadences of speech and for controlling the rambling, inconsequential patterns of conversation is unique in modern fiction. In this all subsequent novelists have learned from him." RF's world is essentially amoral, "yet he confuses ugliness with sin and inexperience with virtue." Jones concludes his enthusiastic review: "His style, his tone and his technique have been vigorously infectious in the work of his successors and although—it is hoped—he will never be considered a 'significant' writer, his novels will continue to be accepted as what they are, minor classics."

In a letter to the editor entitled "Facts on Firbank" (3 December 1961, p. 66), Edward Martin Potoker complains that Jones's review "does the English novelist little service because of the numerous errors" such as writing on blue postcards, paying for his books' publications, and burial next to Keats. Potoker goes on to disagree with Jones's choice of *Inclinations* and *Vainglory* as RF's best works, much preferring *Valmouth* and *The Flower beneath the Foot*.

Listener, 17 March 1988, 22.
A brief review of Picador's reissue: Powell's introduction is "unhelpful and even patronising, and the first two fictions (*Odette* and *The Artificial Princess*) are strictly for the converted. [¶] The thing to do is to make straight for *Vainglory* and take it from there (skipping *Santal* too). Under the mauve coloration, the most radical of modernists is at work, the man who taught Waugh and Huxley and Powell, even the young Hemingway, how it was done. Firbank was a great innovator, a great sweeper away of clutter, and above all a great humorist."

"More Than Just Dandy." *Time*, 10 November 1961, 99.
An overview of RF's life and work (mostly from *Time*'s 1949 review of *Three Novels*). "Firbank's work belongs to the great body of literature which says that life is cruel, beautiful and impossible to explain."

New York Herald Tribune Books, 24 December 1961, 11.
Brief description of contents.

Observer, 31 January 1988, 26.

[Paul, David.] "Butterfly at Large." *Times Literary Supplement*, 28 April 1961, 259.
"He has now reached the stage where the failures (*Odette, Santal, Zoubaroff*) are valuable for the light they throw on the achievement," which is great according to this sympathetic reviewer. "No other novelist has travelled so light, or conveys so much in proportion to weight. . . . He applies the economy of poetry to the novel, proceeds by hiatus. A phrase fills out a paragraph. He took all that verbal wadding out of the novel, and left it, to some eyes, rather bare. . . . His

. . . message? The omnipresence of human folly, uncertainty of anything else."
Aside from a few objections to the editing, Paul finds RF and this edition in
particular splendid. (Also notes the Penguin *Valmouth* omnibus.)

Plomer, William. "Humoresques." *Listener* 65 (18 May 1961): 886, 888.

RF is "a freakish and solitary original and fantast, admittedly, but a master of
ellipsis and innuendo. . . . As a fictionist (the word *novelist* is somehow too
stodgy to apply to so airy a performer) he freed himself completely both from
the soft-focus aestheticism and the commonplace realism of his period. . . . He
devoted himself to his art, and now has won the wider fame he could not have
expected in his lifetime."

Raven, Simon. "The Courts of Cockayne." *Spectator* 206 (28 April 1961): 613-
14.

After tracing (with considerable ingenuity) the development of RF's most
characteristic themes and techniques, Raven comes to two conclusions: "the
Firbankian Court-World . . . is in good part the reverie of a masturbator" in that
it is filled with "endless and loveless self-titillation. . . . But secondly, one medi-
tates that a masturbator, although he may destroy himself, is self-sufficient
while he lasts and cannot be destroyed by others. Paradoxically enough, in
Firbank's case he is even self-perpetuating. For given his emotional indepen-
dence, and then given his brilliance of phrase, his mastery of the rhythms of
dialogue, his ironic love of describing *chic,* his canny relish for human frailty—
given, above all perhaps, his flexible, discriminating, precise yet never quite
pedantic prose—Firbank has succeeded in making an enduring world which has
an atmosphere like no other and to which it is always a pleasure to return. This
world, like its maker and its inhabitants, is indestructible and, in his own terms,
forever valid."

Toynbee, Philip. *Observer,* 1961.

Finds in RF's works "elegance, brilliant invention, economy, wit and beauty."

The New Rythum and Other Pieces
Introduction by Alan Harris
London: Duckworth, 1962
Norfolk, CT/New York: New Directions, 1963

Brophy, Brigid. "Mauve Roots." *London Magazine* 2 (October 1962): 78-81.
Rpt. as "Firbank" in her *Don't Never Forget: Collected Views and Reviews* (Lon-
don: Jonathan Cape, 1966), 243-48. Rpt., abridged and updated, as "Slim
Prancing Novelist" in her *Reads* (London: Penguin/Cardinal, 1989), 37-43.

Begins with the bold declaration: "The three greatest novels of the twentieth
century are *The Golden Bowl, A La Recherche Du Temps Perdu* and *Concerning
The Eccentricities of Cardinal Pirelli,*" and notes "Not only the styles but the
mental attitudes of all three writers have been formed by the aesthete's practice
of continual refinement"—James and Proust by addition, RF by subtraction.
She considers *The New Rythum* "a masterpiece" and contrasts its "excellent"
introduction to Powell's "dreadful" one in *The Complete Ronald Firbank.* She
comments on RF's interest in French culture and flowers, and on the tragic
dimension of his novels, despite his "unparalleled wit" and a combination of
farce and wisecracks that "resemble only Groucho Marx's." RF's novels are a
fusion of nineties decadence and foreign exoticism.

May, James Boyer. "Meaning/s & The WORD: 20th Century Assay." *Trace* 51 (Winter 1963-64): 343.

Notes Firbank's growing prestige and the evidence of his craftsmanship from the ms. materials in *The New Rythum*. Although the title piece is too fragmentary, the early pieces are "excellent entertainment."

Mayne, Richard. "Needlework." *New Statesman* 64 (17 August 1962): 207.

The reviewer quotes several quotable remarks from the book, suggesting it is better to dip into RF rather than read him whole. Only RF's fans will find *The New Rythum* appealing, and even they might find "the tittering, soutanes-and-salacity aspect" of his work tiresome. "Making fun of fashionable gossip-writers, he aped their manner, sometimes, all too well; and his innumerable, brilliantly named 'ladies' . . . too often exude the camp, gushing atmosphere of female impersonations, like the creations of an embarrassed adolescent who has just discovered that his aunts enjoy sex." Nevertheless, "Good jokes are worth a little affectation; and in some of Firbank's tilting at Edwardian manners there was more than just a joke. Moreover, his needle-sharp, allusive and elliptical writing makes a truly astonishing contrast with almost anything comparable at the time." Mayne concludes: "his delicate embroidery, directly descended from Congreve, was in turn the preparation for Aldous Huxley and Evelyn Waugh. This, it's true, severely delimits his achievement; but he wouldn't have scorned the ambiguous credentials of a *petit-maître*."

Mitchell, Julian. "Dot Dot Dot." *Spectator* 209 (17 August 1962): 222-23.

RF's reputation is settled: "We recognise his originality, we acknowledge his limitations, we have absorbed him and we have been amused by him. No one before or since has managed so successfully his satirical-sentimental *mélange adultère de tout*, with its high-flown High-Camp-High-Church-High-Society, its Wildean heights of wit and its choirboy snigger. He is a miniaturist: if we recognise that his attempts to go beyond himself end in flatulence, we are happy to add that his rows of dots are more eloquent than some novelists' chapters. All this is agreed, except by those who find him wholly unreadable; for them we are sorry." RF's literary sources were, "primarily, the writers of the Nineties, salted with French decadence and flavoured by herbs from the middle ages, the whole stirred by Maeterlinck." RF's technical innovations can be traced to the last-named author, and similarities can be found with contemporaries such as Eliot and Pound. But RF never fully broke with the Nineties, as *The New Rythum* demonstrates. "But it is only a draft, and he was dying as he wrote. One is grateful for many small felicities."

New Yorker, 20 July 1963, 91-92.

"Although none of these pieces show Firbank at his best, all of them display that fastidious wickedness—that combination of naughtiness and whimsy, bite and nonsense—that made him a kind of improbable link between Lewis Carroll and Edward Gorey, Oscar Wilde and Evelyn Waugh, and a splendid fop and artist in his own right."

[Paul, David.] "Fabergé of Fiction." *Times Literary Supplement*, 3 August 1962, 555.

Although RF marked many of these pieces "not to be published," he destroyed none. "What clearer invitation could there be to posthumous printing?" Some of the pieces "suggest Maeterlinck and rose-water," others Saki or Beerbohm. Of the extracts, "those from a one-act play, *A Disciple from the Country*, seems the most tantalizing," while the unfinished novel "proves some-

thing of a disappointment. . . . Either, one feels, the author would have drasti-
cally cut, concentrated, re-injected the whole piece, or else abandoned it, saving
a few fragments for some other confection. [¶] But the book as a whole gives us
an invaluable perspective on the life-and-work. . . . And, whatever the ups and
downs of its contents, it confirms too that Firbank remains the one and only
Fabergé of fiction—a whole Ukiyoye school of mood and mannerism in himself."

Plomer, William. *Listener* 68 (9 August 1962): 218.
   A brief description of the contents. Plomer wonders if the strawberry-pick-
ing incident in *The New Rythum* could have been suggested by that in Austen's
Emma and praises RF's "exactitude. It is not his queerness but his mixture of
playfulness and crystalline precision that has made him last."

Potoker, Edward Martin. "Eccentrics in a Mirage." *New York Times Book Review,* 2 June 1963, 5, 26.
   Describes the background to this collection and laments "Firbank did not
live to finish his [New York] book, because the substantial fragment he left us
reveals some of the best qualities of his writing: the sensuous and elliptical style,
the satirical bite, the infallible instinct for rendering social behavior. . . . The
other pieces in this volume date from the author's youth and are largely interesting for the light they shed on his methods and sources."

Willis, Katherine Tappert. *Library Journal* 88 (15 May 1963): 2008.
   A brief description with a recommendation "for all literary collections."

Complete Short Stories
Edited by Steven Moore
Elmwood Park, IL: Dalkey Archive Press, 1990

Anderson, David. *Lambda Book Report* 2 (January 1991): 35.
   RF's "languorous, exquisitely told tales are reminiscent of the daydreams of
Molina in *Kiss of the Spider Woman.* The stories feature "a rich, comic array of
characters" and are written "with a sense of style and a mastery of language rare
for any college-age writer." RF's later novels are "more accomplished works and
more important for their influence on other writers. . . . But reading these
charming short stories will wile away an evening or two. Such entertaining
period pieces shouldn't always be passed up for something edifying."

Aubrey, Bryan. *Library Journal,* 15 September 1990, 78.
   "This book will be of interest to students and scholars of Firbank—it enables
his literary development to be seen more completely—but the general reader,
particularly if unfamiliar with Firbank's novels, is unlikely to find the stories of
great interest."

Barnhill, Sarah. "Firbank's Juvenilia." *English Literature in Transition, 1880-
1920* 34.4 (1991): 489-92.
   Hopes another Firbank revival will soon be under way, but doesn't feel this
book will help. A more accurate title would be "Selected Juvenilia of Ronald
Firbank," and the reviewer has doubts whether the book should have been published. "The merit in *Complete Short Stories* is that which is commonly found
when any writer's juvenilia is unearthed—the discovery of the seeds of style and

theme that will grow to fruition in later work. . . . To the student of the Firbank canon, what is of greatest interest in this early fiction is the appearance of a character type best described as the Sensual Saint, that character who is torn between the taking of the veil at a convent and the taking of tea at the Savoy." The reviewer feels an introduction and more textual notes would have improved the edition, and wishes that she were reviewing instead the Viking Portable Firbank that W. H. Auden wanted to edit.

Brosnahan, John. *Booklist,* 1 October 1990, 255.
    The stories "foreshadow the extravagance" of RF's "astonishing novels," "but also encapsulate much of Firbank's perfumed and precious approach to life and art."

Davis, Robert Murray. *World Literature Today* 65.3 (Summer 1991): 494.
    The juvenilia shows where RF had been rather than where he would go, but one can see him working toward "tales about people whose sophistication and naïve longing clash with comic effect."

Dirda, Michael. "The Triumph of Frivolity." *Washington Post Book World,* 16 December 1990, 6.
    Only the penultimate paragraph deals with the stories, half of which "are pastels in prose, saccharine bits of whispy fluff" and only a few of which "provide the genuine Firbank tang." The rest of the review recounts RF's life, career, reputation, influence, and quotes some of RF's more memorable lines. Dirda concludes: "Ronald Firbank's books, blessed with insouciance and daring, may not be for everybody but they do possess one of the true elements of a classic: They can be read again and again with ever-deepening pleasure. In the right mood they are very nearly the most amusing novels in the world."

Kirkus Reviews, 1 August 1990, 1025.
    "The world could get along without half" of these stories, "but at least six are flawless marvels of delicate pastoral satire. . . . The successes spin webbed silver." Singles out "Lady Appledore's Mésalliance" for particular praise, and summarizes the book as "Glowworms caught in an ostrich feather."

Pekar, Harvey. "Rediscovering an Overlooked Oddity." *San Diego Tribune,* 7 September 1990, C-3, C-18.
    Begins by summarizing RF's influences and the novelists that he, in turn, influenced (Waugh, Huxley, Compton-Burnett, Powell, Spark, Coward) and notes that the present collection "varies widely in tone and quality." Some stories "are embarrassingly affected and precious," but "When Widows Love" and "A Tragedy in Green" are cited for their "accomplished wit."

Phelps, Donald. "Unassembled Parts of a True Eccentric." *Chicago Tribune,* 17 September 1990, "Tempo," 3.
    RF's mature style was "a masterpiece of orchestration. . . . Tapping his own hidden vein of occult discipline, Firbank brought forth a style both loose-jointed and sure-footed, a mischievous, tender, stately melding and meshing of tones that offers a glass for viewing the Edwardian world as a Fairground of Folly. The sometimes riotous contradictions of his writings, the lush colors and fragrances that festoon his paragraphs, serve as counterpoint to the appraisal— ironic, rueful, sometimes touched with affection—of a case-hardened tourist in the guise of a rudderless dilettante." In such stories as "When Widows Love," "Her Dearest Friend," and "A Study in Opal," "the masochism of the Wilde

imitations is purged and rendered as mature pity. . . . This valuable and well-edited book is a restorative for lovers of Firbank and an eye-opener for both old and new acquaintances."

Publishers Weekly, 13 July 1990, 42.

A brief but positive review of the book's contents, concluding: "Despite his fanciful subjects . . . it is not Firbank's plots that fascinate but rather his *art pour l'art* rendering of a world peopled by beautiful grotesques."

Publishers Weekly, 2 August 1991, 70.

A note on the paperback edition, quoting from its 1990 review.

Williamson, Chilton, Jr. *Chronicles,* July 1991, 38.

"*The Complete Short Stories* confirms Firbank as a master of what is called today 'irreverence,' combined with the pithy moral judgment based on a system of traditional values." Most of the stories are "clever and original. Brilliant with an artificiality that they at once reflect and condemn, they are the product of an exquisitely aesthetic imagination that delights in revealing the vanity of the aesthetic imagination." The stories anticipate not only RF's later novels but Waugh's as well ("'A Study in Opal' reads like a clear prophesy of Waugh's greatest novel, *A Handful of Dust*").

The Early Firbank
Edited by Steven Moore. Introduction by Alan Hollinghurst
London: Quartet Books, 1991

Breakwell, Ian. "Thistledown Jewels." *New Statesman,* 2 August 1991, 56.

RF is "one of the greatest English prose stylists and black humourists. His intricate collage-narratives anticipate William Burroughs' cut-up routines, Joe Orton's amoral satires of social pretension, and Harold Pinter's unnerving meanings, hidden in seemingly inconsequential conversation." The stories and playlets include both "brittle sketches of high society" and "outmoded mood pieces." The reviewer questions the ethics of publishing juvenilia against an author's wishes, but concludes: "if the nascent talent, fitfully displayed, encourages reading of his adult masterpieces, then its publication will serve a welcome purpose."

Curtis, Anthony. "A Legend out of His Lifetime." *Financial Times,* 24-25 August 1991.

Recounts the Firbank legend and notes some of those who have written about RF. *The Early Firbank* "is a volume all Firbankians will wish to possess," and he notes the "several, dominant, manipulative, aristocratic women in these stories who lament, in polished epigrams, their lot as widows or wives of boring men," agreeing with Hollinghurst that these are "fictional manifestations of Lady Firbank." He concludes by noting the resemblances between RF and female impersonator Barry Humphries, who owns the manuscripts of two of the stories published here.

Gale, Patrick. "Seraphic Lust." *Daily Telegraph,* 3 August 1991.

Discusses RF's relation to Saki and E. F. Benson—and finds him more daring and unsettling than either—and reports that much of *The Early Firbank* "is of interest solely as a series of revealing teenage *homages* to influences on the greedily bookish and self-consciously European writer." The stories "offer scattered clues to Firbank's adolescent psychology, such as numberless looking-glasses and pervasive imagery of somnolence and death," and the novelist-reviewer recommends that "Firbank-virgins and casual dippers should turn to the later, more polished offerings, 'Lady Appledore's Mésalliance' . . . and 'A Study in Opal.'"

Parker, Peter. "Firbank in Embryo." *Times Literary Supplement*, 30 August 1991, 18.

Discusses the influence of Wilde's *Salomé* on the two plays published here and of Wilde's fairy tales on several of the stories. *A Disciple from the Country*, "A Study in Opal," and "A Tragedy in Green" "are particularly welcome additions to the published canon." The editing is "conscientious but erratic," the introduction "brief but alert." Overall, a "fascinating edition of juvenilia."

Taylor, D. J. "A Hothouse Atmosphere." *Spectator*, 27 July 1991, 32.

Describes the contents and notes that "these pieces are marked by a style that has not quite tugged free of its origins. . . . Firbank's early work is 'decadent' in the strictest sense, which is to say that his analogies tend to be taken from art rather than nature. . . . It is a tiny, tightly circumscribed orbit of reference, governed by a curiously inhuman sense of beauty." Singles out "When Widows Love," "Lady Appledore's Mésalliance," and "A Study in Opal" for praise, and concludes: "For all the camp air of suppressed naughtiness, there is something sharp and hard about these fragments—and about their creator. 'A certain steely something,' Hollinghurst calls it. Even here, as a very young man, aloof-ness and watchful self-possession were the distinguishing marks of Firbank's character. The result may be juvenilia, but of a rare and scintillating sort."

The opening of this review is quoted by Quentin Oates in the *Bookseller* (2 August 1991, 341) in a discussion of Taylor's review of another book.

Complete Plays
Edited by Steven Moore
Normal, IL: Dalkey Archive Press, 1994

Davis, Robert Murray. *World Literature Today* 68.4 (Autumn 1994): 821.

Regards the plays "as apprentice work at the bejeweled workbench of Oscar Wilde. Fortunately, in the years between *The Mauve Tower* . . . and *A Disciple from the Country* . . . he moved from the wholly pernicious influence of *Salome* to *An Ideal Husband*. By 1920, when he published *The Princess Zoubaroff: A Comedy*, he was at least in the vicinity of *The Importance of Being Earnest*."

[Dirda, Michael.] *Washington Post Book World*, 17 July 1994, 13.

Less a review of this book than a brief recommendation of RF's works: "Though Firbank's comic novels, with their fey characters, twee plots and campy humor, may seem as light and inconsequential as souffles, they are built to last."

Lambda Book Report 4.4 (May/June 1994): 45.

A brief description of the contents.

Kennelly, Louise. *English Literature in Transition* 38.2 (1995): 278.

A brief notice, taken from the jacket copy.

Miller, Howard E. *Library Journal,* 15 May 1994, 74.
    A brief description of contents, derived largely from the jacket copy. Of *Princess Zoubaroff,* the reviewer says: "Its openly gay and lesbian scenes and theme mark it as one of Firbank's most daring pieces."

Olson, Ray. *Booklist,* 1-15 June 1994, 1735.
    "The principal English bearer of camp sensibility between Wilde and Coward," RF dramatizes in his plays the "camp characteristic of being enthusiastic about serious things for the wrong reasons." *The Mauve Tower* is dismissed as juvenilia; "*Disciple* offers just enough glib superciliousness to be utterly amusing; *Zoubaroff,* though it has its moments, rather too much."

Pekar, Harvey. "Butterfly on a Rack." *San Francisco Bay Guardian: Literary Supplement,* May 1994, 20.
    Notes RF's mixed critical reputation, despite his being "one of this century's finest and most original British writers." He dismisses *The Mauve Tower* as "an affected juvenile effort," but praises *A Disciple from the Country* and *The Princess Zoubaroff.*

Publishers Weekly, 13 June 1994, 52.
    Brief description of RF's career and contents of the new volume.

Part 2

Books about Firbank
(and their reviews)

Ifan Kyrle Fletcher, *Ronald Firbank: A Memoir*
London: Duckworth, 1930
New York: Coward McCann, 1932

Fletcher's biography of RF (pp. 13-100) is followed by personal reminiscences by Vyvyan Holland, Augustus John, Osbert Sitwell, and Lord Berners (101-50). Together, the memoirs constitute the basis not only of the Firbank biography but of the Firbank "legend," for here are recounted for the first time many of the eccentricities of RF that have been repeated by reviewers and critics ever since. Only 1500 copies were printed, and many of these were destroyed by enemy action in World War II. The entire contents of the volume were reprinted (with some emendations) as Part 1 of *Ronald Firbank: Memoirs and Critiques,* edited by Mervyn Horder (London: Duckworth, 1977). Since this edition is more accessible, page references will be to it rather than the original edition.

Fletcher's biographical sketch (3-56) begins with an overview of RF's family background, continues with his boyhood and education, and notes the influence of French literature, Roman Catholicism, and travel on the young writer. RF's first book was "tiresomely precious, lacking the humour which farced his novels" (9-10) and his other early writings clearly show his indebtedness to Maeterlinck. By "the end of 1905 his was a developed personality" (11). RF's time at Cambridge (1906-9) is described in some detail, and his friendships (especially with Rupert Brooke) noted. After Cambridge began the pattern of travel, reading, and writing that occupied RF until his death. Fletcher details his travels and the publication of his books, their critical reception, and offers his own views of them. He records memories of RF (from book-sellers to writers like Aldous Huxley) and offers a broad literary context (from Congreve to the Harlem Renaissance) for understanding RF's work. Although superseded by later biographies, Fletcher's pioneering essay remains invaluable.

Vyvyan Holland (56-63) writes of RF's Cambridge days, his friendships there, and the aborted attempt to introduce RF to Ada Leverson. He saw little of RF in later years. "I always think of Ronald Firbank as an unhappy man who, luckily for him, had the power of expressing himself through his books" (63).

Artist Augustus John (64-65) recalls the times RF sat for his portrait. "Firbank believed in himself. He knew he could write beautifully" (65).

Osbert Sitwell's contribution (65-82) is an expanded version of his biographical memoir in vol. 1 of *The Works.* It is a leisurely and engaging account of how he first learned of RF and, upon befriending him, of his habits and personality. "Virtuosity and manner were for him the chief merits of literature" (72). (See part 3 for the numerous reprinted versions of this essay.)

Lord Berners (82-85) recalls his first meeting with RF, the difficulty of being his friend, and recounts RF's death in Rome.

*

[Brooks, E. H. J.] "Ronald Firbank." *Times Literary Supplement,* 15 January 1931, 40.

The five selections "paint a single if not especially attractive portrait; a personality, if rather less than a man, emerges. . . . For with one possible minor exception, nothing is recorded of him which is not, in essence, simply silly." The unsympathetic reviewer concludes that "to-day he appeals only to those others who are young enough to believe that a negative attitude is more important than a positive purpose. Technical skill in literature he certainly had, but the validity of his achievement and his experiments has already been questioned in these columns (March 21, 1929 [West's review of *The Works*]). He was, as a writer at least, that dreariest of beings—an artist without values. Like Wilde, he pretended to be concerned not with vice and virtue, but with vulgarity and elegance, forgetting, or refusing to acknowledge, that elegance can upon occasion be the acme of vulgarity."

In a letter to the editor published a week later (22 January, p. 60), Fletcher corrects the reviewer's impression RF was a wealthy man. "I suggest that much of the truth about Firbank is concealed in a very real fear of poverty. Decreases of dividends kept this fear alive until the very end. Acting on a pathologically nervous system this induced the condition of elegance which your reviewer detests."

New Statesman 36 (31 January 1931): 498.
"The little book on Firbank is not autobiographical, but his friends were sufficiently impressed by him to step aside and let us see him pose, pirouette, exclaim and tremble. He leaves the impression of a telephone bell, detached, the ringing of which no one can stop, and so it goes on, and the company can pay attention to nothing else, and yet from it get no real communication."

Orrick, James. *Bookman* 75 (December 1932): 864.
The reviewer finds Fletcher's style careless, Holland "charming but vague," John brief, and Sitwell the best of the contributors: "Here, if anywhere in this volume, one feels the real Firbank."

Saturday Review 150 (20 December 1930): 838.
"That Ronald Firbank had charm, that he could win affection, this book proves, and it abundantly shows the reason why he was so lonely, was so disliked by many, suffered so greatly. An æsthete, intensely self-conscious, intensely nervous: driven by his temperament to do, as also to be, just what aroused the maximum of attention, the maximum of disapprobation from that great multitude that is suspicious of beauty and merciless to decadence."

Soskin, William. *New York Evening Post,* 5 November 1932, 7.
Calls RF a "strange, hot-house bloom that rose incongruously out of the simple, healthy, prosaic Public School soil of England . . . [a] most decadently delicate, mauve-tinted youth who, hidden in his silken-robed room and surrounded by his incense burners, his jade and Egyptian figures, produced work which Carl Van Vechten described rather extravagantly."

Wright, Cuthbert. *Nation* 133 (9 September 1931): 262.
The reviewer praises this "courageous attempt to capture, without apology, the unbelievably rare and defiant soul of Ronald Firbank. Our only criticism of this rather enticing book is that, inevitably perhaps, it lacks the gossamer humor befitting any treatment of its utterly fantastic subject."

Jocelyn Brooke, *Ronald Firbank*
London: Arthur Barker, 1951; rpt. 1970
New York: Roy, 1951

A hundred-page introduction to the life and work, written in the late forties (before the reprinting of RF's novels) to rescue RF from critical neglect. An introduction makes distinctions: Huxley may have had RF in mind when describing the tales of Knockespotch in *Crome Yellow*, but Brooke feels RF was less a revolutionary than a reactionary, harking back to the 1890s. His temperament combines a fin-de-siècle sensibility with cynical self-mockery, and his fiction has more in common with music than art: Debussy is a good parallel, as is jazz. The economy of his novels has "a very simple explanation: Firbank simply left out the parts which he found boring to write" (13). To the obvious influences (Maeterlinck, Beardsley, Wilde) Brooke adds Baron Corvo, "late-Victorian lady-novelists such as Ouida and Marie Corelli" (16), and "the earliest Eliot (*Prufrock*) and the Edith Sitwell of the *Façade* poems" (17). His work is "innocent" in the sense that it lacks either moral judgment or immoral purpose.

Chapters follow on "The Life and Legend" (largely drawn from Fletcher's *Memoir*), "Juvenilia and the Early Works (1905-1915)," "The Middle Period (1916-1921)," and "The Last Novels (1923-1926)." The early works are feeble but contain elements that are essential features of his mature work. *Vainglory* is the turning point: better than its predecessors, but different from its successors. *Inclinations* "falls flat" (61), *Caprice* is more successful (Sarah Sinquier may be a projection of RF himself), and *Valmouth* is his "masterpiece, far and away better than anything he wrote" (67). Both *The Princess Zoubaroff* and *Santal* are failures. RF's last novels are, after *Valmouth*, his most satisfactory: *The Flower beneath the Foot* is "vintage Firbank" and the one most people probably have in mind when using the adjective "Firbankian"; *Prancing Nigger* may be RF's most conventional novel, but it is a successful one; *Cardinal Pirelli* is "Firbank's final fling, a gesture of defiance directed at the smug middle-class morality which he despised" (89). Although not "great" or "important" in the boring way some writers are, RF will never "be quite forgotten," Brooke concludes; "one will continue, now and again, to come across *Valmouth* or *Vainglory* on the special shelf which people keep for those books which they read purely for pleasure" (97).

*

Listener 45 (28 June 1951): 1055.
A brief review with some comparisons between Proust's world and RF's (prompted by Brooke's references to Proust on pp. 20-21).

MacCarthy, Sir Desmond. "Butterfly on the Wheel." *Sunday Times*, 6 May 1951, 3.

[Powell, Anthony.] "Portrait of Firbank." *Times Literary Supplement*, 1 June 1951, 339.
"Ronald Firbank is not an easy subject for a brief biography," but Brooke "discusses convincing reasons for considering him a writer who will always be of interest to those concerned with the technique of dialogue and the free play in a novel of the unconscious mind."

Webster, Harvey Curtis. "Each in His Way Knew How to Tell a Story." *New York Times Book Review,* 9 November 1952, 30.

In this group review of five volumes of Roy's English Novelists Series, Brooke's is singled out as one of the better ones, "though neither he nor anyone else would claim that this most fascinating eccentric of the twentieth century is 'important,' has to be read, or is a great writer."

Jocelyn Brooke, *Ronald Firbank and John Betjeman*
London: Longmans, Green, 1962

RF discussed on pp. 5-24, a distillation of Brooke's 1951 book.

Miriam J. Benkovitz, *A Bibliography of Ronald Firbank*
London: Rupert Hart-Davis, 1963
2nd ed. Oxford: Clarendon, 1982

A descriptive, annotated bibliography of primary (and selected secondary) materials, not only listing all of RF's published works, but giving details of their physical appearance and extensive background notes on their composition and process of publication. Section B, traditionally reserved for an author's contributions to books, was left blank in the first edition because Firbank made none, but in the second edition contains eleven books in which RF's letters and novels are quoted.

Between the first and second editions Benkovitz issued a limited edition *Supplement to "A Bibliography of Ronald Firbank"* (London: Enitharmon, 1980), all of which was incorporated into the expanded second edition.

*

Adams, Bernard. *British Book News,* May 1982, 280-81.

A descriptive review of the second edition, adding "Professor Benkovitz's annotations make very good reading since she enlivens them with numerous bibliographic asides." Adams notes RF's important role in the physical production of his books, and concludes: "This consolidated and amended edition is surely the last word in Firbank bibliography."

Davis, Robert Murray. *Books Abroad* 38 (Autumn 1964): 435.

Praises the first edition as "not only a landmark but virtually the first signpost in Firbank scholarship," largely because Benkovitz "is the first to draw information not from highly colored reminiscences or gossip but from the solid evidence of Firbank's correspondence."

[Hobson, Anthony.] "Studies in Firbank." *Times Literary Supplement,* 28 June 1963, 484.

A brief but favorable review; a few errors and omissions are noted, but the reviewer pronounces it "a first-class bibliography" and warmly recommends it to RF's admirers.

Horder, Mervyn. *Book Collector* 12 (1963): 380, 383.

This is more than just a bibliography: "indeed it is a new and essential piece of glass in the Firbank kaleidoscope." Horder points out a few omissions and agrees with Benkovitz's reluctance to assign RF's authorship to *Count Fanny's Nuptials*.

James, Elizabeth. *Library* 5.4 (December 1983): 438-39.
A brief, positive notice, with special attention given to the Grant Richards material.

Watson, John Gillard. *Notes and Queries* 30.6 (December 1983): 556-57.
Reviewing the second edition, Watson notes that a number of errors in the first that Brigid Brophy had pointed out were not corrected, but praises the work nonetheless, especially for its accounts of RF's relationship with Grant Richards.

Miriam J. Benkovitz, *Ronald Firbank: A Biography*
New York: Alfred A. Knopf, 1969
London: Weidenfeld and Nicolson, 1970

The first full-scale biography of RF, invaluable for its quotations from RF's unpublished letters, manuscripts, and notebooks, and for organizing all of the available facts of RF's life in a straightforward manner. It is not a "critical biography"; Benkovitz's remarks on the books themselves are usually limited to their circumstances of composition and publication, though she occasionally offers some critical remarks on them. (The exception is an extended analysis of *Cardinal Pirelli* on pp. 276-84.) Throughout the book, she insists that RF was a serious, innovative writer—not merely the eccentric exquisite recalled by his contemporaries—and that "No one in the history of English letters has been more dedicated to the literary vocation than Ronald Firbank." As can be seen below, the book struck many as somewhat pedestrian and unimaginative, but it remains the standard biography.

*

Adams, Phoebe. *Atlantic*, June 1969, 117.
A short note complaining that RF's "personal life" remains in shadow despite Benkovitz's best efforts.

Allen, Trevor. "Ronald Firbank, Sophisticates' Idol." *Contemporary Review* 216 (February 1970): 110-11.
A brief overview of the life and qualified praise for "an illuminating biography detailed enough to be definitive."

Booklist 66 (15 September 1969): 96.
A brief description of "a penetrating study."

Books and Bookmen 15 (April 1970): 19.

Cushman, Keith. *Library Journal* 94 (15 April 1969): 1623.
Finds Benkovitz's insights "acute and illuminating. This seems the definitive biography of an interesting minor writer."

Davis, Robert Murray. *Journal of Modern Literature* 1 (1971): 787-90.
A summary of Benkovitz's findings; Davis approves of her decision "not to

try to find the man in the works but to rely upon objective evidence" and, with some reservations, commends her perceptions of Firbank's technical achievements (especially on *Cardinal Pirelli*). Although the book "comes just short of being definitive," Davis is grateful for her construction of "a new and more accurate portrait of Firbank the artist and complex human being to replace the caricature extant in the minds of most who have heard of him at all."

Ewart, Gavin. "Discomfirter of Fools." *London Magazine* 10.3 (June 1970): 94-96.
   Describing it as "indispensable as background to serious students," Ewart summarizes the biography, praises RF for finding a new language, and concludes "Firbank's novels are seminal to the comic novel as we know it."

Freedman, Richard. "Next to Him, Max Beerbohm Reads Like Mailer." *Book World* (*Washington Post/Chicago Tribune*), 18 May 1969, 4.
   The reviewer hopes this "solid but readable" biography widens RF's readership, though he issues a caveat: "Unlike Wilde or Saki, whom he also resembles, Firbank's style is so tortuously involuted, so crammed with epigram and far-out metaphor, above all, so artificial, as to put off all but the hardiest reader. Affectation is so extreme with him as to cease to be affectation at all, but to become a unique voice. His tales are like the artifacts 'of hammered gold and gold enamelling' in Yeats's Byzantium, specifically designed to irritate the Common Reader but to delight the connoisseur." Prof. Freedman concludes by identifying RF as "a fascinating link between Yeats's 'Tragic Generation' of the 1890s and the glittering Mayfair of the 1920s—between the worlds of Wilde and Waugh."

Hafley, James. *Arizona Quarterly* 26 (Spring 1970): 83-85.
   "The shortcomings and the triumph of Miss Benkovitz's book are to be found in her adherence to providing 'the facts.'" Hafley feels she relies too heavily upon letters (which may have been written with ulterior motives) and avoids conjecture, which is often necessary "to make the data yield a personality." He repeats his 1956 thesis that the novels "are actually stringent critiques—like the drawings of Beardsley—of the frivolity they celebrate," and comments on RF's homosexuality, business acumen, and "utter loneliness."

Harcourt-Smith, Simon. "Too Shocking, Too Soon." *Evening Standard,* 7 April 1970, 25.
   Tells of visiting RF (with Osbert Sitwell): see Brophy's *Prancing Novelist,* 154, 177.

Heppenstall, Rayner. "The Light Touch." *Encounter* 34 (June 1970): 55-56.
   The novelist frankly admits "I can do without Firbank altogether," but "for Miss Benkovitz's book I have nothing but praise. It is so scholarly it hurts. No fault of Miss Benkovitz's that Firbank comes out so unattractive a personality and quite uneducated. The lack of charity is entirely mine."

Hodgart, Matthew. "Good Camper." *New York Review of Books,* 11 September 1969, 26-27 (with a David Levine caricature of RF on 26).
   In this review of both the biography and New Directions's reissue of *Five Novels,* Hodgart states RF "was not always exact" but, as the biography demonstrates, was "extremely painstaking" in composing his books, producing "that economical dialogue from which Evelyn Waugh learned so much." Thus RF's "later work, which looks so casual, must be taken seriously as craftsmanship."

Benkovitz corrects many of the misapprehensions surrounding this "mythical figure," but "she has failed to add any story or fact that adds anything striking to one's impression of Firbank," except for Cunard's reminiscences. Hodgart then discusses high camp ("of which Firbank is the outstanding exponent") and concludes with a brief evaluation of *Cardinal Pirelli* (which contains, he believes, a parody of Proust at one point): "The blending of learning and triviality throughout is perfect. It would be unFirbankian and pompous to call *Pirelli* a fable for our times; yet apart from his wonderful clowning, Firbank treats the theme of disorder and decay with melancholy Yeatsian grandeur."

Humphries, Barry. "Dainty Legends." *Spectator* 224 (31 January 1970): 148-49.

   "Unfortunately," Humphries laments two-thirds through this quirky and amusing review-reminiscence, "Firbank is a literary personality who survives in the popular imagination, not so much by his works, as by the fabric of anecdote," and it is from such fabric this review is woven. There are curious and inconclusive references to Simon Arrow, "Jocelyn Quilp," Quilp's chauffeur Dorothy ("a fount of anecdote" on RF), Michael Arlen, Carl Van Vechten, and Lord Alfred Douglas.

Kirkus Reviews 37 (1 April 1969): 412.

   RF's wit is purer than that of Wilde and Shaw, "the wit of fancy and eccentricity, a sensibility at once artificial and thoroughly idiosyncratic." This is a "finely-wrought and sensitive biography"; despite the gloom of his life, RF "created works of dazzling humor, wickedly gleaming personages and landscapes, a truly tonic double-entendre vision of joy and despair."

Manchester Guardian Weekly, 21 February 1970, 18.

Martinetti, Ronald. "Cackle and Confusion." *Wall Street Journal,* 29 May 1969, 18.

   Calls the book "a prime exhibit of poor academic writing" and gives an overview of the life and work. (Also includes notice of the reissue of *Five Novels.*)

Miller, Clyde. *Denver Quarterly* 5.3 (Fall 1970): 97-98.

   Notes that RF's amusing "legend" has damaged his standing with academic critics, and thus praises Benkovitz for "advanc[ing] the cause of Firbank criticism immeasurably by clearing away the superficialities of legend and revealing the growth of the artist in the man."

Mitchell, Julian. "Aide-de-Camp." *New Statesman* 79 (6 February 1970): 191-92.

   Mitchell calls RF "the patron saint of literate screaming queens, and one of the funniest English writers of this century," but Benkovitz offers little to what is already known and less literary insight than her predecessors. He adds Noël Coward to those probably influenced by RF and concludes with some reflections on literary camp.

Natale, A. Stephen. *Cithara* 10.1 (December 1970): 103-4.

   Because of the complexity of her subject, Benkovitz's achievement is all the more commendable. "*Ronald Firbank* does more than report the various peculiarities of his behavior; it discusses the reasons for them, speculates as to their origin, and places them in proper biographical perspective." Natale goes on to praise her brief analyses of the novels and her "tact, taste, and genuine empathy."

New Yorker, 2 August 1969, 76.
A brief, superficial note.

Observer, 1 February 1970, 29.

Potoker, Edward M. *Saturday Review,* 7 June 1969, 31-32.
"*Ronald Firbank* is not a definitive biography" because of still-living relatives and limited access to materials. "Nevertheless, Miriam Benkovitz has produced a work of art. . . . [RF] would have admired her sense of drama, her 'staging.' Most importantly, Ronald Firbank here emerges as a revolutionary writer. . . . Firbank's central theme is the dilemma of the sensitive individual who wishes to be honest but is isolated and then destroyed by the world." Potoker goes on to comment on RF's technical innovations and the influence he had on later writers, and predicts the timeless quality of his work "will continue to guarantee his reputation among a steadily increasing number of readers who appreciate the most insolent refinements of satire."

Powell, Anthony. *Daily Telegraph,* 1970. Rpt. in his *Under Review: Further Writings on Writers, 1946-1990.* London: Heinemann, 1991; Chicago: Univ. of Chicago Press, 1994. 311-13.
Laments that Benkovitz "writes without a glimmer of humour" and "little that is substantial is added to" Fletcher's *Memoir.* Benkovitz's criticism is "inept," deriving "from an inability to distinguish between comedy and satire." (Powell feels RF was a humorist rather than a satirist.)

Publishers Weekly, 17 March 1969, 54.
A brief but positive note: "Miriam Benkovitz lets her readers know in no uncertain terms that this man had genius, was an *avant garde* writer far ahead of his time, and merits a long-overdue appreciation. . . . Miriam Benkovitz does a service to readers who don't know Firbank's writings or the poignant, lonely life out of which they sprang."

Sheridan, Philip. "Far Away from His Country." *Carleton Miscellany* 11 (Winter 1970): 96-109.
Praises Benkovitz for demonstrating "there is a real basis for the admiration for Firbank" and, given RF's vulnerability, for resisting "the temptation to be malicious." The bulk of this lengthy review is a summary of RF's life, with some concluding remarks on RF's attitudes toward religion, women, and flowers.

Sokolov, Raymond A. "The Last Flower." *Newsweek,* 2 June 1969, 94, 96, 98.
RF's novels "are the last fragile flower of Edwardian refinement gone slightly rank," says Sokolov, who goes on to give a brief overview of the life, concluding with praise for Benkovitz's assiduous research, especially for contacting RF's surviving relatives.

Sykes, Christopher. "Firbankiana." *Listener* 83 (26 February 1970): 286.
Although Benkovitz "has got the record straight in the fullest detail," Sykes still prefers Nicolson's misleading "Lambert Orme" "because it tells more of what one is likely to want to know: namely, what the man was like." An authentic humorist, RF is unfortunate in having a biographer without a sense of humor. "The book is only acceptable if it is treated as a 'Firbank Companion' addressed exclusively to readers who already know his books and want to know further about where and under what circumstances he produced them."

[Taylor, John Russell.] "Baba's Hard-working Boy." *Times Literary Supplement,* 12 March 1970, 285.

Notes that Benkovitz seems to have limited herself merely to "the collection and arrangement of information" on RF, but the book fulfills its purpose. "By putting the pieces together, sorting fact from fiction, and gathering personal information about Firbank while there are still some people around to supply it, Miss Benkovitz has provided us with valuable material for the study of Firbank."

Weintraub, Stanley. *New York Times Book Review,* 11 May 1969, 1, 31.

A summary of the life, legend, and work, with almost no mention of the actual book under review, except to call it "thorough."

John Anthony Kiechler, *The Butterfly's Freckled Wings: A Study of Style in the Novels of Ronald Firbank*
Bern: Francke, 1969

The published version of a dissertation submitted to the University of Zurich in 1967 (unrevised for book publication). After an introduction that summarizes RF's life and critical reception, Kiechler devotes four chapters to RF's style: "Local Colour" (chap. 2), "Reported Speech" (3), "Dialogue" (4), and "Imagery" (5). By "local colour" he means English as spoken by foreigners (Mrs. Yajñavalkya in *Valmouth*), Italian and Arabic in *The Princess Zoubaroff* and *Santal,* respectively, the Franco-Negro dialect in *Prancing Nigger,* Spanish in *Cardinal Pirelli,* and American slang in *The New Rythum.* (Kiechler also notes the gallicisms that appear throughout RF's work.) Chap. 3 discusses RF's use of what linguists call "free indirect speech" to reveal his characters' inner thoughts (as opposed to dialogue for their public thoughts), arguing that in these passages RF reveals his more serious concerns with mortality. (Examples are given from almost all the works except *Inclinations,* where free indirect speech isn't used at all and which, consequently, "contains the least convincing collection of characters.") Chap. 4 on dialogue shows that RF used it not to advance the plot (as most novelists do) but to create atmosphere. He is best at upper-class British speech; less successful when attempting local color (as shown in chap. 2); again, examples are taken from nearly all the works. In chap. 5, Kiechler divides RF's imagery into three groups: synaesthetic (especially crossing color with other sensations), emblematic (especially beast imagery), and aesthetic (especially from literature and music). Examples are taken from all the works; *Vainglory* is singled out for detailed examination, especially its use of personification. In the first of two concluding chapters, Kiechler summarizes his findings and offers further observations on RF's work: "I was repeatedly struck by the fact that French borrowings and neologisms recurred in the passages of heightened eroticism." "Characters emotionally alienated from their fellow-men, establish an emotional rapport with buildings, pictures, music, and books." "Cases of balanced affection are lacking and the emphasis is on the heartless disconnection of one person from another." Kiechler discusses some influences on RF (especially Beardsley), and in the second concluding chapter discusses works that show RF's influence: Cyril Connolly's "Where Engels Fears to Tread," Auberon Waugh's *The Foxglove Saga,* Ivy Compton-Burnett's novels, and Brigid Brophy's *The Finishing Touch*—"really a posthumous monument to him."

James Douglas Merritt, *Ronald Firbank*
New York: Twayne, 1969

Intended for those unfamiliar with RF's work, this 148-page book begins with an overview of his accomplishments and background, then continues with discussions of all the major works (including *The New Rythum*) more or less in chronological order. In his introduction, Merritt disqualifies RF as a satirist because "to be a satirist the writer must exhibit a reasonably strong disapproval of those elements of society which he chooses to satirize, and Firbank does not." Regarding the sexual inversion of many of RF's characters, Merritt says "it is as though Firbank had done away with the whole problem of gender and substituted for it mere sexuality—albeit sexuality handled with kid gloves." He goes on to say "In Firbank's world the reader is always a *voyeur,* watching and over-hearing things which he probably shouldn't see or hear." RF's texts approach Joyce's in density, texture, and use of allusions. RF looked at the world with irony and humor. In his discussions of the novels, Merritt traces RF's development from an imitator of fin-de-siècle, decadent literature to an original artist using all the techniques of modernism. An annotated bibliography concludes this serviceable introduction.

*

Kantra, Robert A. *Journal of Modern Literature* 1 (1971): 790-91.
    The book is self-defeating in its contradictions, weak in its scholarship, and imprecise in its discussions of satire.

Edward Martin Potoker, *Ronald Firbank*
New York & London: Columbia Univ. Press, 1969

A 45-page analysis of RF's work (a condensation of his 364-page dissertation), beginning with "La Princesse aux soleils": admittedly "precious and slight, but with respect to its theme, mood, and imagery it anticipates major elements in his later work" (4). The Princess is RF's "initial version of the victimized innocent. A central theme in his novels is the dilemma of the individual, often a female, who is isolated from the surrounding world and then destroyed by it" (4-5). The Princess also suffers unrequited love, another major theme in RF's novels, beginning with his first, *The Artificial Princess.* "La Princesse" also demonstrates RF's knowledge of the French literary tradition and his love of floral imagery.
    The title of RF's early story "A Study in Temperament" is "meaningful, for all of Firbank's novels are studies in temperament" (7), and the story itself shows the direction RF would take, both in subject matter and technique. Potoker traces a line of development from Monsieur le Curé de Bois-Fleuri (in "Odette d'Antrevernes") to Bishop Bob (in "A Study in Opal"), Monsignor Parr (in *Vainglory*), the Archbishop of Cuna (in *Prancing Nigger*), finally to Cardinal Pirelli. "As Firbank's priests receive successive promotions within the Church hierarchy, they become increasingly abandoned and corrupt" (10). Potoker discusses RF's attitude toward Catholicism ("devious and ephemeral") and sin ("playful"), finding it more aesthetic than devout. He also notes RF's interest in paganism, magic, and superstition, and cites numerous passages from the novels demonstrating this interest. But "Firbank's ironic impulse, the most fundamental element in his nature, forestalled his taking one creed as the only

possible form of truth" (19).

Potoker discusses RF's letters to his mother and to Carl Van Vechten, finding them a more accurate indication of RF's character than the outlandish anecdotes that have circulated. He also notes the critical neglect RF suffered in his day, discusses his aesthetics, his form of humor, and his idiosyncratic style. He discusses in greater detail RF's three principal contributions to the novel: "structure, the art of dialogue, and elements of comic organization" (32). He finds a "striking precedent" for RF's novels in the structure and whimsicality of Sterne's *Tristram Shandy* (38-39) and contemporary parallels in the novels of Waugh and Huxley (especially the latter's *Crome Yellow*). Potoker concludes by underlining the satiric intent that runs through RF's work.

Nancy Cunard, *Thoughts about Ronald Firbank*
New York: Albondocani Press, 1971
Rpt. in Lord Horder's *Ronald Firbank: Memoirs and Critiques*, 122-26.

A 2000-word memoir written in 1954 at Miriam Benkovitz's prompting. She recalls that by 1919 RF was already "legendary," and in person he could be "extremely witty, of particular quickness." She discusses his relationship with Evan Morgan and tells the same story about RF suggesting violets for a homophobic young man's meal as Wyndham Lewis does. "He was like a dipping strand of willow with a nerve of steel, and that 'something' floating, bending but unbreakable in him is, of course, the integrity of the good artist."

Brigid Brophy, *Prancing Novelist: A Defence of Fiction in the Form of a Critical Biography in Praise of Ronald Firbank*
London: Macmillan, 1973
New York: Barnes & Noble, 1973

The longest, most ambitious, and most controversial book on RF to date. Convinced that RF has been underrated because most critics misunderstand the true nature of prose fiction, Brophy devotes the first 87 pages (part 1) to a defense of artistic fiction, which is distinguished from naturalistic fiction by its greater concern with technique, design, and the creative instinct. Part 2 (pp. 93-237) discusses RF's life, personality, and critical reception (with special attention to Fletcher's *Memoir* and Benkovitz's *Biography*). The enormous influence of Oscar Wilde on RF—on both his life and work—is the subject of part 3 (pp. 243-390), and part 4 (pp. 396-568) is an analysis of the writings themselves. Brophy combines close reading with bold speculation to argue that RF was a better, more imaginative writer than previously assumed. (RF's preface to *The Flower beneath the Foot* is reprinted as an appendix.) It is a deliberately provocative, even aggressive book, and predictably received mostly negative reviews. It is essential reading, however, for the Firbank student and a tour de force of creative criticism.

*

[Calder-Marshall, Arthur.] "The Classic Case of Firbank." *Times Literary Supplement*, 30 March 1973, 347-48.

Considers the book a failure on most counts: as a defense of prose fiction, as a work of literary biography and history, and as a commentary on RF's novels, arguing that Brophy's obvious ingeniousness is often over-ingenious and self-defeating.

Choice 10 (October 1973): 1188.
    "The place of Ronald Firbank in the history of English literature continues to be a very minor one and Brophy's 592-page attempt to elevate him to more serious consideration will probably alienate more readers than it will convince." The rest of the short notice continues in this negative vein.

Davis, Robert Murray. *Journal of Modern Literature* 4 (November 1974): 320-21.
    Although annoyed by the book, Davis grudgingly admits "no single aspect is entirely worthless. Her opening arguments, which defend the primacy of art over mimesis in fiction and the virtues of classical form and extol Firbank as modern exemplar of that form, are certainly defensible. But to rest the first two points on the third is to revise literary history in a way that many Firbankians would reject and to make Firbank's very real artistic achievement assume an intolerable burden." Although the middle of the book purports to be a "critical biography," Brophy "adds little to our knowledge of Firbank's external life. Markedly original, however, is her psychological interpretation of this material to illuminate Firbank's motives for writing. . . . Less happily, the psychological approach also leads her to free association, to hit-or-miss interpretation (especially of the significance of characters' names), and to baroque flights of speculation-as-fact." "The conduct and apparatus of Brophy's research in the first three-fourths of the book is even more erratic than her interpretations," as Davis demonstrates with a few examples. But the last fourth of the book is, for the most part, "genuinely illuminating," and Davis feels the interested reader is best advised to skip the first three parts and go directly to the last.

Dougill, David. "Firbank: A Long Look." *Books and Bookmen* 18 (May 1973): 32-36.
    A long essay-review dealing evenly with the faults and virtues of Brophy's book. "Never before have Firbank's life and writing come under such intense and sympathetic scrutiny. . . . But her book goes *too* far, and it goes on far too long." Dougill reviews RF's life, work, and the shifting currents of his critical reputation over the preceding fifty years. He feels Brophy's claim for RF as "the first novelist in English to create a 20th-century aesthetic, idiom and technique" is "nonsense," but finds her analysis of RF's technique to be "quite acute." Brophy's speculations are often illuminating, but just as often "there is a disproportion in the weight she gives to certain incidents." Although she "aims at—and achieves—a deeper insight into Firbank's character than Professor Benkovitz could manage," she is guilty of several scholarly lapses. Yet some of "Miss Brophy's speculations have a note of genius in them" and he praises her for her "detective intuition" in several instances. Dougill recounts (with apparent approval) Brophy's theory of the Wilde influence on RF and her arguments for the psychological importance of RF's artificial Eden, and spends the rest of the review speculating on the Firbank-Benson-Rolfe connection missed by both biographers (and for which he appends a short bibliography).

Furbank, P. N. "Ronald Firbank." *Listener* 89 (29 March 1973): 421-23.
    Furbank finds the book "at once so bad and so good one doesn't know whether to cheer or weep." He finds the first and third sections weak: the first

because it "shows a great innocence of literary history," and the third because it follows out too closely RF's alleged continuation of Wilde's "muddled" aesthetic. But Furbank finds the biographical and psychological material in part 2 absorbing and convincing. RF's work "is adorable and life-giving. . . . His own humour lives on quite another plane from [fin-de-siècle] 'naughtiness': it breathes despair of life but, at the same time, the most ardent love of the created world. . . . And what it extracts from the decadent and 'forbidden' is a heavenly innocence." The reviewer concludes by complaining of Brophy's diction in part 4, comparing it to "Firbank's Miss Sinquier in the Café Royal."

Gish, Robert F. *Modern Fiction Studies* 20 (Summer 1974): 259-60.
    Focuses on Brophy's ubiquitous presence in the book: "being more novelist than biographer she never allows the reader to forget her presence and in fact calls attention to it." Although she sometimes engages in "copious bitchery . . . in the best light, Ms. Brophy's biographical presence is amusing, especially her antagonistic asides to readers and reviewers."

Graver, Lawrence. "The Flower beneath the Footnotes." *New Republic,* 30 June 1973, 25-26.
    Brophy's book is "just the wrong kind of memorial for a writer as precious as Firbank," Graver feels, arguing that RF's fiction can't possibly live up to Brophy's extravagant claims. "About the extraordinary artifice of Firbank's fiction, Miss Brophy has shrewd things to say," but her "effort to establish Firbank as a major pioneer of modernism" is futile. "Firbank's essential limitations stem from the narrowness of his interests and the severity of his estheticism. . . . To escape he lived in his imagination and created in his novels an idiosyncratic secondary world in which wit, exoticism and outrageous affectation banish boredom and diminish pain."

Luckett, Richard. "Flower beneath the Foot." *Spectator,* 31 March 1973, 397-98.
    After summarizing Brophy's various theses, Luckett briefly wonders if the book is "an elaborate spoof" of a Ph.D. thesis, but decides not. He disapproves of her intrusive presence in the book, her "sloppy Freudianism," and her use of RF where a writer like Nabokov would have been better to advance her arguments about the nature of fiction. He concludes that Waugh's 6-page essay on RF (see part 3) is superior to her 600-page book.

Manchester Guardian Weekly, 7 April 1973, 25.

Marvin, John R. *Library Journal* 98 (July 1973): 2105.
    A short but positive review, praising Brophy's closeness to her subject ("all but telepathic") and her documentation "with copious detail (and with apparent omniscience) all that went into Firbank's life and novels."

Observer, 1 April 1973, 37.

Quinton, Anthony. "Anatomy of a Butterfly." *New Statesman* 85 (13 April 1973): 548, 550.
    Feels the massive claims made for RF are not adequately supported by Brophy's book. He has had a discernible influence on "gentleman-novelists" such as Waugh, Powell, and Berners, and Quinton gives qualified praise to Brophy's "prodigies of detection." RF's "great technical gift was concentration, produced, we may suppose, by vigorous cutting-out. But beyond the technique

lies the fact that he had something to cut out from, an idiosyncratic but coherent conception of life and the world, one in which limited expectation of happiness was enhanced by exact perception." Quinton concludes by chiding Brophy
for being unjust to Wilson's *New Yorker* essay on RF, "which makes many of the
points she is anxious to enforce in one-seventieth of the space."

Rosenthal, Michael. "The Fixer of Modern Camp." *New York Times Book Review,* 22 July 1973, 4.

Rejecting Brophy's view that artists "create formal artifacts in which all narrative interest is subordinate to over-all design," Rosenthal cannot "take
seriously Brophy's claims for Firbank. The estimate of Firbank as 'minor' has
nothing to do with the length of his books or his sexual preferences, but with
the simple fact that his novels lack that compelling vision of human experience
that great writers are capable of giving us." Inflating RF "beyond recognition,
she leaves Firbank a swollen, distorted hulk and makes a shambles of the English novel, which she is presumably defending." The book will appeal to
Firbankians, "but those not already committed to Firbank will hardly be
encouraged to sample him by the tendiousness and irresponsibility of much of
this book."

Spurling, John. "Unman the Barricades: Fictions and Factions in Criticism."
Encounter 41 (December 1973): 66-70.

Feeling that unrealistic writers like RF have been unduly neglected by "professional critics," Spurling applauds "the furious energy with which Brigid
Brophy springs to the rescue of her fellow-writer Ronald Firbank. . . . Thus she
presumably hopes to turn the tables on her adversaries, questioning not simply
their assumptions about Firbank, but their assumptions about how to approach
fiction in the first place." Brophy's defense of fiction makes "very good sense,"
but Spurling wonders if championing "innovatory, revolutionary fiction" over
realistic fiction likewise falls short of the ideal of judging writers solely "by the
novels they have written rather than by the theories of writing they are supposed
to exemplify."

Washington Post Book World, 10 June 1973, 15.

A brief, unsigned note worth quoting in full: "Even if you finish Brophy's
592 pages still convinced (against her impassioned arguments) that Firbank is a
minor novelist, the journey to this foregone conclusion is a remarkable one and
enriching. It is tenable that Brophy's true medium is the *obiter dictum* and that
the real function, for her, of an ostensible subject is that of a rack on which to
hang random perceptions."

Mervyn Horder, ed. *Ronald Firbank: Memoirs and Critiques*
London: Duckworth, 1977
Dallas: Duckworth, 1979

An anthology of biographical and critical writings on RF, most previously pub-
lished. Part 1 reprints Fletcher's 1930 book *in toto* ("with a few minor additions
and corrections to the Kyrle Fletcher contribution supplied by Mrs C. A. Kyrle
Fletcher"); part 2 consists of reminiscences by A. C. Landsberg, Grant Richards,
Nancy Cunard, Sewell Stokes, Viva King, Thomas J. Firbank, Maurice Sandoz,
Raisley Moorsom, Forrest Reid, Shane Leslie, Siegfried Sassoon, Vivian de Sola
Pinto, Wyndham Lewis, Harold Acton, Martin Secker, Ernst Goldschmidt,

and John Steegman, along with Harold Nicolson's story "Lambert Orme" and Coleridge Kennard's introduction to *The Artificial Princess*; part 3 reprints Carl Van Vechten's *Excavations* essay, Arthur Waley's introduction to *The Works* and Ernest Jones's to *Three Novels*, book reviews by E. M. Forster and Edmund Wilson, and essays by Evelyn Waugh, Mervyn Horder, and Ellis Waterhouse. All of these items are annotated parts 1 or 3, depending on their first appearance.

Pieces written specifically for this anthology and/or published here for the first time include Horder's "Introduction" (vii-xii), an overview of Firbank's critical reception and of the contents of this anthology, as well as a selection of self-referential passages from RF's novels; A. C. Landsberg's "Firbank at Cambridge" (89-93), the complete text of a letter used in part by Fletcher for his *Memoir*; Viva King's "Ronald Firbank" (134-35), a brief recollection of RF about 1923; Thomas J. Firbank's "Uncle Ronald" (135-38), hazy but insightful recollections of RF, his mother, and sister Heather; Raisley Moorsom's "Reminiscences of Ronald Firbank" (145-46), which quotes a 1922 letter from RF and describes him in Italy in 1921 (Moorsom says he gave RF the idea of writing a novel set in Haiti—*Prancing Nigger*); and the brief, untitled anecdotes from Secker (156), Goldschmidt (156), and Steegman (156-57). On the final page of the book is the text of RF's plaque to the memory of his father and mother (227). In some ways the most satisfying book written on RF.

*

d'Arch Smith, Timothy. "Such Cultured Pearls." *Gay News*, 11 August 1977.

Given RF's elusiveness, it is useful to have this collection of thirty-two views. RF "was as dotty and evasive as his novels. Dotty, and tipsy, and gangling, and, inevitably, homosexual."

Dougill, David. "Eccentricities of an Individualist." *Books and Bookmen* 23 (February 1978): 40-42.

After tracing RF's critical reception over the years, Dougill comments on the omissions from this book (Nina Hamnett, C. R. W. Nevinson, and some of the more influential reviewers) and the easy availability of some of the pieces that were reprinted (unnecessarily, he implies). "However, to give the book its due, there is much useful material in it": Fletcher's memoir is "essential reading," though it skirts the issue of RF's homosexuality; Sitwell's is "the most substantial, full of marvellous anecdote," though it perpetrated the mystery of the blue cards [see Potoker and Braybrooke (1963)]; and Thomas J. Firbank's "is amusing and valuable in the light it throws on Lady Firbank and her daughter Heather." Dougill points out some of the inconsistencies between these accounts, relates some of his favorite anecdotes, and comments on RF's mismanaged burial and his own visit to RF's tomb in 1973. (The reviewer also refers to Duckworth's reprinted editions of *Valmouth, Prancing Nigger,* and *Cardinal Pirelli*.)

Mosley, Nicholas. "Banqueting on a Pea." *Listener* 98 (29 September 1977): 405-6.

Given the degree to which RF's "quaint eroticism" suffuses his work, Mosley is surprised "there is no mention of sexuality" in these memoirs. RF's "art is a masochist's art—it can never quite come to the point, because the point is, that the point [real pain] shall never be come to." RF's books about blacks are written in a style "sensuous, hot, rhapsodic: his descriptions of black boys, black girls, black cities and black landscapes are the cries of someone in love." RF's "distinction is to have made out of masochism something beautiful—his black tempters and temptresses are redolent of a universal exuberance, wit, enchantment."

Sage, Lorna. "Violet Cream." *New Statesman* 94 (19 August 1977): 250-51.

An unsympathetic review of RF's "grotesque life and unnatural fiction." Sage feels the "reminiscences make him out to be so extraordinarily unappetising," and among the critiques only Waugh's and Wilson's "escape the prevailing coy shamateurishness." RF is a cruel "satirist of physical life and naturalism. . . . His place, if he is ever to find one, will be among those writers (Waugh himself, Muriel Spark) who have made the heartless, decorative 'Catholic' rituals of the English upper classes into a metaphor for universal decay. He remains awkwardly poised between their brilliant nastiness and a merely clownish fame."

Firbankiana: Being a Collection of Reminiscences of Ronald Firbank
Madras & New York: Hanuman Books, 1989

This tiny (2 1/2 x 4") hundred-page booklet is merely an abridged edition of Horder's *Memoirs and Critiques* (without any acknowledgment), consisting of short extracts from nearly all the contributors to parts 1 and 2.

*

Moore, Steven. *Review of Contemporary Fiction* 11.2 (Summer 1991): 260.

A brief note on this and another Hanuman publication, pointing out *Firbankiana*'s reliance on Horder's anthology.

Part 3

Essays, Parts of Books, and Other Commentary

Acton, Harold. "Mr. Ronald Firbank and the Eloquence of Indifference." *Cherwell,* 24 May 1924, 78-79.

Criticizes reviewers who have linked RF's works with the 1890s and praises the books as sharp satires of modern life. He quotes several passages from the novels to illustrate RF's "brilliance and wit," but predicts he won't be fully appreciated until the 1980s.

————. *Memoirs of an Aesthete.* London: Methuen, 1948. 105, 107, 182, 201. The Reggie Turner incident on 105 rpt. in Horder's *Memoirs and Critiques,* 155-56.

Contains brief references to "the airy faery Ronald," a butterfly "who belonged to an older generation: his freckled wings had unfolded in an Edwardian conservatory." Acton published a sequel, *More Memoirs of an Aesthete* (1970), which contains only passing references to RF, all inconsequential.

Aercke, Kristiaan P. "Two Decadents' Fragrant Prayers." *Neohelicon* 15.1 (1988): 263-74.

RF satirizes what J. K. Huysmans feared: the bourgeois appropriation of austere religion as operatic entertainment, and the aesthetic appropriation by which religion becomes a cult of beauty. "Firbank's bourgeois mock-religion of the Kitsch is called *Chic,* and it is in order to sacrifice to the cruel God of Chic that the sorority of social climbers that rules Firbankland has transformed churches into opera houses and reduced the secular clergy to the status of salaried entertainers." Treats *Flower beneath the Foot, Prancing Nigger, Valmouth,* and *Cardinal Pirelli.* "Huysmans and Firbank see the dispersal of the clergy in the world and society, and the conception of churches as places of entertainment, as so many signs of the decline of the Mother Church."

Albert, Edward. *History of English Literature.* 1923; 5th ed., revised by J. A. Stone. London: Harrap, 1979. 527.

A brief description of RF's work: "Action is inconsequential, conversation is wittily spectacular, and everyone is highly unconventional."

Alford, Norman W. "Seven Notebooks of Ronald Firbank." *Library Chronicle of the University of Texas* 7 (Spring 1967): 33-39.

A description of the seven *Valmouth* notebooks in the Texas library's collection, with numerous quotations and illustrations from this material.

Allen, Walter. *The English Novel: A Short Critical History.* London: Phoenix House, 1954; New York: Dutton, 1955. 92.

Notes the influence of Beckford's *Vathek* on Beardsley's *Under the Hill* and on RF's novels.

————. *Tradition and Dream.* London: Phoenix House, 1964; in U.S. as *The Modern Novel in England and America.* New York: Dutton, 1964. 39-41.

A brief assessment of this "remarkable" talent, using *The Flower beneath the Foot* for demonstration purposes. "Decadent, frivolous, trivial—the adjectives come hopping off the typewriter—. . . Frivolous, flippant, outrageously affected, written, it seems, *épater la bourgeoisie.*" *Cardinal Pirelli* is "his most outrageously irreverent and most explicitly perverse novel." Allen concludes by noting affinities between RF's work and, "perhaps, the poems of Edith Sitwell and E. E. Cummings. Firbank, too, in his own intensely mannered, muted way is the clown with the broken heart."

[Anonymous.] *Tatler*, 28 April 1915, 108.

Features a portrait of RF by Augustus John and brief remarks on the "shortly to be published" *Vainglory* (published nearly two weeks earlier) and on RF's background.

————, *Tatler*, 30 January 1918, 418.

Published a photograph of RF by Bertram Park in conjunction with the publication of *Caprice*.

————. "Ronald Firbank." *Chicago Evening Post*, 24 September 1926, "Literary Review," 4.

A smart, sympathetic summary of RF's work shortly after his death. "Mr. Firbank could be described, very justly, as a teller of fairy tales for grown-up people. Not that his fairies wander quite so far as do those of Mr. Yeats, nor that they stay young so sempiternally. They are still human enough to need rouge and lipstick. But they are fairy-like, at least, in being beyond good and evil: they live according to the devices and desires of their own hearts—and are by no means lacking in devices." The anonymous critic feels RF's "wit is much more genuine than Wilde's," but wryly fears that RF's work is too daring for American readers; only *Vainglory* "is free from sex situations—which, of course, makes it safe for democracy. But it will be too fine spun for democracy."

————. "Rumor that Ronald Firbank Still Lives Is Denied." *New York Times*, 10 October 1926, 18.

A response to Milton Mackaye's bogus story in the *Post* two days earlier: see below.

————. "Introduction, *The New Rythum*." *Portfolio: A Quarterly of New Ideas Made Visual* 7 (Winter 1963): 56, 58, 112-14.

An overview of RF's life and reputation, with special attention to his critical reception in the U. S. "The key to Firbank is that he satirizes what he loves [and thus] his 'use' of the influences upon him amounts to tender but outrageous parody." The origins of *The New Rythum* are recounted and it is noted that, "Like most of the novels, *The New Rythum* sets out to give a picture of a whole community of characters with one slightly perverse relationship in bas relief in the center." Despite the inauthenticity of some of RF's New York slang, the novel contains "some of Firbank's best descriptions."

————. "Keeping the Camp Fires Burning." *Tatler*, December 1985/January 1986, 34, 36.

To mark RF's centenary, the *Tatler* asked several writers to express their attitude toward him. Angus Wilson counts himself "a devout admirer," but A. N. Wilson has "never been able to read more than about three pages of Firbank—never seen the point of him at all." Sandy Wilson recalls his musical production of *Valmouth*, Alan Bennett confesses knowing next to nothing about RF, and Gavin Ewart considers him the "runner-up" (to Waugh) as the great British comic novelist of this century: "There is also something sad about his books. . . . The cry of the peacock is a sad cry." Michael Frayn considers RF "unreadable," and for Kingsley Amis he "Perfectly sums up in himself what I can't bear about one of the two main kinds of novel I can't bear." Francis King says RF's "tinsel was spun from tungsten. . . . His oeuvre is at once smaller in its entirety than many a single 'serious' novel, and infinitely more durable." Brigid Brophy remains a devoted admirer, as does Harold Acton: "His novels float and flicker as from a moulting bird of rococo paradise." John Braine praises RF's self-sufficiency: "His books are dazzling, juggling feats, but he juggles only for his own pleasure. There hasn't been any writer like him for sheer economy. . . . His work will endure because of its sheer perfection." Ned Sherrin has yet to outgrow his adolescent enthusiasm for RF, and Bryan Guinness, who was an undergraduate at Oxford at the time of RF's death, retains "only a memory of brilliance and brittleness . . . with a tinge of sorrow at the sadness of this invalid's life."

Ansen, Alan. *The Table Talk of W. H. Auden.* Ed. Nicholas Jenkins. New York: Sea Cliff Press, 1989 (ltd. ed.); Princeton: Ontario Review Press, 1990.
     These notes on Auden's conversations (1947) record the poet's informal views on RF: "Firbank is very good. I'm fond of Disraeli, who gives something of the same effect. His characters are so good. I don't see how you can parody him. Firbank is really very tough underneath. His father wasn't Director of the London Northwestern Railway for nothing. He doesn't claim to be the whole world—just a small window on reality" (15). Mozart's *Così fan tutte* "looks a little like Firbank but is ultimately major" (16). He tells Ansen he has tried to persuade Viking to let him "do a Portable Firbank for them. You ought to get in about five novels—no excerpts. Let's see, what would they be? *Santal, The Flower Beneath the Foot, Concerning the Eccentricities of Cardinal Pirelli. . . .* I sometimes think that *Vainglory* is the best of them all" (54). He goes on to say that the daily book critic for the *New York Times,* Orville Prescott, "has sworn a mortal grudge against Firbank" (55; Prescott's enmity is repeated on 67-68). In his annotations, Nicholas Jenkins notes that in the summer of 1947 "Auden went to a party at the Fire Island Hotel dressed as Cardinal Pirelli" (113).

Ash, John. "The Outrageous Stephen Tennant." *Washington Post Book World,* 3 February 1991, 10.
     In this book review of Philip Hoare's *Serious Pleasures: The Life of Stephen Tennant,* Ash devotes a paragraph to comparing Tennant with RF.

Auden, W. H. "Ronald Firbank and an Amateur World." *Listener* 65 (8 June 1961): 1004-5, 1008. (BBC Third Programme.)
     RF's fiction was created more in the amateur spirit of a game than in the professional spirit of obligation or dedicated action. He created a "private vision of Eden," and such an "earthly paradise is no place for literary critics." (Either you revel in RF's world or you don't.) In his world, religion is treated as "an amateur game" and sex is appropriately "infantile and polymorphously perverse. The improprieties in Firbank are those of children playing Doctor." Several extended quotations from RF's novels are given.

————. *A Certain World: A Commonplace Book.* New York: Viking, 1970.
     In this anthology of the poet's favorite passages, RF's works are quoted on pp. 74, 236-37, 307, and 327-28.

Baker, Ernest A., and James Packman. *A Guide to the Best Fiction.* New and enlarged ed. New York: Macmillan, 1932. 174-75.
     A listing of RF's works with brief, bemused annotations.

————. *The History of the English Novel,* vol. 9: *The Day before Yesterday.* London: Witherby, 1939; New York: Barnes & Noble, 1939. 240-42.
     "A belated straggler from the æsthetic rearguard, who astonished an innocent second decade of the twentieth century with his revival of the cynical perversions of Beardsley and Oscar Wilde and his own delicately indelicate jests," RF

possessed "a new and curiously efficient mode of impressionism, rapidly and vividly conveying, without describing anything or telling any story, the attitudes and affectations and the simpering accents of the half-real types in Mayfair society or cosmopolitan pleasure-cities by tropic strands." The authors quote snatches of "agreeable nonsense" from *Caprice* and *Vainglory*, and cite *Prancing Nigger* as "a good example of the story that enacts itself." An exchange of dialogue from this novel is quoted, followed by the critical evaluation: "It is like a talking film."

Barnhill, Sarah. "Method in Madness: Ronald Firbank's *The Flower Beneath the Foot.*" *English Literature in Transition* 32.3 (1989): 291-300.
     Listening to "the voice of despair and loss that can be heard below the surface of his fiction," Barnhill carefully analyzes *The Flower* "to show both the darker, crueler side of the Firbank vision as well as the exile's longing for a place that can never be regained." The nihilistic ending of the novel displays "a desperation commensurate with the cry of the exile and appropriate to the postwar apocalyptic gloom that covered much of Europe in the Twenties."

Bartlett, Neil. *Who Was That Man?: A Present for Mr. Oscar Wilde.* London: Serpent's Tail, 1988. 167, 179.
     RF mentioned and quoted.

Benkovitz, Miriam J. "Ronald Firbank in New York." *Bulletin of the New York Public Library* 63 (May 1959): 247-59.
     A discussion of RF's relationship with Carl Van Vechten; the material was expanded for use in Benkovitz's *Biography* (as were most of the essays that follow).

———. "Ronald Firbank in Periodicals." *Papers of the Bibliographical Society of America* 54 (4th quarter 1960): 295-97.
     Identifies for the first time most of RF's magazine publications. The early ones are juvenilia, Benkovitz admits, yet are interesting because they anticipate RF's later strengths and weaknesses as a writer.

———. "More Ronald Firbank." *Times Literary Supplement,* 18 August 1961, 549.
     In re Horder, *TLS,* 14 July 1961 (see below).

———. "A Chronology of Ronald Firbank." In RF's *Two Novels: The Flower beneath the Foot* [and] *Prancing Nigger.* Norfolk, CT/New York: New Directions, 1962. 351-56.

———. "Notes toward a Chapter of Biography: Lord Alfred Douglas and Ronald Firbank." *Bulletin of the New York Public Library* 67 (March 1963): 143-51.
     A discussion of RF's relation to the older man, expanded in Benkovitz's biography.

———. "Introduction." in RF's *"The Wind & the Roses."* London: John Roberts (for Alan Clodd), 1966. 3-5.
     An overview of RF's juvenilia. Benkovitz believes the actual subject matter of "The Wind & the Roses" is unimportant; RF's true subject, here and elsewhere, "was natural beauty in certain formal aspects," especially the beauty of his childhood home.

———. [Untitled bibliographic note.] In RF's *Far Away*. Iowa City, IA: Typographical Laboratory (University of Iowa), 1966. 9-12.
On the background of this early prose piece.

———. "On 'An Early Flemish Painter' by Ronald Firbank." *Bulletin of the New York Public Library* 72 (December 1968): 653-55.
Background material to RF's only published essay in art criticism.

———. [Untitled introductory note.] In RF's *An Early Flemish Painter*. London: Enitharmon, 1969. 3.
Adapted from the previous entry.

———. "Foreword." In Nancy Cunard's *Thoughts about Ronald Firbank*, 5-7.
A brief discussion of Cunard's relationship to RF.

———. "Foreword." In RF's *Two Early Stories*. New York: Albondocani, 1971. 5-7.
Brief remarks on the composition process for both stories and their first appearance in the Cambridge undergraduate magazine *Granta* in 1906 and 1907. She also notes how they anticipate RF's later work, especially *Vainglory*.

———. "Introduction." In RF's *La Princesse aux soleils & Harmonie*. London: Enitharmon, 1974. xi-xiii.
Gives the composition background to both stories—without, however, explaining what happened to RF's English originals of these works, which had to be translated from his French versions by Edgell Rickword.

———. *Frederick Rolfe: Baron Corvo*. London: Michael Joseph; New York: Putnam's, 1977.
Makes passing reference to RF on pp. 177, 184, and 214.

———. "More about Ronald Firbank." *Columbia Library Columns* 26.2 (1977): 3-12.
On the earliest version of *The Flower beneath the Foot*, more libellous than the published version because of its caricature of Evan Morgan (revenge for Morgan's refusal of RF's dedication of *The Princess Zoubaroff* to him), whose relationship with RF is discussed at length. (The findings are summarized in the 2nd edition of Benkovitz's *Bibliography*, pp. 25-26.)

———. "The Fabric of Biography." *Columbia Library Columns* 29.2 (1980): 23-32.
A discussion of Ifan Kyrle Fletcher and how he assembled his Firbank memoir, based on 127 letters to Fletcher about RF acquired by the Columbia University Library in 1977.

Bermel, Albert. *Farce: A History from Aristophanes to Woody Allen*. New York: Simon & Schuster, 1982. 435.
Enumerates the farcical elements of *The Flower*.

Bezel, Julian. "A Whim of Iron." *Elle* (U.S. ed.), June 1989, 100.
A brief overview of the nature of RF's work—"beautiful, conscienceless, 20 degrees beyond wit"—with particular attention to his dialogue: "not so much social portraiture as language with a life of its own." (The contributor's note reports that Bezel was at work on a biography of RF.)

Bigland, Eileen. *Ouida, the Passionate Victorian.* London and New York: Jarrolds, 1950. 179.

Asserts that Ouida's "*Princess Napraxine* was a novel in advance of its time— if it had been published fifty years later people would have attributed it to Ronald Firbank."

Blackmer, Corinne E. "Firbank's Sapphic Saints." Paper presented at the annual MLA Convention, session 367: "Ronald Firbank: New Readings," San Diego, CA, 28 December 1994.

Notes the influence of Massenet's opera *Thaïs* on RF's aesthetic and his contribution to "Sapphic modernism."

———. "Firbank, Ronald (1886-1926)." In *The Gay and Lesbian Literary Heritage: A Reader's Companion to the Writers and Their Works, from Antiquity to the Present.* Ed. Claude J. Summers. New York: Holt, 1995. 274-76.

A compact, well-informed overview of the life and work. (RF is often mentioned in passing elsewhere in this massive reference book.)

Blamires, Harry. *Twentieth-Century English Literature.* London: Macmillan, 1982. 49-50, 89, 230-31.

A brief, unoriginal discussion of RF's "frivolous febrility."

Bloom, Harold, ed. "Ronald Firbank." In *Twentieth-Century British Literature.* New York: Chelsea House, 1986. 2:617-29.

A mini-anthology of older RF criticism.

Booth, Mark. *Camp.* London: Quartet, 1983.

RF is frequently cited in illustration of various facets of camp behavior.

Boutell, H. S. "Arthur Annesley Ronald Firbank, 1886-1926: A Bibliographical Check List of His Books." *Publishers Weekly* 117 (15 February 1930): 889.

A lightly annotated bibliography.

Bowles, Paul. *In Touch: The Letters of Paul Bowles.* Ed. Jeffrey Miller. New York: Farrar, Straus & Giroux, 1994. 77.

In a letter of July 1931 to Bruce Morrissette, Bowles passes on some opinions of Gertrude Stein's from a recent visit: "Of Firbank. He did it, and no one else can."

Bradford, Sarah. *Sacheverell Sitwell: Splendours and Miseries.* London: Sinclair-Stevenson, 1993; in U.S. as *Splendours and Miseries: A Life of Sacheverell Sitwell.* New York: Farrar, Straus & Giroux, 1993. 90-91.

A brief account of RF's relations to the Sitwells, drawn from Sir Osbert's *Noble Essences.*

Braybrooke, Neville. "Ronald Firbank 1886-1926." *Ramparts* 1.2 (September 1962): 4-12. Rpt. in *Dalhousie Review* 42 (1962): 38-49, and in *Kromek von Kunst un Kultur* (Amsterdam), 23 July 1964. Revised and rpt. as "Firbank Revisited," *Twentieth Century* (Australia) 19 (Summer 1964): 164-76, and (with slight revisions) as "Thorns and Vanities: Ronald Firbank Revisited," *Encounter* 31.3 (September 1968): 66-74.

An overview of the life and work. Locates several key passages to explain RF's work (the description of Claude Harvester in *Vainglory,* Odette's realization that "Life" was "beyond the garden in which she dwelt"), specifically those displaying RF's conflicting impulses toward boldness and shyness, observing and hiding. Similarly, writing novels indulged RF's theatrical impulse for "dressing up" and accounts for their dramatic form and extensive use of dialogue. *Cardinal Pirelli*, if (in a Renaissance sense) "the most bawdy remains in a religious sense the most profound" of his novels. Braybrooke speculates on what RF may have learned from Shaw, Congreve, and Beckford, and—noting the prevalence of roses in RF's work—concludes by paraphrasing the conclusion of "Odette": "Roses are their own parable. Life is sad, the blooms must fall. Life is cruel, there are thorns."

Brennan, Neil. *Anthony Powell*. Rev. ed. New York: Twayne, 1995. 29, 36, 60, 70.
    Notes and dismisses RF's influence ("inevitable" but "invidious") on Powell's early novels.

Bristow, Joseph. "Firbank's Exotic Effiminacy." In his *Effeminate England: Homoerotic Writing after 1885*. New York: Columbia Univ. Press, 1995. 100-126.
    Places RF in a historical context and focuses on his interest in lesbians and, toward the end of his career, in other races. Despite RF's admiration for Wilde, he moved away from him as his career progressed, finding lesbians more to his purpose (i.e., representing artificiality and homosexuality) than Wildean dandies. Notes that RF's "work is expressly modernist in its marked self-consciousness, constantly prompting us to reassess how fiction can set about representing its imaginary worlds." Most of the works are discussed, including the juvenilia, with special attention to *The Artificial Princess, Valmouth,* and *Prancing Nigger*.

Bronski, Michael. *Culture Clash: The Making of Gay Sensibility*. Boston: South End Press, 1984. 64-66.
    Asserting that RF's "style and sensibility would have an important effect upon future gay writers," Bronski describes his novels as "elaborate fantasies filled with invented languages and characters whose names bear no relationship to common English nomenclature. . . . His writings are prime examples of a gay sensibility. By inventing a new reality he could create situations where he could show emotion safely." RF's unusual diction and use of innuendo are a kind of self-protection similar to the "unique manners and speech" of gay men. RF "used elusiveness as much to convey psychological states as to cover for openly homosexual content."

Brooke, Jocelyn. *A Mine of Serpents*. London: Bodley Head, 1949. 124, 126. Rpt. as part 2 of *The Orchid Trilogy*. Introduction by Anthony Powell. London: Secker & Warburg, 1981. 201, 203.
    In this lightly fictionalized memoir Brooke discusses the RF cult in Oxbridge during the 1920s: "Our whole code of manners, indeed, aspired to a condition of complete artificiality; Firbank, Wilde and the early Huxley were our models, even if we hadn't read them yet" (124). Brooke describes a Firbankian student he calls Hew Dallas—his library includes *Valmouth, Vainglory,* and *The Flower beneath the Foot*—who tells Brooke: "'You haven't read Firbank? Oh my dear you *must*—Beardsley in prose, but *much* better . . .'" (126).

Brophy, Brigid. *Baroque-'n'-Roll and Other Essays*. London: Hamish Hamilton, 1987. 147-48.
    In the title essay, Brophy notes "Ronald Firbank did not become, to a literary ear, recognisably himself until he had with flair and hard work fashioned a

modern rococo prose. In it he couched *Vainglory* . . .; into it he adopted and adapted practices borrowed, consciously, from jazz, the great musical rococo contemporary with him; he deepened and solidified his idiom into the baroque masterpiece *Concerning the Eccentricities of Cardinal Pirelli*."

Bryfonski, Dedria, and Phyllis Carmel Mendelson, eds. *Twentieth-Century Literary Criticism*. Detroit: Gale Research, 1978. 224-32.
    Quotes lengthy extracts from several major reviews and essays on RF.

Burkhart, Charles. "Ronald Firbank." *British Novelists, 1890-1929: Modernists*. Ed. Thomas F. Staley. *Dictionary of Literary Biography*, vol. 36. Detroit: Gale Research Co., 1985. 37-41.
    An overview of the life and work of this "eccentric writer who belongs to no school . . . one of the great stylists of the novel and one of its great comedians, artificers, and wits." *Caprice* is characterized by "his typical cold and melancholy irony," *The Flower beneath the Foot* by "brittle and rococo wit," and *Cardinal Pirelli* by "preposterous wit." RF's characters "spend their lives in little intensities," and while his work is better dipped in to than pondered, RF is "one of the rare eccentric flowers of the English romantic tradition."

Burns, Edward, ed. *The Letters of Gertrude Stein and Carl Van Vechten, 1913-1946*. New York: Columbia Univ. Press, 1986.
    In his letter of 22 February 1923, Van Vechten asks whether Stein has read RF and recommends his latest, *The Flower beneath the Foot*. He adds that he'll send RF her latest, *Geography and Plays*, confident "He will love it" (66-67). In his letter of 13 April 1924, Van Vechten recommends *Prancing Nigger* to her (96). She responded 25 June 1924 to say she hadn't seen "Firbank's book but will soon" (103). In her letter of 23 July 1924, she writes Van Vechten: "Have just read Prancing Nigger and am delighted with it. It is sweet and funny, do tell Firbank how much I like it. I would like very much to meet him, I imagine he comes to Paris from time to time" (105). Van Vechten responded on 8 September 1924 to say he had written to RF "that you want to see him & I hope he will call on you someday but he is described by those who have seen him as excessively shy" (106). She responded on 11 October 1924: "Thanks for forwarding my message to Firbank. I heard he was shy the man who came with the faithless Hunter Stagg he never has sent me a copy of the Reviewer I mean Stagg, well [Montgomery] Evans I think his name was turned up again and he said he would bring Firbank sometime he knew him in London so I am hoping to meet him sometime" (107). In her letter to Van Vechten of 3 November 1928 Stein makes a further reference to RF in connection with the Chilean-born painter Alvaro Guevara.

Carens, James F. *The Satiric Art of Evelyn Waugh*. Seattle: Univ. of Washington Press, 1966. 5-10.
    Discusses RF's influence on Waugh, specifically RF's dialogue, his objectivity and detachment, and his invention of counterpoint (though RF "was possibly not entirely conscious of what he was doing"). RF "has no interest in ideas; he is no reformer. Nevertheless, through the indirection of his irony and by means of a montage-like technique, Firbank achieves some intense effects." As late as *Brideshead Revisited*, Waugh was using RF's devices.

Carpenter, Humphrey. *Geniuses Together: American Writers in Paris in the 1920s*. Boston: Houghton Mifflin, 1988. 71.
    Notes that Gertrude Stein "only had good words for writers who had praised

her own work. The sole exception was Ronald Firbank; she was greatly amused by his high-camp fantasies with their sexual ambiguities."

—————. *The Brideshead Generation: Evelyn Waugh and His Friends.* London: Weidenfeld & Nicolson, 1989; Boston: Houghton Mifflin, 1990. 27-28, 138, 152-54, 236-37, and passim.
    The earliest stories by Brian Howard and Harold Acton in the *Eton Candle* were in RF's manner. Carpenter notes RF's influence on Waugh's student film *The Scarlet Woman* as well as on his fiction.

Charney, Maurice. *Joe Orton.* New York: Grove Press, 1984. 6, 12, 125, 130, 134.
    Brief references to RF's influence on the dramatist.

Clark, William Lane. "Degenerate Personality: Deviant Sexuality and Race in Ronald Firbank's Novels." In *Camp Grounds: Style and Homosexuality.* Ed. David Bergman. Amherst: Univ. of Massachusetts Press, 1993. 134-55.
    Situating RF halfway between Wilde's Victorian critique and Susan Sontag's reevaluation (in "Notes on Camp") of moral seriousness, Clark argues that RF's novels challenge the ideology of bourgeois values via "the transgressive aesthetics of camp." Respectability and appearance are frequent targets of his, though RF goes further than Wilde to show that such values, and gender itself, are not pretenses but illusions: "Heterosexuals, homosexuals, and bisexuals in Firbank's society are only so by appearance; all are in drag." RF embodied the "deviancy" and "degeneracy" shunned by Victorian moralists, but "Firbank's fascination with people of color and black culture is that degenerate aspect of the deviant personality most important toward elucidating style and structure in his writing," which Clark proceeds to do by way of RF's use of jazz techniques and the Negro as a figure of sexual liberation. *Valmouth* provides most of Clark's examples, with some references to *The Flower, Prancing Nigger,* and *The Princess Zoubaroff.*

—————. "Something between a Eunuch and a Snigger: Sex and the Church in Firbank." Paper presented at the annual MLA Convention, session 367: "Ronald Firbank: New Readings," San Diego, CA, 28 December 1994.
    On the conflation of the erotic with the religious in RF's novels, specifically on how masturbation is sublimated as institutional flagellation, thereby allowing degeneration to masquerade as respectability.

Clarke, Gerald. *Capote: A Biography.* New York: Simon and Schuster, 1988. 511.
    Notes Capote's regret for "all the dead people who would have loved 54. It's a shame they're not around—people like Ronald Firbank or Toulouse-Lautrec or Baudelaire or Oscar Wilde or Carl Van Vechten. Cole Porter would have loved it." (Studio 54 was a nightclub in Manhattan notorious in the late 1970s.)

Cleto, Fabio. "An Updated Bibliography of Firbank Criticism." *Quaderni del Dipartimento di Linguistica e Letterature Comparate* [University of Bergamo] 9 (1993): 37-51.
    An expanded and updated revision of Davis's 1969 checklist through the summer of 1992.

Connolly, Cyril. "The Novel-Addict's Cupboard." January 1936. Rpt. in his *The Condemned Playground.* New York: Macmillan, 1946. 114-15.

Tells the anecdote of RF meeting Huxley in the Café Royal ("Aldous—
always my *torture*"), then expresses his appreciation of RF as one of those
whose works "attempt, with a purity and a kind of dewy elegance, to portray
the beauty of the moment, the gaiety and sadness, the fugitive distress of
hedonism; . . . He and the early Eliot seem to me the pure artists of the 'twenties, . . . Of course, it is quite useless to write about Firbank—nobody who
doesn't like him is going to like him, and he can be extremely aggravating and
silly—but he was a true innovator, and his air of ephemerality is treacherous in
the extreme."

————. "Anatomy of Dandyism." Chap. 5 of his *Enemies of Promise*. Boston:
Little, Brown, 1939. 45-50; rev. ed. New York: Macmillan, 1948. 33-39.
    Cites RF as an example of dandyism in literature, a tradition stretching back
through the seventeenth century to Horace and Tibullus. Asking "What is his
contribution to modern literature?" Connolly answers not the sexuality in
RF's works but his recognition of "frivolity as the most insolent refinement of
satire" and his use of inconsequence, dialogue, and impressionism. Connolly
concludes with a footnote: "The debt of Firbank to Beardsley's *Under the Hill*
is not here sufficiently stressed. It is the archetype of sophisticated butterfly
impressionism in our tongue. Firbank perhaps was never quite so witty, vicious
or well-informed as the adolescent of genius, however he was more radiantly
preposterous, a humourist of wider calibre."

————. *The Evening Colonnade*. New York: Harcourt Brace Jovanovich, 1975.
6, 16, 198, 380.
    Brief, passing references.

————. *Journals and a Memoir*. Ed. David Pryce-Jones. London: Collins,
1983.
    Contains two references to RF on p. 245 (entry for 15 April 1935) listing
him among "Projects of the moment" and "Authors of the moment."

Cooper, Frederic Taber. "The Twentieth Century Novel." *Bookman* 65 (March
1927): 42-47.
    Includes passing, dismissive references to RF's novels; Cooper guesses "that
Mr. Galsworthy or Mr. Kipling or Joseph Conrad stands a far better chance of
surviving the dawn of the twenty first century than such experimentalists as, let
us say, Mr. Joyce or Mr. Huxley or Ronald Firbank" (43).

Core, Philip. *Camp: The Lie That Tells the Truth*. London: Plexus; New York:
Delilah, 1984. 85-86.
    A biographical sketch of RF as "a sort of clockwork Symbolist dandy" with
only passing reference to "the innuendos and peripatetic bitchiness" of his
novels, which "are inscrutable at an emotional level, due to romantic expression
or, more likely, the author's dislike of his own homosexuality." RF is referred to
throughout this "encyclopedia" as a touchstone of camp (but too inconsequen-
tially to merit detailed citations).

Daiches, David. *The Present Age: After 1920*. London: Cresset, 1958. 274.
    A brief, incomplete bibliography of RF's work, followed by the comment:
"A novelist of sophisticated fantasy, whose stories are full of absurdly brilliant
inconsequential conversation and a desperate brightness. There is an odd mixture of decadence and innocence about his work."

d'Arcangelo, Angelo. *The Homosexual Handbook*. New York: Ophelia Press, 1969. 267-68.

RF called "the best English-language writer to come out of the years of the First World War. The most delicious comic novellas imaginable. Evelyn Waugh parodied him in his *Brideshead Revisited*, under the name of Anthony Blanche." (*Note:* Most critics believe Brian Howard was the inspiration for Waugh's character.)

d'Arch Smith, Timothy. *Love in Earnest: Some Notes on the Lives and Writings of English "Uranian" Poets from 1889 to 1930*. London: Routledge & Kegan Paul, 1970. 56, 58-59.

Suggests that a story in the Oxford literary magazine *Chameleon*, "The Priest and the Acolyte" by John Francis Bloxham, may have inspired *Cardinal Pirelli*.

Davenport-Hines, Richard. "Firbank in Conversation." *Times Literary Supplement*, 4 November 1994, 11.

A book review of Duncan Fallowell's *Twentieth-Century Characters* (Vintage, 1994). Describing a group interview between Fallowell, Quentin Crisp, Caroline Langrishe, and Arnold Schwarzenegger, the reviewer says "the fast-paced chaos reads like dialogue by Firbank."

Davies, Paul. "'The Power to Convey the Unuttered': Style and Sexuality in the Work of Ronald Firbank." In *Lesbian and Gay Writing: An Anthology of Critical Essays*. Ed. Mark Lilly. Philadelphia: Temple Univ. Press, 1990. 199-214.

RF's strategies for expressing his homosexuality in his writings differ from those of other gay writers, first by "taking a homosexual, high-church tradition and transforming it through camp," and second in his continuation of Wilde's aesthetic. Other strategies include using martyrs (Saints Sebastian and Dorothy), writers (Sappho as well as Wilde), and settings (Arcadia, Sodom) that denoted homosexuality. Davies suggests that Firbank's unorthodox spelling, grammar, and punctuation likewise express his unorthodox sexual orientation: "Sexual deviance is made manifest in the text through a strategy of stylistic deviance." Davies concludes with a discussion of *The Princess Zoubaroff*, RF's "most explicit vision of a world of homosexual happiness." The play "dramatises a theme mentioned elsewhere in Firbank—the benefits of a world where the sexes live apart."

Davis, Robert Murray. "From Artifice to Art: The Technique of Firbank's Novels." *Style* 2 (Winter 1968): 33-47.

Though RF's use of dialogue has been regarded as his most important innovation, it was his blending of pictorial and dramatic methods that allowed his dialogue to function. His early worked erred by relying too heavily on the pictorial or the dramatic: "Although there are obvious exceptions, the pictorial method tended to dominate Firbank's writing until 1914, the dramatic that of the period from 1916 to 1920." Only when the two methods were combined did a proper structure for his dialogue emerge, which accounts for the aesthetic satisfactions of the later novels, beginning with *Valmouth*. Davis gives examples from all the works and discusses the influence of Beardsley. Several specific aspects of RF's dialogue are noted—his "babel of voices," the use of "seemingly bland irrelevancy," and contrast in speakers—and RF's ability to combine dialogue and description smoothly is demonstrated. Davis also discusses the pacing and fragmentation of plot in RF's novels. Here, as in all of the essays that follow, Davis—one of the few great Firbank scholars—shows considerable insight and acuity in assessing RF's achievement.

————. "'Hyperaesthesia with Complications': The World of Ronald Firbank." *Rendezvous* 3.1 (Spring 1968): 5-15.

Describes the physical world of RF's novels: its characteristic seasons, climate, scenery, cities, the absence of physical suffering or poverty. RF's characters often consider their surroundings to be like landscape paintings, and themselves try to "achieve the composed and static quality of a work of art." They misuse both art (in the early novels) and religion (in the later) "to furnish a pattern for their lives and to enable them to arrange life as a work of art with themselves as the focus." Freedom vs. control is the central conflict for most of the characters, and "the peace and order of the natural world" becomes, especially in the later novels, an enviable alternative to society.

————. "The Text of Firbank's *Vainglory*." *Papers of the Bibliographical Society of America* 63 (1st quarter 1969): 36-41.

Points out the deficiencies of the *Complete Ronald Firbank* text, with special attention to *Vainglory*. Four tables list variants between the major editions of this novel.

————. "Ronald Firbank: A Selected Bibliography of Criticism." *Bulletin of Bibliography* 26.4 (October/December 1969): 108-11.

An exhaustive listing of reviews and essays on RF up to that time.

————. "On Firbank." In his *Modern British Short Novels*. Glenview, IL: Scott, Foresman, 1972. 153-58. (Preceded by the complete text of *Cardinal Pirelli*: 112-53.)

An overview of RF's work and critical reception, with introductory remarks on *Cardinal Pirelli*.

————. "The Ego Triumphant in Firbank's *Vainglory*." *Papers on Language and Literature* 9 (Summer 1973): 281-90.

Of all RF's novels, "*Vainglory* presents the broadest and most comprehensive picture of prewar England." It shows RF's trust in hints and suggestions rather than explanations, of doing without authorial exposition. Two principles organize the work, one thematic (his characters' need "to dominate others or to ensure the perpetuation of their personalities"), one mathematical (the twenty-four chapters fall into four units of six chapters each, alternating between Ashringford and London). Despite her vainglory, Mrs. Shamefoot is not condemned; she and her quest for permanence "are the objects of ridicule so gentle as to seem almost sympathetic."

————. "Ronald Firbank's Notebooks: '. . . writing books was by no means easy.'" *Harvard Library Bulletin* 25 (1977): 172-92.

RF's notebooks "provided him with the opportunity for self-discipline and self-criticism as well as a place to leave feeble jokes, self-indulgent pursuit of a striking phrase, and the stock characters and situations that naturally if lamentably gather around popular subjects and themes." From the material in his notebooks the novels grew: examples are given mostly from *Caprice* and *Valmouth*. RF left out more than he used from the notebooks, but the unused material "helps to explain how, in very very short novels, he was able to create the effect of a full and busy world."

————. *Evelyn Waugh, Writer*. Norman, OK: Pilgrim Press, 1981. 52-54.

Brief remarks on Waugh's use of RF, especially in *Vile Bodies*, which "clearly shows the influence of Firbank's dialogue. . . . Waugh admitted as much in the preface to the final collected edition (London: Chapman and Hall, 1965)."

Deghy, Guy, and Keith Waterhouse. *Café Royal: Ninety Years of Bohemia*. London: Hutchinson, 1955. 22-24, 165-71, 175-76.

An account of RF's appearances in this legendary bar-restaurant, the people he met there (especially C. R. W. Nevinson), and his use of the Café Royal in *Caprice*. "This short burlesque, *Caprice*, runs the gamut of tired and tiring sophistication from puns that would not pass unpunished in a self-respecting fifth form, to glittering *tours-de-force* of mute comment. It makes for hard, though not unrewarding, reading" (168).

Dickinson, Patric. "A Note on Ronald Firbank." *Windmill* 1.3 (1946): 26-36.

An adoring, at times impressionistic review of RF's life, with many quotations from his books and reported conversation (from Fletcher's *Memoir*). His work has no serious purpose, nor is he a satirist: "No, Firbank's work is an expression of Style, of Taste, of Sheer Æstheticism. He is an original, unique, uninfluenced, absolute." Dickinson feels *The Flower* "is perhaps the most successful, though not the most perfect," while *Prancing Nigger* "is a masterpiece." All of the novels are lovingly praised and quoted.

Dirda, Michael. "Readings." *Washington Post Book World*, 16 July 1995, 15.

Naming "a handful of uncanonical but vastly influential modern books . . . that helped establish the conventions, if not the archetypal patterns, of current popular fiction," Dirda chooses for the category of "Camp comedy: Ronald Firbank's *The Flower Beneath the Foot*. No question here about the master of this genre. Firbank is silly and naughty, and his prose actually minces. . . . But he is also a major influence on a whole line of writers from Evelyn Waugh and Anthony Powell to W. M. Spackman and Alan Hollinghurst. More than just a model of one kind of gay literary sensibility, Firbank taught fiction how to leave out the inessential, to be fast-moving and airy, to reflect the fragmented way people actually talk."

Dock, Leslie. "An Interview with Brigid Brophy." *Contemporary Literature* 17.2 (Spring 1976): 151-70.

Brophy notes that she began reading RF as a child (157) and that her Firbankian novel *The Finishing Touch* owes as much to Colette's Claudine novels as to RF (163).

Dold, Bernard E. "Firbank in Translation." *Annali: Sezione Germanica* [Instituto Universitario Orientale, Naples] 15.1 (1972): 177-88.

Dold spends the first half of his article finding fault with *Cardinal Pirelli*, and the second half finding fault with recent translations of *Cardinal Pirelli* into German and Italian, concluding "Firbank should be read in English or not at all."

————. *Edwardian Fall-out: The Ironic School*. Messina, Italy: Peloritana, 1972. 155-65 and passim.

Contains an unsympathetic, rather ludicrous chapter on RF, comparing and contrasting him to the three other principal subjects of his book (Saki, Wodehouse, Beerbohm). Dold accuses RF of indulging in "automatic writing" (championed by the surrealists) and "free association," which Dold himself indulges in rather recklessly in pursuit of parallels between RF's work and that of others.

Drabble, Margaret, ed. *The Oxford Companion to English Literature*. 5th ed. Oxford and New York: Oxford Univ. Press, 1985. 350-51.

RF has a substantial, appreciative entry. "His use of dialogue, his oblique narration, his highly coloured fantasies, and his intense concentration of language and image are now seen as truly innovative, and some writers have claimed that he did more to liberate the novel from 19th-cent. concepts of realism than Joyce himself."

Duck, David. "Ronald Firbank." In *Frederick Rolfe and Others*. Ed. Lady Margaret Sackville. Aylesford, Kent: St. Albert's Press, 1961. 14-17.

Duck satirizes the attempts to trace influences on RF and argues that he was better read than generally assumed. He places RF in "the long line of English romantics, many of whom were eccentrics as well," partly because of RF's "highly developed awareness of 'place,' and the ability to transfer that feeling to paper in such a way that the reader shares it." He notes the many parallels between RF and romantic eccentric William Beckford and accounts for them "less from filching on Firbank's part than from the fundamental similarity of the two as people."

Duckworth, Gerald, and Co. "Puzzles in Firbank." *Times Literary Supplement*, 27 January 1961, 57.

A letter to the editor announcing the forthcoming publication of *The Complete Ronald Firbank* and inviting solutions to several textual cruxes.

————. "Puzzles in Firbank." *Times Literary Supplement*, 28 April 1961, 263.

Gives solutions offered by correspondents to the cruxes announced in the 27 January issue.

Elliman, Michael, and Frederick Roll. *The Pink Plaque Guide to London*. London: GMP, 1986. 74-75.

A brief overview of RF's life and works—"novels in which yet another exploding jewelled handbagful of aphorisms and epigrams awaits you just over the page"—along with a list of ten London addresses he inhabited.

Ellis, G. U. *Twilight on Parnassus: A Survey of Post-War Fiction and Pre-War Criticism*. London: Michael Joseph, 1939. 216-20 and passim.

Concerning the eccentricities of RF and a body of work "which in method was unique in its mastery of obliquity and nuance; in form, almost among the visual arts in its power to render colour; in wit, more fantastic but far more subtle than anything issuing from the pen of Wilde. . . . Both in appearance and in influence he was a direct link between the Decadence and some of the early post-War writers." But RF, "alone of his contemporaries, returned to Verlaine and Baudelaire."

Fallowell, Duncan. "Butterfly and Cocoon." *London Magazine* 10.12 (March 1971): 57-64.

Musing on the revival of interest in RF, Fallowell makes several interesting distinctions concerning RF's relation to the "Oxford Tradition," his obliqueness (as opposed to discreetness: "Firbank is not a discreet writer. He is rococo, not neo-classical, a tea-cup vampire with a stammer"), his use of satire ("he uses the technique without the [moral] obligation"), and his writing style. If "some of Firbank's magic has faded," Fallowell blames Benkovitz's unimaginative biography.

————. "Ronald Firbank." In *Makers of Modern Culture*. Ed. Justin Wintle. London: Routledge & Kegan Paul, 1981. 166-67.

RF's "audacity had much to do with inventing the modern novel and his influence has been very widespread, though typically oblique, and more practical than theoretical. Writers respect him far more than do academics," Fallowell notes, and goes on to enumerate RF's various modernist techniques and the writers who show his influence.

Fiedler, Leslie. "The Eye of Innocence." In his *No! in Thunder*. Boston: Beacon, 1960. 285-86.

Compares *Cardinal Pirelli* with Mann's *Death in Venice* and sees their protagonists' attraction to "boy-coquettes" as the "sinister embodiment of the Romantic drive toward self-immolation."

Field, Andrew. *Djuna: The Formidable Miss Barnes*. Austin: Univ. of Texas Press, 1985. 26, 90.

Notes resemblances between Barnes's early work and RF's (without, however, suggesting Barnes read him).

Fletcher, Ian. "Inventions for the Left Hand: Beardsley in Verse and Prose." In *Reconsidering Aubrey Beardsley*. Ed. Robert Langenfeld. Ann Arbor: UMI Research Press, 1989. 251.

Notes that in Beardsley's *Under the Hill*, "the subversion of pornography works against the idiom of sophisticated or offhand allusion which anticipates the subtler, more velvet indirections of Ronald Firbank. In Firbank, the bravura [prose] solicits and diverts attention from the dangerous silence of the subtext where the real decrypting occurs. And there is also the violent difference of pace between a Firbank narrative and Beardsley's slow and linear progression."

Fletcher, Ifan Kyrle. "Ronald Firbank: Newport Associations of a Modernist." *South Wales News*, 20 August 1927. Rpt. (abridged) as "A Modern Eccentric: Memories of the Exquisite Work of a True Bohemian." *South Wales Argus*, 6 October 1928.

An overview of the Firbank legend, described in Benkovitz's "The Fabric of Biography" (25).

[Fontaine, Robert.] "Who Is Ronald Firbank." *Writer* 71 (July 1958): 1-2.

Having named RF as his favorite writer in a self-interview in the May issue of the *Writer* (p. 12), the once-popular short-story writer answers a letter to the editor asking if RF is indeed a real person. Fontaine recommends the New Directions omnibuses and recycles some Firbank anecdotes.

Foster, Jeanette H. *Sex Variant Women in Literature*. 1956; rpt. Tallahassee: Naiad, 1985. 268-69.

A brief discussion of lesbianism in *The Flower beneath the Foot*.

Francis, John. "Firbank's Flowering Tributes." *Hortus* 3 (Autumn 1987): 100-107.

According to Peter Parker, "an essentially light-hearted but knowledgeable and championing essay on flowers and gardens in RF's works. It also has something to say about RF's fictional method." (*Hortus* is a quarterly gardening journal published in Wales with an irregular feature on "Gardens in Fiction," of which Francis's is the third.)

————. "Food in Fiction: Dining with Firbank." *Convivium* 1.2 (Summer 1993).

Fraser, G. S. *The Modern Writer and His World.* Derek Verschoyle, 1953; rev. ed. London: Andre Deutsch, 1964; New York: Frederick A. Praeger, 1965; Harmondsworth: Penguin, 1970. 119, 127-29, 183.

"Firbank's life was one of frozen hysteria and sterile self-absorption. . . . His novels must have helped him to retain his precarious balance, and in them he concentrates with an almost religious earnestness on the 'amusing': for him, in life and in literature, to be obvious and to be serious were equal solecisms." Fraser finds a childlike quality in RF's works that offsets "his high, thin, giggling naughtiness." Durrell reminds Fraser of Firbank at times.

Gallup, Donald, ed. *The Flowers of Friendship: Letters Written to Gertrude Stein.* New York: Knopf, 1953. 151.

Contains a letter by Carl Van Vechten dated 22 February 1924 recommending *The Flower beneath the Foot* to Stein.

Glendinning, Victoria. *Vita: The Life of V. Sackville-West.* London: Weidenfeld & Nicolson/New York: Knopf, 1983. 129-30.

Notes RF's portrayal of Sackville-West as the Hon. Mrs. Chilleywater in *The Flower beneath the Foot* and quotes a passage from the novel.

Goldring, Douglas. *The Nineteen Twenties.* London: Nicholson & Watson, 1945. 97-98.

Mentions RF in a survey of 1920s literature, but believes he belongs more to the 1890s. "He was both in the English tradition of Surrealist nonsense and in the equally English tradition of Catholic humour, both 'Anglo' and 'Roman,' which survives in Sandys Wason, Evelyn Waugh and John Betjeman."

————. *Privileged Persons.* London: The Richards Press, 1955. 41.

RF is remembered "standing shyly, with his head on one side, at the entrance to the Café [Royal], looking about for a congenial companion."

Gould, Gerald. *The English Novel of To-day.* London: John Castle, 1924. 166-70.

Slightly revised versions of his *New Statesman* reviews of *Inclinations* and *Caprice.* Gould admits he is not among "those who can whole-heartedly enjoy Mr. Ronald Firbank, an author whose themes, whose scholarship, whose fantasy, suggests some affinity with Mr. Douglas. I cannot think his wit in the same class, but then I often cannot even guess at what he is talking about." Gould goes on to quote some passages from *Inclinations* that he finds incomprehensible but faintly amusing.

Green, Martin. *Children of the Sun: A Narrative of "Decadence" in England after 1918.* London: Constable, 1977; New York: Basic Books, 1977. 16, 64, 77-78, 81, 127, 182, 192, 193, 212, 223-24, 279.

Notes RF's crucial role in transmitting the style of the 1890s to the dandies of the 1920s. Alan Pryce-Jones is quoted as saying "that in his time at Oxford the test of whether a man was really an aesthete was whether he owned any Firbank books" (77-78).

Greif, Martin. *The Gay Book of Days.* Secaucus, NJ: Lyle Stuart, 1982. 25, 101, 106, 172.

RF noted under entry for 17 January (his birthday) and in entries for Beau Brummell, Carl Van Vechten, and Charles Ricketts.

Griffin, Jasper, ed. *Snobs.* Oxford: Oxford Univ. Press, 1982.
Four quotations from RF's work (two from *Flower beneath the Foot,* one from *Inclinations,* one from *New Rythum*) are included in this anthology.

Gross, John. *The Rise and Fall of the Man of Letters: English Literary Life since 1800.* 1969. New ed. London: Penguin, 1991. 315.
"Some authors lend themselves more appropriately to academic study than others. The idea of a graduate seminar on Ronald Firbank would be Firbankian."

Haddow, G. C. "Featherpate of Folly." *University of Toronto Quarterly* 24.2 (January 1955): 191-96.
An appreciative if condescending overview of the life and work. Like Milton, RF is valued only by a small audience, but unlike the Puritan poet he is unaware of good and evil and lacks moral judgment or righteous indignation. There is no serious purpose in his work; "Firbank never deviates into sense, and rarely into dullness." Haddow feels *The Flower* is RF's finest work, though *Prancing Nigger* "perhaps comes closest to technical perfection." Echoing (if not plagiarizing) Pritchett five years earlier, Haddow concludes: "With the eyes and ears of a gossip columnist, a feminine delight in the chic and modish, a temperament incurably frivolous, and a sublime sense of the ridiculous, he saw life neither steadily nor whole but in glittering bits and pieces. . . . Yet Firbank has his niche in the permanent gallery of English comic writers."

Hafley, James. "Ronald Firbank." *Arizona Quarterly* 12 (Summer 1956): 161-71.
RF's work displays "the quality of high-seriousness, or, if you like, moral awareness." In *The Flower beneath the Foot* this quality emerges from "a careful juxtaposition of traditional religious and moral order with another order, or disorder, that completely denigrates it and that it in turn condemns." Similar criticisms of lives in disorder are to be found in *The Artificial Princess, Vainglory, Caprice, Valmouth, Prancing Nigger,* and *Cardinal Pirelli* (the last concluding with "a hymn of praise for one conception of cosmic order"). Consequently, RF is closer to a writer like Graham Greene than Beardsley and the decadents. RF, like Proust, achieves "the immutable in terms of the most ephemeral . . . by the continual ambiguous interplay of faith and folly."

Hamnett, Nina. *Laughing Torso.* London: Constable, 1932; New York: Ray Long and Richard P. Smith, 1932. 264-65.
Relates two meetings with RF, who was nervous and tongue-tied both times.

————. *Is She a Lady? A Problem in Autobiography.* London: Allan Wingate, 1955. 142-43, 157.
One day in the Swiss Bar a man named George Lovelace "said that Ronald had given him many of his books, most of which he had destroyed. This sounds fantastic," Hamnett explains, "but when they first appeared during the 1914-18 war, had anyone understood what they were all about? They were written long before their time and it is only comparatively recently that he has come in to his own" (143). She also records that in 1949 a reporter for the *Daily Graphic* told her: "I am writing an article on [the popular novelist] Ouida. When did she write the 'Princess Zoubouroff'?" (*sic*)(157).

Harris, Alan. "Introduction." In RF's *New Rythum,* 9-17.

Describes the circumstances in which these writings came to light and notes the obvious influences (Maeterlinck, Wilde) on the young RF. Though incomplete, *The New Rythum* is "the authentic thing . . . everything definable that his faithful votaries have a right to expect is there." Harris concludes with humorous comments on the photographs of RF published in this volume.

Hastings, Selina. *Evelyn Waugh: A Biography.* London: Sinclair-Stevenson, 1994; New York: Houghton Mifflin, 1995. 93, 171-72, 209, 316.

Notes both that Harold Acton introduced Waugh to RF's novels and their influence on *Decline and Fall* and *Vile Bodies.*

Heath, Jeffrey. *The Picturesque Prison: Evelyn Waugh and His Writing.* Kingston: McGill-Queen's Univ. Press, 1982. 42, 60-61, 68, 81, 123, 227, 296 n29, 297 n14.

Brief references to Waugh's adaptation of RF's "structural use of innuendo and allusion" and Waugh's preference of RF's "baroque" over Wilde's "rococo."

Hemingway, Ernest. *A Moveable Feast.* New York: Scribner's, 1964. 27.

In his account of his years in Paris in the 1920s, Hemingway notes: "In the three or four years that we were good friends I cannot remember Gertrude Stein ever speaking well of any writer who had not written favorably about her work or done something to advance her career, except for Ronald Firbank and, later, Scott Fitzgerald."

Hewitt, Douglas. *The Approach to Fiction: Good and Bad Readings of Novels.* London: Longmans, 1972. 9.

Cites RF as an example ("in a more extreme way") of a writer whose metaphors depend for their effectiveness on the reader's conscious realization that dissimilarities are being yoked together.

Higgins, Patrick, ed. *A Queer Reader.* London: Fourth Estate, 1993. 302-3.

A brief reference to RF.

Hoare, Philip. *Serious Pleasures: The Life of Stephen Tennant.* London: Hamish Hamilton, 1990. 116-17, 133, 367.

Notes the parallels between RF and Tennant, "the last professional exquisite," who struck some, like Harold Acton and Cecil Beaton, as a character out of one of RF's novels. Tennant was Siegfried Sassoon's lover, and RF's relationship with Sassoon is retold. Tennant began reading RF in 1928, and Hoare traces the influence of RF's works (especially *Caprice*) on Tennant's own writings (see part 4).

Hobson, Anthony. [Description of RF's mss.] In *Sotheby & Co.'s Catalogue of Nineteenth-Century & Modern First Editions, Presentation Copies, Autograph Letters & Important Literary Manuscripts.* London: Sotheby & Co., 1961. 3-27. Rpt. (with some omissions) in *The New Rythum,* 127-35.

Includes extensive quotations from RF's unpublished works.

Holland, Vyvyan. *Son of Oscar Wilde.* London: Rupert Hart-Davis, 1954; New York: Dutton, 1954. 160-61, 172-74; Oxford/New York: Oxford Univ. Press, 1988. 181-82, 194-96.

A distillation of his memoir in Fletcher (see part 2).

Hollinghurst, Alan. "Vibro-message." *Times Literary Supplement,* 28 May 1982, 583.

A review of John Dexter's production of Sandy Wilson's musical adaptation of *Valmouth* at the Chichester Festival Theatre. Though the production captures only the "vulgar" in RF's own description of the novel ("Vulgar, cynical & horrid"), Hollinghurst believes RF would have loved it, if only because of his devotion to the earliest jazz. Finally, however, the play betrays the novel by abandoning its ending for a "deplorably coarse" alternative, indicating "a failure to come to terms with the true nature of the novel," which has to do with "the entrancing yet humiliating nature of the sexual imagination, the hunger for an elsewhere—in religion, culture, love—that can never be attained."

————. "Introduction." In *The Early Firbank,* vii-xi.

RF's early writing is largely about his mother and *The Early Firbank* can be divided broadly into "those pieces written for her and those written about her. The former are by and large insipid or religiose, linguistically dead to modern taste and drawing heavily on the *Symbolistes* and on the precious rhetoric of Wilde's fairy-tales." The latter, "the society tales, are marked by the sharpness of their exposure of self-delusion in female behaviour and falseness in female relationships." Comparisons are made with Jane Austen, and Hollinghurst concludes: "for all the Wildean wit and coruscating inconsequence of these tales, their abiding atmosphere is melancholy . . . the tone that belongs uniquely to Firbank, the poet of solitude and singleness, of the workings of the mind left to its own frail or feverish devices."

Hooker, Denise. *Nina Hamnett: Queen of Bohemia.* London: Constable, 1986. 43, 143, 155, 178.

Brief anecdotes about RF, derived from Benkovitz's *Biography* and Hamnett's own memoirs.

Horder, Mervyn. "More Ronald Firbank." *Times Literary Supplement,* 14 July 1961, 440. Rpt. as "A Firbank Manuscript" in his *Memoirs and Critiques,* 209-10.

On the recently discovered manuscript of *The New Rythum,* with some general observations on RF. Benkovitz wrote a long letter to the editor challenging Horder's short note: see her "More Ronald Firbank" (1961).

Inge, M. Thomas, ed. *Truman Capote: Conversations.* Jackson: Univ. Press of Mississippi, 1987. 28.

In his *Paris Review* interview of 1977 (reprinted here), Capote states: "To some degree all writers have style . . . Ronald Firbank, bless his heart, had little else, and thank God he realized it."

Irwin, W. R. *The Game of the Impossible: A Rhetoric of Fantasy.* Urbana: Univ. of Illinois Press, 1976. 80-81, 114-19, and passim.

Praises RF's "linguistic virtuosity": "Firbank's effort was to give an imitation in language of dandyism. His style is part of his whole game, and for all that it is mannered, it is also disciplined" (80-81). Irwin aligns RF with the fantasy tradition in literature and discusses his techniques, with special attention to *The Flower beneath the Foot* (115-19).

Jebb, Julian. "The Art of Fiction: Evelyn Waugh." *Paris Review* 30 (Summer-Fall 1963): 77, 80.

In this interview, Waugh admits *Vile Bodies* "was second-hand too. I cribbed

much of the scene at the customs from Firbank" (77) and goes on to say that
he no longer read RF and thought there would be "something wrong with an
elderly man who could enjoy Firbank" (80).

John, Augustus. *Chiaroscuro: Fragments of Autobiography.* London: Jonathan
Cape, 1952; New York: Pellegrini & Cudahy, 1952.
    Among the patrons of the Eiffel Tower, "The evasive Ronald Firbank
struggles almost manfully with his asparagus and a bottle of wine, while following intermittently the bird-like flights of the Honble. Evan Morgan" (137). On
p. 210, John wishes RF had been able to join him in Venice: "How *he* would
have enjoyed it all! and how I would have enjoyed his enjoyment."

Jones, Ernest. "Introduction." In RF's *Three Novels,* vii-xx. Rpt. in Horder's
Memoirs and Critiques, 185-95.
    Argues that RF "is a better and a more serious writer than it has ever been
fashionable to suppose" and that his achievement is greater than that of his
more stolid, realistic contemporaries. A brief account of his background is
followed by comments on RF's characteristic settings and themes (ennui,
homosexuality, pretentiousness). Everything for RF was a subject for comedy:
sex, religion, homosexuality, culture. "He was afraid of feeling, a fear which
seriously limited the range of his fiction, but which is directly responsible for
his delightful ironies and flippancies." Jones shows that artistic influences on
RF are just as important as the often-noted literary ones, especially the methods
of the Impressionists. His fantastic, eccentric characters are not that far re-
moved from their real-life counterparts in pre-1914 café society, and much of
his writing resembles "the private sensibility, a private witticism, typical of the
fashionable talk of a tiny set." His novels "burlesque themes popular in nineteenth-century fiction" and, in novels like *Valmouth, Santal,* and especially
Prancing Nigger, "achieved comedy by imposing English lower middle class
values on a half-civilized society." RF's conception of Evil is actually mere
naughtiness, a transgression "in terms of the moral atmosphere of the middle
class into which he was born. . . . There are no Stavrogins in this fiction." Jones
concludes that RF is essentially "a comic writer; his chief device is a kind of
romantic irony. . . . There is a consistent satiric intent in his novels, aimed at
the usual objects of satire. . . . One has only to read a page or so of Firbank at
random to note his awareness of the transience of all the earthly beauty he loved
so well, an awareness which makes these novels, with their curious materialism,
their praises of the rich and the exotic, moving as well as comic."

Karl, Frederick R. *A Reader's Guide to the Contemporary English Novel.* New
York: Farrar, Straus & Giroux, 1962. 10, 169, 239.
    Passing references to RF's "fruity nonsense" and its influence on Waugh and
Powell.

Kellner, Bruce. *Carl Van Vechten and the Irreverent Decades.* Norman: Univ. of
Oklahoma Press, 1968. 185-88 and passim.
    An account of RF's relationship to Van Vechten, with several quotations
from RF's letters.

————. "Valmouth." In *Reference Guide to English Literature.* Ed. D. L. Kirk-
patrick. 2nd ed. Chicago and London: St. James Press, 1991. 3:1918-19.
    Valmouth is quintessential Firbank, Kellner argues, who compares it to his
other works and summarizes the plot.

Kennard, Sir Coleridge. "Introduction." In RF's *The Artificial Princess*, vii-x. Rpt. as "Introduction" to RF's *Extravaganzas*, 7-11, and in Horder's *Memoirs and Critiques*, 107-11.

When Kennard knew RF at Cambridge, he noted his habit of writing phrases that pleased him on strips of paper, and hoarding them until they could be assembled into a book. "Behind the seemingly incoherent pages of his prose were months of toil, of conscientious selection and revision carefully hidden from every eye." Though early, *The Artificial Princess* "is a mature and typical work. In it the faint, shadowy Court, the Conder-like figures, the ceremonial, the stifled twilights and whispered innuendos that were to form the background of his later books are sketched for the first time." Firbank hesitated publishing this in later life because he realized he used some of its phrases for later work (Kennard gives some examples), and sent it to Lord Berners for his opinion, who in turn passed it along to Kennard. He concludes with a charming account of the first time he met RF in Cambridge.

Kiernan, Robert F. "Aestheticism Empurpled: Ronald Firbank." Chap. 4 of his *Frivolity Unbound: Six Masters of the Camp Novel*. New York: Continuum, 1990. 49-65.

Complaining "it is a scandal of letters that Firbank's densely wrought fictions are not generally recognized as milestones in the effort of the twentieth-century novel to free itself from nineteenth-century realism," Kiernan finds RF at the heart of the "camp enterprise" and examines three of the novels, which "form an interesting trilogy as well, for *The Flower Beneath the Foot* is a camp vision of paradise, *Prancing Nigger* a vision of paradise on the verge of ruin, and *The Eccentricities of Cardinal Pirelli* a vision of paradise lost." Kiernan comments on the use of ellipsis in *The Flower* and feels the "aesthetical mischievousness" in the novel outweighs any "satiric instinct." RF's "amateurish rendering of the patois [in *Prancing Nigger*] is a surrealistic technique," and comparisons are made to Jane Austen's world. *Cardinal Pirelli* is concerned with "the mindscape where religion, social éclat, and sexual promiscuity come together." Kiernan concludes: "So definitive, so purely camp, are Firbank's novels that all subsequent works of literary camp seem to defer to them."

King, Viva. *The Weeping and the Laughter*. London: Macdonald and Jane's, 1976. 89-90.

A brief recollection of RF in the early twenties; rpt. in Horder (134-35).

Kirkup, James. *I, of All People: An Autobiography of Youth*. New York: St. Martin's Press, 1988. 11, 15, 152, 174, 191, 192, 210, 217.

RF is mentioned/cited a half-dozen times as someone Kirkup admired and even imitated in appearance.

―――. *A Poet Could Not But Be Gay: Some Legends of My Lost Youth*. London: Peter Owen, 1991. 42-43, 51, 71, 79, 121-23, 145, 157.

A sequel to the above, with more passing references to RF. Kirkup often visited RF's grave in Rome ("Ronald lies next to someone for whom he would have felt the utmost horror, and whom he would have satirized in his scintillating novels—Una, Lady Troubridge") and even stayed in the same Roman hotel room in which RF died.

Knight, Grant C. *The Novel in English*. New York: Richard R. Smith, 1931. 72, 262, 365.

Contains brief references linking RF's work to that of Sterne, "madcap literature," and comic opera.

Knoll, Robert E. *McAlmon and the Lost Generation*. Lincoln: Univ. of Nebraska Press, 1962. 175-76.
    Reprints McAlmon's account in *Being Geniuses Together* (see below) of meeting with RF. (A brief biographical note on RF appears on p. 373.)

Kopelson, Kevin. *Love's Litany: The Writing of Modern Homoerotics*. Stanford: Stanford Univ. Press, 1994. 49-73.
    In chap. 2, RF is paired with Gide to demonstrate how two "frustrated pederasts" dealt with the traditional erotic notion of "complimentary merger" (i.e., opposites attract). Working mostly with *Cardinal Pirelli* (and with references to *The Artificial Princess* and *The Princess Zoubaroff*), Kopelson investigates disrobing as an act of both self-revelation and disempowerment, RF's rejection of Wilde's constructionist rejection of an essential self (without, however, fully embracing essentialism), and "the use of Narcissus as a trope for libidinal investment in the ego."

Kunitz, Stanley, ed. *Twentieth-Century Authors: First Supplement*. New York: H. W. Wilson, 1955. 326.
    Notes the revival of interest in RF in the late forties and early fifties.

————, and Howard Haycroft, eds. *Twentieth Century Authors*. New York: H. W. Wilson, 1942.
    An overview of RF's life and work, with an emphasis on his personality.

Lahr, John. *Prick Up Your Ears: The Biography of Joe Orton*. New York: Knopf, 1978. 105-8.
    Discusses the influence of RF on the dramatist, repeated from Lahr's introduction to Orton's *Complete Plays* (see part 5).

————. *Dame Edna Everage and the Rise of Western Civilisation: Backstage with Barry Humphries*. London: Bloomsbury, 1991.
    Notes the influence of RF on the Australian dandy, female impersonator, and Firbank collector.

Lane, Christopher. "Re/Orientations: Firbank's Colonial Imaginary and the Sexual Nomad." *Literature Interpretation Theory* 3.4 (1992): 271-86. Rpt. in his *The Ruling Passion: British Colonial Allegory and the Paradox of Homosexual Desire*. Durham, NC: Duke Univ. Press, 1995.
    In this significant essay on colonialism in RF's works, Lane argues that RF displaces male homosexual desire by focusing instead on lesbianism and on the attraction of exotic cultures. "Firbank's emphasis on travel, and fascination with indigenous cultures, provides an additional exit from the demand for a normative sexuality because his fantasy offers alternative positions and pursuits that fall under the sway of an effusive—though normally allusive—homosexuality." Although works like *Prancing Nigger* or *Valmouth* may appear racist, in them "race works as a metonym for homosexuality, without effacing or substituting for it. Firbank may be said to offer an analogy that makes 'race' the metaphorical expression of homosexuality because they share similarities as marginal and repressed components within colonial society." Though RF frequently exploits racial stereotypes, he just as frequently undermines them: his attitude is ambivalent and complex. (*Santal* and *Cardinal Pirelli* are also discussed.)

Lee, Patricia. "The Play of Obscenity: Ronald Firbank's *The Princess Zoubaroff.*" Paper presented at the annual MLA Convention, session 367: "Ronald Firbank: New Readings," San Diego, CA, 28 December 1994.

The failure of marriage and heterosexuality occupies the stage in RF's play, while the success of homosocial bonds occurs offstage; thus "the conventional center is not the center of our attention," and conventional bonds (marriage, heterosexuality) are thereby displaced. Examining British conventions in an Italian setting is a further act of displacement. RF dramatizes "the arbitrariness and obscenity of centers. . . . For, in *The Princess Zoubaroff,* what is conventional is obscene; it is what we would see center-stage that Firbank will not have us watch."

Lees-Milne, James. *William Beckford.* NJ: Allanheld and Schram, 1979.

Describes Beckford's prose as antedating that of 20th-century writers like RF and Waugh.

―――. *Harold Nicolson: A Biography.* London: Chatto & Windus, 1980. 24-26, 51.

Describes Nicolson's mixed feelings toward RF.

Leslie, Shane. *The Film of Memory.* London: Michael Joseph, 1938. 322-23; rpt. in Horder's *Memoirs and Critiques,* 149-50.

Brief remarks on RF at Cambridge. "He wrote a number of orchidaceous books, whose style and texture grew more and more like himself. He was a harmless and pathetic being, and died like a lily which had always been trying to break its window-box."

―――. "Ronald Firbank and the Faith." *Tablet* 198 (22 September 1951): 194-95.

A letter to the editor responding to a review of Brooke's *Ronald Firbank* (by a Mr. Bates; untraced); Leslie contests the reviewer's claim that, though converted, RF didn't practice as a Catholic. He recounts RF's involvement with Catholicism under Mgr. Benson at Cambridge.

Lewis, Wyndham. "The 'Blessings of the Sophisticated School of Literature.'" *The Enemy* 2 (September 1927): 111.

Announces his intention to write a blistering critique of what a catalogue called "the sophisticated school of literature," beginning with Norman Douglas's *South Wind* and moving on to Huxley, RF, Van Vechten, and Michael Arlen. The critique was never written; as Lewis explains in *The Enemy* 3 (1929): 97-98, he found *South Wind* unexpectedly enjoyable.

―――. *Men without Art.* London: Cassell, 1934; corrected ed. Santa Rosa, CA: Black Sparrow, 1987.

Contains two brief references to RF (61, 149), both grouping him with other "exotic" writers and artists.

―――. *Blasting and Bombardiering.* London: Eyre and Spottiswoode, 1937. 225-29. 2nd, rev. ed. London: Calder & Boyars, 1967; Berkeley: Univ. of California Press, 1967. 224-28. Rpt. in Horder's *Memoirs and Critiques,* 152-55.

Considered RF "the very *genius loci* of the 'post-war,' and the reincarnation of the Nineties—Oscar Wilde, Pater, Beardsley, Dawson [*sic*] all rolled into one, and served up with *sauce créole.*" Recalls how difficult it was to draw RF with his writhing and constant need to monitor the process, but thinks the result "the best head that was ever done of him." (Two portraits by Lewis, dated 1922, are reproduced in Benkovitz's *Biography,* plate VI). Despite his impatience with him as a sitter, Lewis didn't object to RF. "On the contrary. He seemed to me a pretty good clown—of the 'impersonator' type. . . . I had such relations with him as one might have with a talking gazelle, afflicted with some nervous disorder." He concludes with an anecdote about dining with RF and an American college boy at Stulik's.

————. *Letters.* Ed. W. K. Rose. Norfolk, CT: New Directions, 1963. 415.
    Reprints a letter to the editor of *TLS* (27 September 1947) responding to a review of three novels by William Gerhardi; Lewis disassociates his novel *Tarr* from satires like "*South Wind* and *Antic Hay* or the books of Ronald Firbank— a very 'ninetyish company," and goes on to say: "The *Apes of God* on the other hand I should not classify as a novel, but as satire, for as satire it was written, and not as a realistic narrative, as was *Tarr,* though I think it would make a volume of Firbank's somewhat uncomfortable, if it were jammed up against it on a bookshelf, as a result of a misunderstanding regarding their consanguinity."

Locher, Frances C., ed. *Contemporary Authors,* vol. 104. Detroit: Gale Research, 1982. 148-49.
    A brief overview of RF's career.

Lodge, David. "The Fugitive Art of Letters." In *Evelyn Waugh and His World.* Ed. David Pryce-Jones. London: Weidenfeld and Nicolson/Boston: Little, Brown, 1973. 183-217. Rpt. in Lodge's *Working with Structuralism: Essays and Reviews on Nineteenth- and Twentieth-Century Literature.* Boston: Routledge & Kegan Paul, 1981.
    Brief remarks on RF's influence on Waugh.

Long, Richard A., and Iva G. Jones. "Towards a Definition of the 'Decadent Novel.'" *College English* 22 (January 1961): 245-49.
    Includes a brief discussion of RF as a "decadent" novelist, and remarks on the tragic note in his later works. "He stands as the best practitioner of this genre" (248).

Lueders, Edward. *Carl Van Vechten and the Twenties.* Albuquerque: Univ. of New Mexico Press, 1955. 22, 60-61, 85, 117.

————. *Carl Van Vechten.* New York: Twayne, 1965. 44, 53, 54, 72, 87, 90, 109.
    Brief points of comparison between the novels of RF and Van Vechten.

MacInnes, Colin. *"No Novel Reader."* London: Brian & O'Keeffe, 1975. 20, 22.
    The novelist includes RF in his discussion of innovators like Proust and Joyce because "he seems to me, though a minor artist, to have turned the novel upside-down far more radically than did any of the more portentous English imitators of James Joyce." None of these writers can be called a "novelist" in the traditional sense: "if one said that *Caprice,* or *The Flower beneath the Foot,* were the works of a 'novelist,' the very shade of Firbank would surely shudder" (20). They don't have traditional elements of the novel (plot, character development) "Yet they have a logic, a lucidity, a 'meaning' even, all their own: which seems to be that life is exquisite, only when it is momentary; ecstatic, only because really tragic." His prose is musical in a literal sense, "and for a writer whose tone is apparently so casual, it is sinewy, pared prose at that" (22).

Mackaye, Milton. "Firbank, Sophisticates' Idol, Dead? or Alive and Well?" *New York Evening Post*, 8 October 1926.

Subheaded "Evening Post Learns Proof of Writer's Death is Lacking— Manuscripts Missing, No Trace of Body, and Publishers are Baffled." A trumped-up story that was rescinded in the following day's *Post*.

Madden, David, ed. *Rediscoveries.* New York: Crown, 1971. 316.

Prancing Nigger included in "A Partial List of Other Fiction Worthy of Rediscovery."

Mais, S. P. B.

In her Firbank biography (p. 97), Benkovitz quotes this popular British novelist and critic's opinion that RF was "the Mercutio of our time." Source unknown.

Manguel, Alberto, and Gianni Guadalupi. *The Dictionary of Imaginary Places.* New York: Macmillan, 1980. 367.

Contains a page-long entry for Tacarigua, the Caribbean island setting of *Prancing Nigger*.

Mannin, Ethel. *Young in the Twenties: A Chapter of Autobiography.* London: Hutchinson, 1971. 91-95.

Compares RF with Michael Arlen (to RF's disadvantage) but notes how attractive RF's "wickedness" and "Wildean decadence" were to Mannin in the twenties: "a certain *chic* attached to an enjoyment of them."

Mansfield, Katherine. *Letters to John Middleton Murray: 1913-1922.* Ed. John Middleton Murray, 1958. 451.

In a letter dated 7 January 1920, the short-story writer asks Murray *not* to praise *Valmouth* in the *Athenæum*.

Maschwitz, Eric. *No Chip on My Shoulder.* London: Herbert Jenkins, 1957. 36.

In the songwriter and theatrical producer's autobiography, he mentions knowing RF in the early 1920s, and quotes from the obituary he wrote for him: "A thin man with a black felt hat . . . a narrow man and restless—writhing like a basket of serpents. Clutching at the lapel of his coat, dipping his head like an embarrassed governess. Always paying for drinks . . . 'My dear! I saw a crossing sweeper in Sloane Street to-day with the eyes of a startled faun!' . . . 'My dear, when you talk like that you give me a distinct feeling of plush!'"

———. *These Foolish Things.*

In their *Café Royal* (pp. 175-76), Deghy and Waterhouse quote apparently from this memoir a description of RF as glimpsed there by Maschwitz.

McAlmon, Robert. *Being Geniuses Together.* London: Secker and Warburg, 1938; rev. ed., ed. Kay Boyle. Garden City, NY: Doubleday, 1968. 84-85, 88-90. London: Michael Joseph, 1970. 76-81.

Describes meeting RF in 1923 and records some of his conversation.

McCarthy, Shaun. "Firbank's *Inclinations* and the *nouveau roman*." *Critical Quarterly* 20.2 (Summer 1978): 64-77.

The isolated, self-absorbed nature of most of RF's characters is conveyed by his use of dialogue, a private language often difficult for the reader to comprehend, and which is exhausted of meaningful content. The lack of communication between RF's characters anticipates the exercises in non-communication to be found in such *nouveaux romanciers* as Robbe-Grillet (whose *L'Année dernière à Marienbad* is quoted) and Resnais. The undated quality of his work, its lack of historical perspective, challenges "the fundamental question of *temporality* in fiction." RF's "work introduces to narrative prose some of the techniques appropriate to modern poetry. It requires, hence, a more substantial effort at imaginative interpretation than has been commonly accorded it." RF is also compared and contrasted to Eliot, Compton-Burnett, and Murdoch.

McCartney, George. *Confused Roaring: Evelyn Waugh and the Modernist Tradition*. Bloomington: Indiana Univ. Press, 1987. 71-74, 78, 98, 102, 104, 121.
    Details Waugh's technical debts to RF. "Waugh found in Firbank's novels a way to avoid both the restrictive conventions of realism and the psychoanalytic excesses of modernism. His elliptically evanescent narratives provided an avant-garde strategy that never lapsed into self-absorbed solemnity" (71). "Firbank's absurd subject matter, weightless characters, and elliptical wit—in sum, his gossamer inconsequence—were congenial to Waugh's satiric temperament" (73). Waugh's use of cinematic techniques was adapted from RF's, borrowing "Firbank's method in order to construct a narrative equivalent of film edited in staccato montage" (102).

————. "Satire between the Wars: Evelyn Waugh and Others." In *The Columbia History of the British Novel*. Ed. John Richetti. New York: Columbia Univ. Press, 1994. 878-80.
    A distillation from his book (above) on RF's influence on Waugh.

McCormick, John. *Catastrophe and Imagination*. London: Longmans, Green, 1957. 74-75, 286-88, 298-301.
    Despising RF's "neuter giggle" and "tasteless burlesques," McCormick traces his negative influence on Huxley, Waugh, L. P. Hartley, and other "immediate and distant imitators: all the Sitwells, Cyril Connolly, William Sansom, and Angus Wilson; and in America, Truman Capote, Tennessee Williams, Paul Bowles, and Frederick Buechner. The majority of these writers share with Firbank a taste for excessive stylization, an adolescent desire to shock, a fondness for exotic paraphernalia, and an inadequately reasoned and therefore irresponsible attack on social shibboleth." McCormick suggests RF was influenced by Henry James, though RF "actually takes the Jamesian formula and turns it inside out; his characters (*Prancing Nigger* excepted) are Jamesian, and his situations are grotesque burlesques of James's; it is as though some blasphemer had written a musical comedy on the story of the Crucifixion." RF and his followers fail as satirists because they "attempted to eliminate the traditional strength that satire derived from the assertion of morality; without morality, their work became expressions of disgust or unconvincing buffoonery."

McDonnell, Jacqueline. *Waugh on Women*. New York: St. Martin's Press, 1985. 34-39.
    Discusses RF's influence on Waugh's early work and makes distinctions: "where Firbank has a delightful but irresponsible grasshopping mind, Waugh hops as effectively but with more responsibility. Very often he points a social moral, which Firbank does not."

Melchiori, Giorgio. *The Tightrope Walkers: Studies of Mannerism in Modern English Literature*. London: Routledge & Kegan Paul, 1956. 198, 208.
    In a chapter on Henry Green, RF is twice cited as a precursor.

Meyers, Jeffrey. *The Enemy: A Biography of Wyndham Lewis*. London: Routledge & Kegan Paul, 1980.

Despite his genial account in *Blasting and Bombardiering*, Lewis "clearly disliked" RF, was "actually revolted by him" (116).

Michel, Walter. *Wyndham Lewis: Paintings and Drawings*. Berkeley: Univ. of California Press, 1971.

Contains technical details on Lewis's two drawings of RF (382) and reproduces one of them (plate 59).

Monk, Leland. "Postcards from the Edge." Paper presented at the annual MLA Convention, session 367: "Ronald Firbank: New Readings," San Diego, CA, 28 December 1994.

Takes the story of RF's composition on postcards (which Monk sees no evidence for) as a metaphor—via Derrida's book *The Postcard*—for RF's habit of organizing his narratives into "picture postcards" (i.e., set pieces and dialogues), often "dirty" ones.

Moore, Steven. *William Gaddis*. Boston: Twayne, 1989. 7, 9, 49, 63.

Notes RF's influence on the American novelist, especially in the use of dialogue and satire.

———. "Textual Notes." In RF's *Complete Short Stories*, 157-70; rpt. (with additional material) in *The Early Firbank*, 209-23.

A historical and bibliographic account of RF's early work.

———. "Introduction" and "A Note on the Texts." In RF's *Complete Plays*, vii-xiii and 129-30.

A discussion of RF's interest in the drama and of the writing of his own three plays.

Mortimer, John. "Introduction." In RF's *The Flower beneath the Foot* (Penguin, 1986), 5-12.

Opens with a comparison of RF's dialogue with that of Wodehouse and Waugh and insists that RF, while never as popular as them, is just as accomplished. A brief overview of the life is followed by the suggestion that RF's religious background resulted in his becoming "the most elegant writer of ecclesiastical comedy since Trollope." His "chief stylistic gambit . . . was the juxtaposition of the ornate and the banal, continually puncturing his most pretentious moments." *The Flower* "has some of his best and most economical comic passages, with dialogue which might also have occurred to the creator of Jeeves."

Muir, Percy H. "A Bibliography of the First Editions of Books by Arthur Annesley Ronald Firbank (1886-1926)." Supplement to the *Bookman's Journal* 15.4 (1927): 1-8.

A checklist, with brief comments.

Neill, S. Diana. *A Short History of the English Novel*. London: Jarrolds, 1951. 249.

Contains a brief, favorable evaluation of RF's work, aligning him with Wilde and Beardsley. "Firbank was an impressionist whose object was to evade formal narrative; his characters have the iridescent glitter of moral decay and their gossamer talk is compounded of cynical wit and nonsense. He makes a cunning use of dialogue to convey his indelicate humour in a series of brilliant pastiches."

Nevinson, C. R. W. *Paint and Prejudice.* London: Metheun, 1937; New York: Harcourt, Brace, 1938. 120-21, 171, 216
   Brief accounts of encounters during the war with "that weird writer who was the originator of so much in modern literature."

Nichols, Beverly. *The Sweet and Twenties.* London: Weidenfeld and Nicolson, 1958. 130-33.
   Features an anecdote concerning RF's brief passion for Harry Pilcer (not recorded by RF's biographers). Nichols compares the "fabulous" novelist to "a moth who had fluttered from between the pages of Beardsley's *Under the Hill* to land on Norman Douglas's shoulder."

Nicolson, Harold. *Journey to Java.* London: Constable, 1957. 201-2.
   Nicolson recalls being approached by Col. Thomas Firbank's wife for advice on what to do with RF's papers and manuscripts. Nicolson cites Havelock Ellis (although not in conversation with Mrs. Firbank) to support his conviction that Heather Firbank (the previous owner of the papers) was insane.

[O'Brien, Edna.] "Edna O'Brien Talks to David Heycock about Her New Novel, 'A Pagan Place.'" *Listener,* 7 May 1970, 616-17. (From a broadcast on the BBC 2's *Review.*)
   Asked what she means by the word *literary,* the novelist explains (apparently having just read Benkovitz's *Biography,* published a few months earlier): "I suppose Ronald Firbank was a very literary and mandarin writer and he had the wisdom to recognise it himself. He said of his own work that it was mere thistle-down. Well, I'd rather write thistle, to tell you the truth."

Orton, Joe. *The Orton Diaries.* Ed. John Lahr. London: Metheun, 1986.
   In his introduction, Lahr quotes Peter Willes on some of Orton's manuscripts of the 1960s as "very pseudo-Ronald Firbank" (12), and in Orton's diary for March 1967, upon finishing *Caprice,* Orton notes : "Firbank is the only impressionist in the English novel" (124).

Osborne, Charles. In *The Penguin Companion to English Literature.* Ed. David Daiches. Harmondsworth: Penguin, 1971; New York: McGraw-Hill, 1971. 183.
   In his entry on Firbank, Osborne calls him "the most unusual talent amongst 20th-century novelists. That he is a minor novelist cannot be denied, that he will remain a minority taste is probable, but that his novels are superb works of art and of artifice is beyond question." There follows brief summaries of the novels—"whose plots are wispy, whose dialogue is fragmentary and as though imperfectly overheard, and whose characterization is, to say the least, impressionistic"—with *Caprice* singled out as "one of Firbank's finest and most characteristic achievements." Osborne believes that RF's "homosexual sensibility allied with his *fin-de-siècle* aestheticism creates a kind of pre-absurdist approach to the novel."

Ousley, Ian, ed. *The Cambridge Guide to Literature in English.* Cambridge: Cambridge Univ. Press, 1993. 332.
   A shorter version of the entry in Stapleton (see below).

Panter-Downes, Mollie. "Letter from London." *New Yorker,* 9 December 1961, 228, 231.
   An account of the impending Sotheby's sale of RF's surviving papers, and a

description, based on the notebooks, of how he wrote his books.

Parker, Peter. "'Aggressive, witty, & unrelenting': Brigid Brophy and Ronald Firbank." *Review of Contemporary Fiction* 15.3 (Fall 1995): 68-78.
A well-informed essay on Brophy's book on RF and on his influence on Brophy's own novels.

————, ed. *The Reader's Companion to the Twentieth-Century Novel.* London: Fourth Estate/Helicon, 1994; in U.S. as *A Reader's Guide . . .* New York: Oxford Univ. Press, 1995.
RF has a biography entry (688-89) and individual entries for five of his novels—*Inclinations* (69), *Caprice* (74), *Flower* (96-97), *Prancing Nigger* (99-100), *Cardinal Pirelli* (111-12)—all appreciative.

————, ed. *The Reader's Companion to Twentieth-Century Writers.* London: Fourth Estate/Helicon, 1995.
Contains an entry on RF, who is mentioned in several other entries (e.g., on Waugh).

Paul, David. "Time and the Novelist." *Partisan Review* 21 (November-December 1954): 636-49.
In this essay on how various novelists handle the passage of time in their work, RF is discussed briefly as a writer who, like Sterne, ignores the dimension of time, resulting in "a degree of decorative flatness . . . as mannered and as effective as it is in Beardsley." Paul goes on to say "Firbank's Mrs. Shamefoot, in *Vainglory,* is his Madame Bovary, and her life consists of one motive and one event" (640).

Pearson, John. *Façades: Edith, Osbert, and Sacheverell Sitwell.* London: Macmillan, 1978. 69, 133, 163, 176.
Brief references to the family's acquaintance with RF.

Pinto, Vivian de Sola. *The City That Shone: An Autobiography.* London: Hutchinson, 1969; New York: John Day, 1969. 252, 254. Rpt. in Horder's *Memoirs and Critiques,* 152.
Recalls the party held by the Sitwells and Sassoon in February 1919 for RF, at which he read from the forthcoming *Valmouth.*

Plomer, William. "An Alphabet of Literary Prejudice." *Windmill* 1.2 (1946). Rpt. in his *Electric Delights.* Ed. Rupert Hart-Davis. Boston: David R. Godine, 1978. 15-16.
On *Vainglory* (which Plomer considers his best) and RF's insight into dialogue: "he noticed that people don't listen much to one another, that in conversation they pursue their own thoughts rather than other people's, and that much of what they say is calculated to advertise their own importance, beauty, cleverness, knowledge or taste. . . . Sometimes the talk in his books reminds one of Swift's *Polite Conversation,* but that is recorded rather than invented, and Firbank invents rather than records."

Potoker, Edward Martin. "Facts on Firbank" [letter to the editor]. *New York Times Book Review,* 3 December 1961, 66.
On alleged errors in Alun Jones's review of *The Complete Ronald Firbank* (see part 1).

————. "Firbank, (Arthur Annesley) Ronald." In *Encyclopedia of World Literature in the 20th Century*. Ed. Wolfgang Bernard Fleischman. New York: Ungar, 1967. 1:386-87.

Brief overview of the life and work. RF's "best novels, teeming with brilliant dialogue and meticulously patterned prose, offer no explicit messages but much sardonic artistry and a unique vision of the absurd."

————. "Introduction." In RF's *When Widows Love & A Tragedy in Green*. London: Enitharmon, 1980. 9-14.

Gives the background to both stories and notes how they anticipate RF's later work.

————, and Neville Braybrooke. "The Mystery of the Blue Cards (an exchange of letters)." *Ramparts* 1.5 (March 1963): 53-55.

Potoker writes to point out "numerous misstatements and distortions" in Braybrooke's 1962 *Ramparts* essay, and in particular questions the existence of the blue cards on which (according to Sir Osbert Sitwell) RF wrote down phrases for later use.

Braybrooke responds that he has Sitwell's word that the blue cards exist ("at Renishaw") and deals with Potoker's other complaints.

Powell, Anthony. "Introduction." In *The Complete Ronald Firbank*, 5-16.

After a bemused summary of RF's background and life, Powell recalls how he first heard of him (he worked at Duckworth's in the late 1920s and recommended reprinting his novels). He argues that RF "is not a writer to be critically imposed by argument. He must be approached, as Rilke advocates for all works of art, in a spirit of sympathy." He goes on to warn that "it would be a mistake to claim too much" for him: "Ronald Firbank's range is limited; his narrative devious; his characterisation stylised." RF is worth reprinting, however, because of "his mastery of technique" and "the fact that his daydream is a more popular one than might on the surface be expected." Powell praises his innovation in dialogue and notes the influence on RF of Maeterlinck, Huysmans, Kipling (*Plain Tales from the Hills*), and Saki, and, less obviously, Henry James, Shakespeare, "and that side of Thomas Hardy which might be said in some degree to derive from Shakespeare's clowns and grotesque situations." (He quotes a passage from *The Return of the Native* to substantiate this claim.) Powell discusses each of the novels briefly—*Caprice* "is in some ways, I think, the best he wrote"—and notes the "fundamental melancholy that is at the heart of the Firbankian world." (This introduction is excluded, for unstated reasons, from both of Powell's collections of reviews and introductions, *Miscellaneous Verdicts* and *Under Review*.)

————. *Messengers of Day. To Keep the Ball Rolling: The Memoirs of Anthony Powell*, vol. 2. London: Heinemann, 1978; New York: Holt, Rinehart & Winston, 1978.

Notes the difficulty the proofreader of *The Works* had with RF's "sometimes hazardous Latin" (8); his role in persuading Duckworth to issue *The Works* (75); and RF's treatment of dialogue: "influenced, it seems to me, by Hardy's renderings of Wessex peasant talk" (110).

Praz, Mario. "Introductory Essay." in *Three Gothic Novels*. Ed. Peter Fairclough. Harmondsworth & New York: Penguin, 1968. 7-34.

Notes that "more than once" William Beckford's *Journal in Portugal and Spain* "calls to mind the *Eccentricities of Cardinal Pirelli*" (24).

Pritchett, V. S. *Complete Collected Essays.* London: Chatto & Windus/New York: Random House, 1991.

In addition to his essay-review of *Five Novels* (see part 2), Pritchett alludes to RF briefly in some of these essays. He notes the influence of *Tristram Shandy* on him (497), also of Ouida (540), RF's "mad" comic characters (549), his relation to Saki (645), Waugh (993), and Wodehouse (1244), and his appeal to Connolly (1282).

Prokosch, Frederic. *Voices: A Memoir.* New York: Farrar, Straus & Giroux, 1983. 10, 43.

Twice the novelist mentions his early interest in RF's work.

Putnam, Samuel. *Paris Was Our Mistress: Memoirs of a Lost and Found Generation.* New York: Viking, 1947. 126.

Describes the failed attempt of Ford Madox Ford's secretary to "initiate" him into RF's work, implying that it was RF's homosexuality that put Ford off.

Quennell, Peter. *The Sign of the Fish.* London: Collins, 1960; New York: Viking, 1960. 143-44.

Describes a comic incident between RF and Edward Marsh.

————. *A History of English Literature.* Springfield, MA: Merriam, 1973. 466.

Contains a paragraph on RF, whose novels "might perhaps be described as improper fairy-tales, intended for exceptionally knowing adults—satirical glimpses of a world where the sexes are often confused, and wit is the only indispensable virtue."

Reid, Forrest. *Private Road.* London: Faber and Faber, 1940. 55-58. Rpt. in Horder's *Memoirs and Critiques,* 147-49.

Memories of RF at Cambridge. Reid found him unreal, charming, and talented, but not an original writer: "he never wrote anything that had not before been better done by somebody else. . . . There is nothing in his books that is not in *The Importance of Being Earnest* and *South Wind.*"

Reynolds, Stanley. "Prancing Firbank." *Punch,* 29 January 1986, 49-50.

Notes that RF's centenary went unmarked by most people and magazines except for the *Tatler* (see "Keeping the Camp Fires Burning" above, under "Anonymous"), which he summarizes. Reynolds feels many readers are put off by RF's fiction because it seems to lack "a purpose," missing the point that people read him because RF "is very funny for people who think that he is funny." RF was a "literary pioneer" like Hemingway (Powell and Waugh also found similarities between the two) and developed the technique of cinema before cinema itself developed it. RF's work is "beautifully written," and "if the worse comes to the worse Firbank will be remembered as forming a link between the chi-chi writing of Oscar Wilde and Aubrey Beardsley (*Under the Hill*) and the more everyday but still rather grand styles of Evelyn Waugh and Anthony Powell." Reynolds ends by noting the reissues of *Valmouth and Other Novels* and *The Complete Firbank.*

Rice, Thomas Jackson. *English Fiction, 1900-1950.* Detroit: Gale Research Co., 1979. 1:317-28.

A lightly annotated bibliography of primary and secondary sources.

Richards, Grant. *Author Hunting by an Old Literary Sports Man.* London: Hamish Hamilton, 1934; New York: Coward-McCann, 1934. 248-60; 2nd ed. London: Unicorn Press, 1964. Rpt. in Horder's *Memoirs and Critiques,* 111-21.

An account of Richards's publishing relations with RF. "I have never been quite sure in my secret mind that he really deserved the appreciation that he secured both here and in America," but the first manuscript RF brought him, *Vainglory,* "had some curious fascination for me." He doubted it would sell well, but after RF offered to finance production costs, he became his publisher. RF told him *Vainglory* was an attempt "to do something like Beardsley had done in the illustrations to *The Rape of the Lock.*" RF "was the most nervous man I have had dealings with, and in some ways he was both cunning and suspicious." He goes on to describe several adventures in lunching with RF. He was never able to convince RF that 500 copies of each new book of his was more than enough to meet the demand, and the efforts of "that tall and solid imp of mischief, Carl Van Vechten," only created false expectations in RF. He quotes some posthumous reviews of RF's work, but again states "I myself should have been much surprised if Firbank had written something of lasting value." He concludes with the story of Evan Morgan taking offense at RF's proposed dedication of *The Princess Zoubaroff* to him.

Richardson, Sallyann. "Firbank, [Arthur Annesley] Ronald." In *Twentieth Century Writing: A Reader's Guide to Contemporary Literature.* Ed. Kenneth Richardson. New York: Newnes, 1969. 208-9.

A concise, positive evaluation of RF's work. "His fertile wit, his outrageous statements and occasional startling sexual innuendo, and above all his unerring ear for words and languages, give great vigour to his writing, . . . The close, hot-house impression left by the pervasive sexual depravity and perversion of his characters is sometimes relieved by the freshness and beauty of the natural setting." The novels "seem certain to endure as wry, delicate *fleurs du mal.*"

Riggs, Thomas, Jr. "English Literature since 1910." In *The Voice of England: A History of English Literature.* Ed. Charles G. Osgood. New York: Harper and Bros., 1952. 612.

Contains a paragraph on RF as "a special case of the modern baroque. . . . The strangely persuasive world of his novels is brightly colored, glittering, decadent, artificial, more closely related to the *commedia dell'arte* than to anything in the history of the novel. It is a world without 'morals' but not without values." *Prancing Nigger, The Flower beneath the Foot,* and *Cardinal Pirelli* are singled out for special praise.

Robinson, Herbert Spencer. "Ronald Firbank 1886-1926." In *Authors Today and Yesterday.* Ed. Stanley Kunitz. New York: H. W. Wilson, 1933. 236-39.

One of the earliest reference books to include RF.

Robson, W. W. *A Prologue to English Literature.* London: Batsford, 1986. 191.

Sandoz, Maurice. *The Crystal Salt Cellar.* See part 6, section 3.

Sassoon, Siegfried. *Siegfried's Journey, 1916-1920.* London: Faber and Faber, 1945. 135-37; New York: Viking, 1946. 201-3. Rpt. in Horder's *Memoirs and Critiques,* 150-52.

Recounts going with the Sitwells to visit RF in Oxford in February 1919. He found him "as unreal and anomalous as his writings" and had difficulty conversing with him. "His most rational response to my attempts at drawing him out about literature and art was 'I adore italics, don't you?'" Sassoon regarded RF's early books "as the elegant triflings of a talented amateur," but "in his later works I found a sort of opulent beauty and decadent gaiety."

Severi, Rita. "Words for Pictures: Notes on Iconic Description in Pater, Wilde, and Firbank." *Comparatistica: Annuario italiano* 1 (1989): 83-102.
    A discussion of the description of art objects in fiction; of her three authors, Severi declares RF "the most competent, profuse and versatile user of iconic descriptions" and gives examples on pp. 100-103. RF often uses art objects in a metonymic way to elucidate his characters.

————. "Niggers/Negroes: From Reality to Myth in Anglo-American Fiction (Firbank, Van Vechten, Stein)." Paper delivered at the 17th Convention of the Associazione Italiana di Anglistica, Bologna, Italy, 17 February 1995.
    On *Prancing Nigger,* Van Vechten's *Nigger Heaven,* and Stein's "Melanctha" and *Four Saints in Three Acts.*

Seymour-Smith, Martin. *Guide to Modern World Literature.* London: Wolfe, 1973. 277-78. Rev. ed.: *The New Guide to Modern Literature.* London: Macmillan, 1985. 287.
    A brief, dismissive evaluation. RF's work influenced others and *Sorrow in Sunlight* added to the cult of the Negro in the twenties. "Firbank's work, always valetudinarian, hovers between the ingenuous and the cunning; its tittering nihility has no more than a touching, childish quality."

————. *Who's Who in Twentieth Century Literature.* New York: Holt, Rinehart and Winston, 1976. 166-67.
    Another brief, less dismissive evaluation. "He did what he could with his decadence and lack of robustness, so that his best stories are not merely homosexual in-jokes but elegant wisps of fantasy graced with wittily absurd dialogue (he had a superb ear for the inconsequential)."

Shepherd, Simon. *Because We're Queers: The Life and Crimes of Kenneth Halliwell and Joe Orton.* London: GMP, 1989. 130.
    A brief reference to RF.

Sitwell, Osbert. "Biographical Memoir." In *The Works of Ronald Firbank,* 1:12-34. An expanded version has been reprinted many times with slight variations: as "Ronald Firbank" in Fletcher's *Memoir,* 117-44 (65-82 in Horder's *Memoirs and Critiques*), q.v.; in his autobiographical *Great Morning!* (1948), as the "Introduction" in RF's *Five Novels,* vii-xxxi, and as "Ronald Firbank" in his *Noble Essences: A Book of Characters.* London: Macmillan, 1950. 68-88; Boston: Little, Brown, 1950. 77-100.

Slater, Ann Pasternak. "Waugh's *A Handful of Dust:* Right Things in Wrong Places." *Essays in Criticism* 32.1 (January 1982): 48-68.
    RF's influence on Waugh is discussed on pp. 52-53.

Sontag, Susan. "Notes on 'Camp.'" *Partisan Review* 32.1 (Winter 1965): 515-30; rpt. in her *Against Interpretation and Other Essays.* New York: Farrar, Straus & Giroux, 1966. 278, 281.
    Includes the novels of RF in "the canon of Camp." Although RF is mentioned only in passing, this influential essay identifies a number of facets of RF's aesthetics.

Speedie, Julie. *Wonderful Sphinx: The Biography of Ada Leverson*. London: Virago, 1993.

Stannard, Martin. *Evelyn Waugh: The Early Years 1903-1939*. London: Dent, 1986; New York: Norton, 1987. 207-10 and passim.
	Waugh's interest in RF came from Harold Acton, who told Stannard that RF's "was a voice which, in spite of the language, parodied" the social snobbery implicit in the art of the 1890s. "It's the last gasp of the 1890s but he's laughing at them all the time" (92). Waugh's 1929 essay on RF is discussed at length (207-9), and Stannard links "Waugh's love of the early English Gothic Revival . . . with his earlier advocacy of the novels of Firbank" (381).

————, ed. *Evelyn Waugh: The Critical Heritage*. London: Routledge & Kegan Paul, 1984.
	An anthology of reviews of Waugh's work. Stannard refers to RF's influence in his long introduction (pp. 4, 7, 14, 16, 19, 23), and RF is occasionally cited by Waugh's reviewers (79, 92, 109, [112 n.], 131, 161-62, 424, 459, 488, 500). V. S. Pritchett, for example, calls Waugh "our present master of the hardened school of English comedy, the heir of Firbank's slashing grace" (424).

Stapleton, Michael. *The Cambridge Guide to English Literature*. Cambridge: Cambridge Univ. Press, 1983. 308.
	A brief, routine entry on RF, concluding: "Firbank's novels almost defy description and his wit exists only in their context . . . certainly his work has the stamp of another time upon it."

Stevens, Wallace. *Letters*. Ed. Holly Stevens. New York: Knopf, 1966. 287.
	In a letter to Ronald Lane Latimer dated 22 October 1935, Stevens answers: "I have read Firbank's novels, but have long since sent the lot of them to the attic. There may be some similarity between his work and mine, but certainly there is no relation between the two things. This is extremely interesting. It raises the question why one writes as one does. To my way of thinking, there is not the slightest affectation in anything that I do. I write as I do, not because that satisfies me, but because no other way satisfies me. It is curious to think of the possibility that Firbank wrote in the way he wrote for the same reason."

Stevenson, Lionel. *The History of the English Novel*, vol. 11: *Yesterday and After*. New York: Barnes & Noble, 1967. 159-63 and passim.
	A cogent overview of the life and work, with capsule descriptions of each of the novels: *Vainglory* has "spontaneous charm," but *Inclinations* is weaker (especially in contrast to Forster's *Where Angels Fear to Tread*, with which it "has a slight resemblance"); "the unexpected catastrophe" at the end of *Caprice* "lends a sudden bitter significance to all the inconsequential levity that went before"; *Valmouth*, a "Gothic grotesque," is remarkable for its early insight into "the new awareness of social and psychological problems involving race relations"; *Santal* is a failure; *Flower* ushers in RF's "final mature period" and has "a tone of sincere feeling that is new in Firbank's work"; *Prancing Nigger* is technically his best novel but superficial; *Pirelli* is RF's "least decorous" work. "Apparently the awareness of imminent death provoked him to be as outrageous as possible. . . . Nevertheless the book includes passages of Firbank's best absurdity." Stevenson concludes with two interesting insights: "Firbank seems to have been innately a romantic visionary who felt obliged to protect his sensitive dreams with a contemptuous sneer; an elusive wraith of poetic beauty haunts his wilfully decadent worldliness and the esoteric mysticism of his teen-age story *Odette* lingers under

the surface of his persiflage. The recurrent figure of an immature and innocent victim of heartless selfishness is probably (though often in feminine guise) a projection of his secret self."

Stevenson, Randall. *The British Novel since the Thirties*. London: B. T. Batsford, 1986; Athens: Univ. of Georgia Press, 1986. 27, 53, 58, 59, 139.
    Brief references to RF's work and its influence on later writers like Waugh, Compton-Burnett, and Powell.

―――――. *A Reader's Guide to the Twentieth-Century Novel in Britain*. Hemel Hempstead: Harvester Wheatshead, 1993; Lexington: Univ. Press of Kentucky, 1993. 12, 50-51, 94.
    Brief remarks on RF's novels, which share "some of the celebration of wit and hedonism in Norman Douglas's *South Wind* (1917) and look back to Oscar Wilde and the 1890s" (51); also notes similarities between RF's novels and Compton-Burnett's.

Stokes, Sewell. *Personal Glimpses*. London: T. Werner Laurie, 1924. 80-84, 89.
    Describing RF as "a Futurist novelist who writes for a pseudo-cultured few," Stokes describes RF's personal and writing habits, and how they first met at C. R. W. Nevinson's. He notes the animosity of journalist Hannen Swaffer for RF's works, but concludes: "It is those who do not know him that talk so unkindly about him." Expanded for his *Pilloried!*

―――――. [Letter to the editor.] (London) *Observer*, 9 May 1926.
    Concerns Firbank's relation to Siegfried Sassoon; the material was later used in Stokes's "A Recent Genius" (below).
    The letter is quoted in William Reese & Co.'s catalog 103 (1991), item 314. The clipping was inside Sassoon's copy of *Cardinal Pirelli*, who added a post-script to Stokes's clipping, noting RF's description of Sassoon as "a Tolstoy in galoshes" and himself as "a butterfly, waiting for caterpillars to drop from the trees" was "made to G. Atkin on June 28th, 1921, at a Pavlova performance at Queen's Hall. I first met R.F. in Feb. 1919, at Oxford."

―――――. "A Recent Genius." In his *Pilloried!* London: Richards Press, 1928; New York: Appleton, 1929. 219-30. Rpt. (revised and expanded) as "Reminiscences of Ronald Firbank" in Horder's *Memoirs and Critiques*, 127-33.
    An entertaining character sketch, useful for its quotations from others who knew RF (Cyril Beaumont, Edward Marsh). He quotes RF's remark "All women are funny" and notes how apparent that conviction is in his novels. "It was the little, everyday actions [of women] he found so intensely funny; never the flamboyant gestures of the artist," specifically "goddesses" like Duse, Mrs. Patrick Campbell, Marie Tempest, Isadora Duncan, and Florence Mills. RF "was surprisingly familiar with certain best-sellers" (he didn't think much of Marie Corelli but admits Ouida "*knew* her world").

―――――. "Reminiscences of Ronald Firbank." BBC Third Programme, 24 February 1957. Tape no. TLO 25131.

Swaffer, Hannen. *The People* [newspaper], untraced.
    In his "Reminiscences of Ronald Firbank" (in Horder's *Memoirs and Critiques*, 133), Sewell Stokes tells how upset RF was at a journalist named Hannen Swaffer, "who, having read one of Firbank's novels, wrote in his Sunday paper: 'It is a piece of decadence which I am surprised to see published. What the

censor of books can have been thinking about when he let this pass, I do not know. With pleasure I will show my copy to any policeman who cares to call at the office and see it.'" (Cited also in Stokes's *Personal Glimpses,* 80).

Swann Galleries. *Modern Literature: Sale Number 1421.* New York: Swann Galleries, 1986.

Part 2 is the Miriam J. Benkovitz Collection, auctioned on 11 December 1986. Extensive quotations and illustrations from RF's published and unpublished work.

Symons, A. J. A. "A True Recital of the Procedure of the First Banquet Held by the Corvine Society" (1929). Appendix 2 in his *The Quest for Corvo.* East Lansing: Michigan State Univ. Press, 1955.

Citing a fictitious "Report upon the Present State of Corvine Studies," Symons states, "The first fifteen pages are taken up by an analysis of the works of Mr. Ronald Firbank, Mr. Shane Leslie, and the late Robert Hugh Benson, showing that all three owe most of their ability, and a considerable number of their epigrams, to a profound study of Corvo's books" (289).

Tindall, William York. *Forces in Modern British Literature: 1885-1956.* New York: Vintage, 1956. 103-4.

Suggests RF's probable indebtedness to Beardsley's *Under the Hill* and notes "his prose, however precious, is not only glittering but functional. All conspires to create a vision of what is most unlike the postwar world. Firbank's creation may seem what Mallarmé called an *'aboli bibelot d'inanité sonore,'* but this complicated emptiness is a form for presenting an inverted reality" (104).

Toynbee, Philip. "Experiment and the Future of the Novel." In *The Craft of Letters in England: A Symposium.* Ed. John Lehmann. London: Cresset, 1956; Boston: Houghton-Mifflin, 1957. 60-73.

Contains brief remarks on RF as an experimental novelist.

―――. [interview with Graham Greene.] *Observer,* 15 September 1957.

Toynbee feels a young man writing like RF in the 1950s would be impossible, but Greene welcomes the possibility. "A modern Firbank would certainly be a rather different Firbank. There would inevitably be a difference of tone in his books."

Tyler, Parker. "The Prince Zoubaroff: Praise of Ronald Firbank." *Prose* 1 (1970): 135-52, and 2 (1971): 155-69.

An enthusiastic, if unfocused, essay on RF, ranging from RF's use of dialogue and class relations in his work, to his form of monkhood, to an analysis of various photographs of RF, to (in part 2) an extended discussion of *The Princess Zoubaroff.* Unlike more recent critics who find RF's fiction filled with loss and despair, Tyler finds it "gently sad" at worst, but more often filled with "sweet versions of Arcadian life." RF "and his characters inhabit the held ground of the traditional Paradise, enchanting, if a bit grotesque, with fresh landscaping." Tyler mentions nearly all the novels at one point or another.

Van Leer, David. *The Queening of America: Gay Culture in Straight Society.* London/New York: Routledge, 1995. 27-31, 37-39.

Discusses RF's "equation of homosexuality and stylization," the absence of overtly gay sexuality or self-affirmation in his work, and his influence on Van Vechten.

Van Vechten, Carl. "Ronald Firbank." *Double Dealer* 3 (April 1922): 185-86.

A spirited account of how he first learned of RF and an ecstatic recommendation of his novels to America's flaming youth: "Sophisticated virgins and demi-puceaux will adore these books. Married or unmarried persons over thirty will find them either shocking or tiresome. . . . [Van Vechten was 42 at the time.] These mad romances are a Uranian version of Alice in Wonderland. . . . He is the Pierrot of the minute. *Plus chic que le futurisme.* Aubrey Beardsley in a Rolls-Royce. Sacher-Masoch in Mayfair. '*A Rebours' à la mode.* Aretino in Piccadilly. Jean Cocteau at the Savoy. . . . At last Peter Pan receives an affirmative reply to his long unanswered question."

————. "Pastiches et Pistaches." *Reviewer* 3 (May 1922): 454-59.

On pp. 458-59 is a two-paragraph note on RF entitled "Satirist or Decadent?" The first reads: "A few have become aware of the sensational submarine exploits of Ronald Firbank. Whether this brilliant performer will undertake to fly in an aeroplane depends to a large extent on the state of the atmosphere. His work is sufficiently baffling. Is Valmouth to be considered as a slap at the sexual and psychoanalytic schools of fiction, a burlesque of the method of D. H. Lawrence, showing how little further this method has to be carried to become completely ridiculous? or is it a mystico-religious satire? or is it a complacent picture of modern English life?" The second paragraph gives bio-bibliographic facts.

————. "Pastiches et Pistaches." *Reviewer* 3 (October 1922): 632.

Contains a bibliographic note on *Odette* and notes that RF has been painted often, "more recently, by Guevara, 'a perfectly brutal little study of me,' he [RF] writes, 'huddled up in a black suit by a jar of orchids, in a décor suggestive of opium.'" Van Vechten adds that RF is "at present sojourning in Cuba."

————. "An Icing for a Chocolate Éclair." Preface to RF's *Prancing Nigger*, v-xi.

After noting the circumstances under which RF wrote *Prancing Nigger*, Van Vechten praises its setting and suggests "there is possibly more beauty in this book than in any other by this author, and certainly no less humour." RF's "treatment of the Negro is his own; he owes nothing" to forerunners, and after naming some of his favorite scenes, the novelist states: "the whole book hovers delightfully between a Freudian dream and a drawing by Alastair, set to music by George Gershwin." Although reviewers frequently praise writers for having a "light touch," RF is the "only one authentic master of the light touch, a man who might be writing with his eyelashes or the tips of his polished finger-nails." RF is also "the only purely Greek writer we possess today. There is no sentimentality or irony in his work; hardly even cynicism. . . . He does not satirize the things he hates. He flits airily about, arranging with skilful fingers the things he loves." He is incomparable: "He is unique, a glittering dragon-fly skimming over the sunlit literary garden, where almost all other creatures crawl." Van Vechten concludes with his bio-bibliographic note from the October 1922 *Reviewer* (see above).

————. "Ronald Firbank." In his *Excavations: A Book of Advocacies*. New York: Alfred A. Knopf, 1926. 170-76. Rpt. in Horder's *Memoirs and Critiques*, 161-65.

A composite of his earlier essays and his review of *The Flower beneath the Foot*.

————. *Letters*. Ed. Bruce Kellner. New Haven & London: Yale Univ. Press, 1987. 42-44, 46-47, 58, 70.

Contains the texts of five letters to RF, along with brief references to him in a few letters to others. His letter to RF of 12 March 1922 warns him "there is some danger of your becoming the rage in America" and asks for more facts. To Mabel Dodge Sterne he writes: "Firbank is a gay new idiot. . . . You will *love* Firbank. He lives at Fiesole and writes me letters in purple ink." In his letter to RF of 30 October 1923 he proposes changing the title of *Sorrow in Sunlight* to *Prancing Nigger:* "beyond a doubt the new title would sell at least a thousand more copies." A letter to Gertrude Stein, dated 8 September 1924, states: "I have written Firbank that you want to see him & I hope he will call on you someday but he is described by those who have seen him as excessively shy."

In a footnote, the editor quotes these later thoughts from a letter to him from Van Vechten dated 15 February 1952: "Almost all of Firbank is quaint reading and enough to make your hair, even pubic hair, stand on end once you understand it" (42, n4).

Vines, Sherard. *Movements in Modern English Poetry and Prose*. Tokyo: Ohkayama, 1929. 278-82 and passim.

A general overview of the works, with many complimentary observations—one of the earliest positive critical evaluations after RF's death. He "issues from and at the same time repudiates the 'Nineties' as post-impressionism does impressionism; and his relation to the outlook of the earlier period may be gauged by a study of his *Princess Zoubaroff* together with *The Importance of Being Earnest*. The fact that he can say elegantly what Wilde would no doubt have rendered coarsely is but a single clue out of many." RF's lyrical, sensuous style is applauded (and illustrated with a quotation from *Valmouth*). Unlike Joyce, RF "has nothing to say of or to everyday life but creates an ornate and opulent yet delimited life, as the sixteenth century fashioned rich conceits, to convey a rare experience. . . . His work stands as a protest against the realist heresy that 'life' means drunken persons in a garret by Zola or Wessex yokels by Hardy." With *Pirelli* RF "brought his technique to perfection." His wit is superior to Bernard Shaw's, but RF should not be classed with Norman Douglas: "Mr. Firbank is of no nation, and he is but lightly bound by place and time."

————. *A Hundred Years of English Literature*. London: Duckworth, 1950. 149-50, 254.

A distillation of his remarks on RF from his earlier book (above).

Waley, Arthur. "Introduction." In *The Works of Ronald Firbank*, 1:1-11. Rpt. in Horder's *Memoirs and Critiques*, 166-74.

Notes that the critics' charge of "silliness" has forestalled serious literary study of RF's work, and argues he "is important because he is the first and almost only Impressionist in English fiction, the earliest writer to discard the load of realistic lumber under which the modern story is interred—to do in writing what Cézanne, Matisse, Renoir did in painting." He rejects the idea that RF was a satirist: "there is no sign that he disapproved of or in any way condemned the vapid society that he depicts." Waley then discusses the books in order of publication, quoting his favorite passages; he considers *The Flower beneath the Foot* and *Sorrow in Sunlight* to be the best. Though not blind to RF's defects—"frequent incoherence and lack of construction"—Waley prefers RF over most "of our 'great' contemporary novelists."

Ward, A. C. *Longman Companion to Twentieth Century Literature.* 1970. 2nd ed. London: Longman, 1975. 203.

A routine entry on RF, concluding that his novels "are at once extravagantly artificial, fragile, and bizarre, a throwback to the 1890s and a realization in prose of the delicacy and degeneracy of Beardsley's art at its most ambiguous."

Waterhouse, Ellis. "Ronald Firbank." *Alta: The University of Birmingham Review* 3 (Summer 1967). Rpt. in Horder's *Memoirs and Critiques,* 211-22.

After finding fault with the essays on RF by Waley and Forster, Waterhouse discusses all of the novels in chronological order (with most of his attention on the first two). RF is indeed, as Sitwell first suggested, a war writer; in *Vainglory,* "he might almost be explaining the Great War as a reasonable outcome of the frivolously directed aims of pre-war society." RF was satirizing this society, often by way of his characters' aesthetic interests: "For Firbank there was no distinction between an aesthetic and a moral judgment." In both *Vainglory* and *Inclinations* there are parodies of "the sillier or more popular writing of the day," though these are difficult to detect at this distance. He considers the re-written dinner scene in *Inclinations* inferior to the original, and suspects RF felt in 1925 "that he must address a larger but less subtly attuned audience: indeed it seems to have been written with an American edition in mind." The first three novels are fairly realistic, especially the dialogue. Waterhouse finds parodies of D. H. Lawrence and Henry James's late manner in *Valmouth* as well as a theme that would occupy RF in his later books, i.e., "the nature of the values, the more simple values, of Negro society, and the clash of this scale of values on the extremely sophisticated (and specifically Roman Catholic) society of the other world in which Firbank moved." *The Princess Zoubaroff* is a novel written in dramatic form and "is brilliantly funny on the stage, though over-artificial in reading." Waterhouse feels "there is nothing to be said for *Santal*" but the next, *The Flower beneath the Foot,* "is one of the best of the books." The real-life counterparts of its characters are easily identified, and again the book is not entirely unrealistic: "Anyone who has lived much in a Mediterranean capital will perceive that it is by no means as frivolous or fantastic as it seems." Of the final two books, *Cardinal Pirelli* is funny but *Prancing Nigger* "has qualities of the heart and the imagination which are new in Firbank" and is the one that "shows a promise of development which he never lived to fill." Waterhouse concludes by suggesting it is the "studious indirectness" of RF's moral judgments that exempts him from charges (by Forster and others) of irresponsibility.

Waters, John. *Crackpot: The Obsessions of John Waters.* New York: Macmillan, 1986.

The cult filmmaker names RF in a chapter entitled "Puff Piece (101 Things I Love)" (59). Elsewhere he wonders why other magazines don't adopt *National Enquirer*-style articles, so that the gay *Advocate* could run a piece entitled "Ronald Firbank Didn't Have to Die" (87).

Waugh, Evelyn. "Ronald Firbank." *Life and Letters* 2 (March 1929): 191-96. Rpt. in Horder's *Memoirs and Critiques,* 175-79. Rpt. in Waugh's *A Little Order.* Ed. Donat Gallagher. London: Eyre Methuen, 1977; Boston: Little, Brown, 1980. 77-80. Rpt. in *The Essays, Articles and Reviews of Evelyn Waugh.* Ed. Donat Gallagher. London: Methuen, 1984; Boston: Little, Brown, 1984. 56-59.

To dislike RF's work implies "distaste for a wide and vigorous tendency in modern fiction." Waugh notes that RF's debts to Beardsley and Baron Corvo are superficial, but his "progeny is unmistakeably apparent. In quite diverse ways Mr Osbert Sitwell, Mr Carl Van Vechten, Mr Harold Acton, Mr William Gerhardi and Mr Ernest Hemingway are developing the technical discoveries upon which Ronald Firbank so negligently stumbled." Although his subject matter is similar to Wilde's, his "wit is ornamental; Firbank's is structural. Wilde is rococo; Firbank is baroque." RF is important because he was the first modern writer to solve "the aesthetic problem of representation in fiction; to achieve, that is to say, a new, balanced interrelation of subject and form." Waugh describes the fleas at the Ritz rumor in *The Flower beneath the Foot* to show how RF's seemingly inconsequential dialogue provides structural cohesion to his work.

————. *Letters*. Ed. Mark Amory. London: Weidenfeld & Nicolson, 1980; New Haven & New York: Ticknor & Fields, 1980. 35, 53, 588.

RF mentioned thrice: in a letter to novelist Henry Green, Waugh praises his *Living* and notes: "The thing I *envied* most was the way you managed the plot which is oddly enough almost exactly the way Firbank managed his" (June 1929). Writing from London, Waugh tells Patrick Balfour "Shops dont [*sic*] seem to want Firbank" (12 July 1931). And on 4 July 1962, Waugh sent a postcard to Anthony Curtis, literary editor of the *Sunday Telegraph*, saying: "I am sorry to say that your kind invitation to review *The New Rhythm* [*sic*] reaches me 30 years late. In youth I was fascinated by Firbank. Now I can't abide him." (Curtis recalls this exchange in his review of *The Early Firbank*.)

Weintraub, Stanley. *Beardsley: A Biography*. New York: Braziller, 1967. 247-48. Rev. as *Aubrey Beardsley: Imp of the Perverse*. University Park: Pennsylvania State Univ. Press, 1976. 263-64.

Notes Beardsley's influence on RF, especially on *The Artificial Princess*. "Brilliant, precious, baroque, Firbank survives as a minor modern classic, a satirist who wrote elegant improvisations on a theme by Beardsley, whether he titled them *Caprice* or *Concerning the Eccentricities of Cardinal Pirelli.*"

West, Paul. *The Modern Novel*. London: Hutchinson, 1963; New York: Hillary House, 1965. 79-80, 86, 120.

"A dedicated writer owing much to the example of Henry James, [RF] constructed a world of *malaise* in which perversion was the normal thing. . . . *The Artificial Princess* (1934), his rococo cushion for Salome, *The Flower Beneath the Foot* (1923), a perverse account of a saint (compare with Waugh's *Helena*), and *Valmouth* (1919), his attempt at a *Brideshead Revisited*, are well worth a careful reader's time. His work deserves to be seen as more than a freak fiesta. He has something in common with both Waugh and Huxley, as well as with analysts of other wastelands." West sees parallels between RF's style and Lawrence Durrell's, and concludes: "Fear is Firbank's principal drive: he externalizes what look like nightmares and so has something in common with the surrealists" (79-80).

Whissen, Thomas Reed. *The Devil's Advocates: Decadence in Modern Literature*. Westport, CT: Greenwood Press, 1989. xx, 13-14, 17, 25-26, 32, 45, 48.

Brief references to *The Flower beneath the Foot*'s place in decadent literature and RF's influence on Paul Rudnick's *Social Disease* (see part 4).

White, Edmund, ed. *The Faber Book of Gay Short Fiction*. Boston and London: Faber and Faber, 1981.

In his foreword, White notes "the fantasists who found silvery comedy in the tragic seriousness of marriage are Oscar Wilde and Ronald Firbank" (xi). This anthology reprints the conclusion to *Cardinal Pirelli* (48-57) and includes a brief biographical sketch of RF (581).

Wiley, Paul L. *The British Novel: Conrad to the Present.* Northbrook, IL: AHM, 1973. 36-37.
    A brief primary and secondary checklist.

Wilson, Angus. *Diversity and Depth in Fiction.* Ed. Kerry McSweeney. London: Secker & Warburg, 1983; New York: Viking, 1983.
    Scattered references, all brief but favorable, to RF, who "was irresponsible, adolescent and fantastic; he was utterly unconcerned with the health of society, yet I cannot imagine a novel more in love with life, or indeed more likely to make its readers in love with life than *Prancing Nigger*" (138).

Wilson, Edmund. "Firbank and Beckford." *New Republic* 48 (8 September 1926): 70-71. Rpt. in his *The Shores of Light.* New York: Farrar, Straus & Young, 1952. 264-66.
    Feels *Cardinal Pirelli* is RF's best, but that "in their subjects themselves, Firbank's novels seem to reflect some fundamental maladjustment"; his characters "are as unfortunate as possible; possessed by a bizarre variety of passions," and finds Cardinal Pirelli's career to be symbolic of RF's own fate. Wilson notes parallels between RF and the author of *Vathek*: "Beckford and Firbank both have the same cool and trivial, but suspiciously sadistic-sounding cruelty, which we might speak of as feminine, if it were not so plainly something distinct. And in their sensibility, their subtle intelligence, their exquisite taste for fine and gorgeous things, as well as in their malice, their eccentric manias and their incurable silliness, they have much in common with the uncomfortable character of Proust's M. de Charlus."

————. *The Fifties.* Ed. Leon Edel. New York: Farrar, Straus & Giroux, 1986. 298.
    Meeting Edith and Osbert Sitwell in 1955, Wilson told them he "would like to see something done about Ronald Firbank's letters and papers. 'Oh [Edith replied], we don't care about Firbank anymore—we think he's silly now.' Then, turning to Osbert: 'You don't care for Firbank anymore, do you?' I did not hear his curt reply, but it was evidently in the negative."

————. *The Sixties.* Ed. Lewis M. Dabney. New York: Farrar, Straus & Giroux, 1993. 792.
    In the entry for 11 May 1969 he records his opinion of Benkovitz's biography: "full of more or less interesting facts . . . [but] no real evocation of the atmosphere of the period. I was glad that I had taken the precaution of bringing all my Firbank duplicates up here [to Talcottville, upstate New York]: I was able to look up passages and dip into stories. I found reading him and about him reassuring as Firbank himself said about *Under the Hill*." (Wilson used the first half of this entry in his 1971 book *Upstate*.)

Woodward, A. G. "Ronald Firbank." *English Studies in Africa* 11.1 (March 1968): 1-9.
    An appreciative overview of the life and works, solid if unoriginal—except for a comparison between RF and Rudyard Kipling: both had the rare gift of being able "to create a wholly self-sufficient imaginative world," and "both of them offended the progressive intelligentsia of the period between the two wars. . . . If Kipling was too serious, in the wrong kind of way, Firbank was not

serious enough" (3). The second half of the essay focuses on *Valmouth*.

Woolf, Virginia. *Leave the Letters Till We're Dead.* Ed. Nigel Nicolson and Joanne Trautman. London: Hogarth Press, 1980; in U.S. as *Letters, Volume VI: 1936-1941.* New York: Harcourt Brace Jovanovich, 1981. 526.

In a letter to Mary Hutchinson dated 6 May 1929, Woolf writes: "I should provide you with the works of Ronald Firbank which I am reading with some unstinted pleasure."

Wyndham, Violet. *The Sphinx and Her Circle.* London, 1963; New York: Vanguard, 1964. 87, 100

Brief references to Ada Leverson's meetings with RF.

Young, Ian. *The Male Homosexual in Literature: A Bibliography.* 2d ed. Metuchen, NJ: Scarecrow, 1982. 237.

The Flower beneath the Foot satirizes "the passionate uncertainties of Vita Sackville-West's involvement with Virginia Woolf and the detached interest taken by her bisexual husband, diplomat Harold Nicolson."

Part 4

Creative Works

Acton, Harold. *Cornelian*. London: Chatto & Windus, 1928.

Martin Green says this "could be called a post-Oxford novel, drawing as it does on Firbank for its handling of the social scene and Beardsley for its style" (*Children of the Sun*, 211-12).

Amis, Kingsley. *The Alteration*. London: Jonathan Cape, 1976.

Philip Gardner notes that the opening of this novel about a castrato echoes that of *Cardinal Pirelli* and that the novel "is a sort of 'square' version of Firbank's rococo fantasy" (*Kingsley Amis* [Boston: Twayne, 1981], 84). In his dissertation, Terrance Shults agrees that novel "intertwines religion and Aesthetics in the Firbank manner." But for Amis's low opinion of RF, see part 3 (under Anonymous), *Tatler*, December 1985/January 1986.

Apffel, Edmund. *Last Days at St. Saturn's*. New York: Holt, Rinehart & Winston, 1981.

A novel with Firbankian characters and ambience.

Auden, W. H., and Louis MacNeice. *Letters from Iceland*. London: Faber and Faber, 1937.

There are two references to RF in Auden's poem "Letter to Lord Byron" in this volume: in part 3 (p. 101: "Firbank, I think, wore just a just-enough"), and in part 4 (p. 202):

> . . . You must ask me who
> Have written just as I'd have liked to do.
> I stop to listen and the names I hear
> Are those of Firbank, Potter, Carroll, Lear.

In the revised version of the poem that appears in Auden's *Collected Poems* (New York: Random House, 1976), the first reference appears on p. 89 but the second is dropped.

Beckett, Samuel. *More Kicks than Pricks*. London: Chatto & Windus, 1934.

In his review in the *Spectator* in 1934, Arthur Calder-Marshall detects "a little too much Firbank" in this collection of short stories.

Beerbohm, Max. "Enoch Soames." In *Seven Men and Two Others*. London: Heinemann, 1919. Rpt. in various collections, such as *Selected Prose,* ed. David Cecil. London: Bodley Head, 1970; Boston: Little, Brown, 1970. 55-86.

Though set in the 1890s, the story has a protagonist who has struck some as a parody of RF.

Benson, Robert Hugh. *The Conventionalists*. London: Hutchinson, 1908; St. Louis: Herder, 1908.

Shane Leslie (in *The Film of Memory*) says this novel "enshrined a strange apparition from our midst: Ronald Firbank," and David Dougill (in his review of Brophy's *Prancing Novelist*) agrees that the principal character Algy Banister was modeled on RF.

Betjeman, John. *Summoned by Bells*. Boston: Houghton Mifflin, 1960. 81.

In section 8 of this autobiographical poem, the poet lists *Prancing Nigger* among the furnishings of his Oxford room.

Betjeman once wrote: "The polished work of Ronald Firbank is like a jewelled and clockwork nightingale singing among London sparrows" (*Daily*

Herald, date unknown).

Breakwell, Ian. *The Artist's Dream.* London: Serpent's Tail, 1989.
    The front cover of this book of stories and surrealist photographs describes it as "Franz Kafka meets Ronald Firbank in Bexhill-on-Sea!," with an additional note on the back cover: "Among the author's loves are Goya, Kafka and Ronald Firbank; to say that his fictions combine elements of all three alerts the reader to the varied pleasures ahead."

Brophy, Brigid. *The Finishing Touch.* London: Secker & Warburg, 1963; rpt. with an introduction by the author: London: GMP, 1987. First published in U.S. as the second of half of an omnibus with *The Snow Ball*: Cleveland & New York: World Publishing Co., 1964. 183-253.
    In her *Prancing Novelist,* Brophy describes this as "my novel in a superficially Firbankian idiom" (49). *TLS* commented: "Firbank is almost too obviously both the inspiration and the victim of Miss Brophy's waspish and witty tale."

————. *Palace without Chairs.* London: Hamish Hamilton/New York: Atheneum,1978.
    Like *The Flower beneath the Foot,* a modern-day fairy tale set in an imaginary Eastern European monarchy.

Capote, Truman. *The Grass Harp.* New York: Random, 1951.
    Critic John McCormick notes with disapproval RF's apparent influence on this novel about a group of people who live in a tree house (*Catastrophe and Imagination,* 299).

Clark, Laurence. *Kingdom Come.* London: Centaur, 1958.
    The anonymous reviewer for *TLS* described this novel as "a delightfully absurd, almost Firbankian day-dream on the tribulations of the Anglo-Indian military man" (19 December 1958, 733).

Cloud, Maurice B. "Jazz Vamp." In *The Vampire in Verse: An Anthology.* Ed. Steven Moore. New York: Dracula Press, 1985. 158-60.
    Many of Firbank's characters are mentioned in this poem (and identified as such in the editor's note on p. 193).

Connolly, Cyril. *The Rock Pool.* Paris: Obelisk, 1936; New York: Scribner's, 1936; London: Hamish Hamilton, 1947.
    Several critics have noted the apparent influence of Firbank (and Waugh) on this satiric novel set in an expatriate colony on the French Riviera.

————. "Where Engels Fears to Tread." First published in *Press Gang.* Ed. Leonard Russell. London: Hutchinson's, 1937; rpt. in Connolly's *The Condemned Playground,* 136-53.
    A spirited mock book review that parodies several trends and writers of the time, including RF (who is named on pp. 147 and 149).

Crisp, Quentin. [works]
    In his fiction and autobiographical writings, especially *The Naked Civil Servant* (1968), Crisp writes in what Robert L. Caserio has called "the contrasting style of Wildean and Firbankian aphorisms" (*The Gay and Lesbian Literary Heritage,* ed. Claude J. Summers [New York: Holt, 1995], 256).

Day, Wesley. "I Have Never Read Ronald Firbank." *TriQuarterly* 6 (1966): 118.
    A prose poem in RF's manner.

Ducornet, Rikki. *The Stain.* London: Chatto & Windus, 1984; New York: Grove Press, 1984; rev. ed. Normal, IL: Dalkey Archive Press, 1995.
    Reviewing the British edition of this novel for the *Guardian,* novelist Robert Nye wrote: "Imagine *Cold Comfort Farm* revamped by Ronald Firbank . . . and you may have some small notion of its outrageous flavour."

Fairbanks, Lauren. "Firbank's Friend." In *Muzzle Thyself.* Elmwood Park, IL: Dalkey Archive Press, 1991. 51-52.
    A poem.

————. *Sister Carrie.* Normal, IL: Dalkey Archive Press, 1993.
    A novel containing a character named Valmouth and some Firbankian phrases and images.

Gaddis, William. *The Recognitions.* New York: Harcourt, Brace, 1955; London: Macgibbon and Kee, 1962.
    In the final chapter, largely set in Italy, a female American tourist is seen reading *Cardinal Pirelli* (918, 925). Throughout the novel, Gaddis uses clever, unattributed dialogue in a manner similar to RF's.

Gordon, Karen Elizabeth. *The Transitive Vampire: A Handbook of Grammar for the Innocent, the Eager, and the Doomed.* New York: Times Book, 1984; rev. as *The Deluxe Transitive Vampire.* New York: Pantheon, 1993.
    On the cover of the British edition (London: Severn House, 1985), Frank Muir is quoted as saying: "Just what we have all been needing for years—a high-camp Grammar text-book. *The Transitive Vampire* is an extraordinary work, like Hall and Norman's Algebra rewritten by Ronald Firbank; extremely bizarre, amusing yet educational. And the illustrations are wonderful." Gordon's other books employ Firbankian sentences and characters (*The Well-Tempered Sentence* [1983], *Intimate Apparel* [1989; rev. as *The Red Shoes and Other Tattered Tales* (1996)]), but the author claims not to have read RF previously.

Gorey, Edward. [works]
    Gorey's self-illustrated booklets are filled with Firbankian characters and share a similar atmosphere of Edwardian decadence. Gorey once told an interviewer that RF was "the greatest influence on me . . . because he is so concise and so madly oblique" (Alexander Theroux, "The Incredible Revenge of Edward Gorey," *Esquire,* July 1974, 146). Gorey illustrated the Albondocani Press editon of RF's *Two Early Stories* (1971).

Green, Henry. *Concluding.* London, 1948; New York: Viking, 1950.
    Critic-biographer Peter Parker calls this Green's "most Firbankian novel. . . . It occurs, of course, that it is merely the setting of this novel that *makes* it Firbankian; but the ravishing obliquity of Green's prose seems here, more than in any other of his novels, indebted to Firbank" ("'Aggressive, witty, & unrelenting': Brigid Brophy and Ronald Firbank," 73). Other critics have perceived RF's influence on other Green novels.

Harris, Bertha. *Lover.* New York: Daughter's, Inc., 1976; rpt. New York: New York University Press, 1983.

In her introduction to the 1993 reprint of her novel, Harris cites "the ethere-ally discrete [*sic*] fiction of Ronald Firbank" as an early influence (p. xxv).

Heppenstall, Rayner. [novels]
This innovative British novelist has been called "as inquisitive as Anthony Powell, as odd as Firbank, as minute as Sterne" (*TLS*).

Hollinghurst, Alan. *The Swimming-Pool Library.* London: Chatto & Windus; New York: Random, 1988.
A novel in which RF is frequently mentioned and discussed, especially pp. 54-55, 152-54, 166-68, 170, 174, 216-17, 242, 282, 284-87. The narrator had imagined RF "to be a supremely frivolous and silly author. I was surprised to find how difficult, witty and relentless he was. The characters were flighty and extravagant in the extreme, but the novel [*Valmouth*] itself was evidently as tough as nails" (54). In a section purporting to be an aristocrat's journal and dated 23 June 1925, RF is depicted in the Café Royal, reluctantly receiving the admiration of some undergraduates (152-54); later the narrator says RF's adult characters "don't have any dignity as adults, they're all like over-indulged chil-dren following their own caprices and inclinations" (242), and the novel ends with a description of some unearthed film footage featuring RF in Italy at the end of his life.
For a discussion of Hollinghurt's use of RF, see Ross Chambers, "Messing Around: Gayness and Loiterature [*sic*] in Alan Hollinghurt's *The Swimming-Pool Library,*" in *Textuality and Sexuality: Reading Theories and Practices,* ed. Judith Still and Michael Worton (Manchester: Manchester Univ. Press, 1993), 207-17.

Huxley, Aldous. "Happy Families." In his *Limbo.* London: Chatto & Windus, 1920. 211-44.
The setting of this short play is one "of Firbankish grotesqueness" according to George Woodcock (*Dawn and the Darkest Hour: A Study of Aldous Huxley* [New York: Viking, 1972], 70).

————. *Crome Yellow.* London: Chatto & Windus, 1921.
Several critics have not only noted RF apparent influence on Huxley's early novels, but that in this particular novel Huxley seems to have had RF in mind when referring to a writer named Knockespotch. "It was Knockespotch," a character named Mr. Scogan says, "the great Knockespotch, who delivered us from the dreary tyranny of the realistic novel." Scogan's description of the *Tales of Knockespotch* sounds like RF's work (except for the "immense erudition"): "Fabulous characters shoot across his pages like gaily dressed performers on the trapeze. There are extraordinary adventures and still more extraordinary specu-lations. Intelligences and emotions, relieved of all the imbecile preoccupations of civilised life, move in intricate and subtle dances, crossing and recrossing, advancing, retreating, impinging. An immense erudition and an immense fancy go hand in hand. All the ideas of the present and of the past, on every possible subject, bob up among the Tales, smile gravely or grimace a caricature of them-selves, then disappear to make place for something new. The verbal surface of his writing is rich and fantastically diversified. The wit is incessant." Compare Huxley's more subdued review of *Valmouth* (see part 1).

Keenan, Joe. *Putting on the Ritz.* New York: Viking, 1991.
In this Wodehousian novel, there is a brief appearance by a minor character named Milo Fessendon, "a drooping young poet and semiotician, apparently

possessed by the ghost of Ronald Firbank. So exquisite and ethereal was his nature that one gruff staffer was moved to bluntly inquire to his face if he ever consumed actual food or if he got by all right on photosynthesis" (264).

Kirkup, James. "A Character from Ronald Firbank." *Time and Tide*, 22 March 1952. In *A Correct Compassion and Other Poems*. London: Oxford Univ. Press, 1952. 36.
    A poem describing a woman in "elegant decay."

Lessing, Doris. "The Day Stalin Died." In *The Habit of Loving*. London: Macgibbon & Kee/New York: Crowell, 1957. 189-94.
    While visiting a photographer ("a charming young man in a black velvet jacket") the narrator notices RF's *Prancing Nigger*. "Do you read our Ron?" the photographer asks her, and after the narrator answers "From time to time," he states: "'Personally I never read anything else,' he said. 'As far as I am concerned he said the last word. When I've read him all through, I begin again at the beginning and read him through again. I don't see that there's any point in anyone ever writing another word after Firbank.'" The narrator thinks to herself: "This remark discouraged me, and I did not feel inclined to say anything" (199).

Lewis, Wyndham. *The Apes of God*. London, 1930; rpt. Santa Barbara: Black Sparrow, 1981.
    "In substance Lewis's sophisticated satire is related to those of Firbank in its concern with male homosexuals," writes Jeanette H. Foster in *Sex Variant Women in Literature* (1956), "and his writing about them has something of Firbank's zany touch" (292).

Mackenzie, Compton. *Extraordinary Women*. London: Secker, 1928.
    Peter Parker wonders if there isn't "a very faint whiff of *Inclinations*" in this "execrable" novel about a group of lesbians on the Mediterranean island of Sirene (letter to me, 18 May 1993).

MacKiernan, Elizabeth. *Ancestors Maybe*. Providence, RI: Burning Deck, 1993.
    In his review of this novel, Dennis Barone asked: "What if Ronald Firbank, Flann O'Brien, and Richard Brautigan found themselves forced by circumstances to seek employment with one of Hartford, Connecticut's large insurance companies? Let's say they all worked in the same office in the same building for the same company. Throughout the day via their computers and perhaps during lunch hours of drinks and marbles they'd collaborate on a novel. *Ancestors Maybe* resembles what might have resulted from such a collaboration" (*Review of Contemporary Fiction* 14.1 [Spring 1994]: 221).

Massie, Allan. *Change and Decay in All Around I See*. London: Bodley Head, 1978.
    French critic Colette Daube sees RF's influence in this novel.

Mathews, Harry. *Tlooth*. Garden City, NY: Doubleday/Paris Review Editions, 1966.
    In "A Conversation with Harry Mathews" (*Review of Contemporary Fiction* 7.3 [Fall 1987]: 21-33), John Ash begins by comparing the opening of RF's *Vainglory* with that of *Tlooth*, and Mathews admits that RF influenced him. "Of course Firbank was *the* great formal innovator," Mathews says. "He invented modernism, more so than Joyce really . . . and it's almost a source of irritation

that there are so many things one can't do without sounding like him" (21). Mathews expands upon these remarks in an interview published in Warren Leamon's *Harry Mathews* (New York: Twayne, 1993), 16-17.

Maupin, Armistead. *Sure of You*. New York: Harper & Row, 1989. 49.
   Chiding a gay man for teasing a lesbian for not knowing who Sappho was, Mrs. Madrigal reminds him she "had to explain Ronald Firbank to you." The man replies, "Well . . . Firbank is much more obscure than Sappho."

McCourt, James. *Mawrdew Czgowchwz*. New York: Farrar, Straus & Giroux, 1975.
   In his review of this novel in the *New York Times Book Review* (26 January 1975, 6), John Yohalem wrote: "The style keenly recalls Ronald Firbank, whose appeal is a specialized one, despite recent claims for his universality. . . . McCourt has Firbank's vast supply of improbably stylish phrases, his knack for sketching a character lightly but complexly, his eye and love for nonsense in the name of social amenities. But he is less far out. He has not Firbank's taste in perversity. . . . Firbank's novels are perceived through a hazy scrim of non sequiturs, compared with which McCourt's prose is straightforward."

————. "Summer Buses, Summer Fugues." In *Summer*. Ed. Alice Gordon and Vincent Virga. Reading, MA: Addison-Wesley, 1990. 229-38.
   This short story contains an allusion to *Sorrow in Sunlight* (237).

————. *Time Remaining*. New York: Knopf, 1993.
   Alexander Theroux said of McCourt's third book: "nowhere, except perhaps in Ronald Firbank, can be found writing more arch or wickedly precious" (*Review of Contemporary Fiction* 13.3 [Fall 1993]: 207). In my review of the novel for the *Washington Post Book World* (20 June 1993, 5) I too compared McCourt's fiction to RF's.

Murdoch, Iris. *Under the Net*. London: Chatto & Windus, 1954.
   John McCormick finds the unfortunate "suggestion of Firbank fantasy" present in the novel's "haphazard symbolism of the down-at-the-heel hero backstage in a pantomime theatre making love to an elusive mistress amidst masks, a bear-skin and other theatrical props" (*Catastrophe and Imagination*, 301).

Nicolson, Harold. "Lambert Orme." In his *Some People*. London: Constable, 1927. Rpt. in Horder's *Memoirs and Critiques*, 94-107.
   In this semi-fictitious, semi-autobiographical sketch, Nicolson recalls meeting nineteen-year-old RF in Madrid and describing the impact he made on most people. "It would be impossible, I feel, to actually be as decadent as Lambert looked," it begins, and Nicolson goes on to describe his walk, physical appearance, and mannerisms with a mixture of bemusement and disapproval. The narrator meets Lambert again back at Oxford, living in fabulous rooms and writing his novel *Désiré de St. Aldegonde* in the manner of Maeterlinck: "a style which, in English, tastes like bananas and cream." Though still repelled by him, the narrator is also curiously attracted to him until a kindly don "cures" him of his attraction with a copy of Pater's *Marius the Epicurean*. In later years the narrator realizes Lambert "represented my first contact with a literary mind." But "I am still quite unaware whether I regard Lambert as ridiculous, as tragic, or as something legendary."

O'Hara, Frank, and Bill Berkson. "Letters of Angelicus & Fidelio Fobb." *Z* 4 (1975): 90-109.

These fictitious letters, writes Marjorie Perloff, "seem to be modeled on the prose of Ronald Firbank or Evelyn Waugh" (*Frank O'Hara: Poet among Painters* [New York: Braziller, 1977], 217, n12). Earlier in her book she notes O'Hara's early fondness for RF's work, especially *Vainglory* and *The Flower beneath the Foot* (33).

Oke, Richard. *Frolic Wind*. London: Gollancz, 1929; New York: Payson & Clarke, 1930.

In his *Ronald Firbank,* Jocelyn Brooke says *Frolic Wind* "may be singled out as one of the best novels written under Firbank's influence" (78 n1).

————. *Wanton Boys*. London: Gollancz, 1932.

Colette Daube agrees with Brooke that RF's influence can be seen in Oke's *Frolic Wind* and in this later novel as well.

Orton, Joe. *Complete Plays*. Ed. John Lahr. London: Methuen, 1976. 13

In his introduction, Lahr notes that Orton learned of RF from his lover Kenneth Halliwell and that the two of them wrote a number of unpublished novels showing RF's influence. "Orton's humour was more robust and gregarious than Firbank's rarefied fantasies. He shared Firbank's obsessions and adapted many of Firbank's comic manoeuvres to a much more aggressively popular dramatic form."

Powell, Anthony. *Venusberg*. London: Duckworth, 1932.

Critic D. J. Taylor believes "the origins of *Venusberg* (1932), which must rank as one of the most substantial productions of mid-period English modernism, are there for any literary sleuth armed with his copy of Firbank and his knowledge of the Tannhäuser myth to view" (*Times Literary Supplement,* 20 January 1995, 6).

Powell, Dawn. [novels]

Novelist/critic Gilbert Sorrentino once wrote: "Dawn Powell is a kind of disheveled Ronald Firbank" ("Beliefs Reasonable, Unreasonable Beliefs," *Conjunctions* 21 [Fall 1983]: 328).

Pumphrey, Arthur [pseud. of Alan Pryce-Jones]. *Pink Danube*. London: Secker, 1939.

In his *New Statesman* review, Brian Howard wrote: "*Pink Danube* lies in what, to me, is the most comforting of modern fiction countries. To the north, lies the new, industrial town of Isherwoodstadt, and to the south, the vast, old, lazy pleasure-cities of Comptonia and Normanville, from which, on fine days, one may descry Firbank Island" (quoted in Marie-Jacqueline Lancaster's *Brian Howard: Portrait of a Failure* [London: Anthony Blond, 1968], 399. Elsewhere in this book, Howard is quoted advising Bryan Guinness to read *Cardinal Pirelli:* "I think, on the whole, it is the wittiest book ever written. A triumph of indecent sophistication" [172]).

Purdy, James. *Malcolm*. New York: Farrar, Straus & Giroux, 1959.

In a review of Serpent's Tail reissue of this novel about a fifteen-year-old boy, Paul Binding noted "the Firbank of *Valmouth* is somewhere in the background" (*Times Literary Supplement,* 7 April 1995, 25).

————. *Out with the Stars*. London: Peter Owen, 1993; San Francisco: City Lights, 1993.

In its review of this novel (loosely based on the relationship between novelist Carl Van Vechten and composer-novelist Coleman Dowell), the *Observer* described Purdy as "The most eminent modern successor to Ronald Firbank."

Raven, Simon. *An Inch of Fortune*. London: Blond & Briggs, 1980.

A copy of *Caprice* is found in Mrs. Fairweather's house.

Robson, Jeremy. *Blues for the Lonely*. EP, date unknown (1960s).

British record collector Chris Long describes this as "Allen Ginsberg-type poems but in an upper-class British accent like Sir Laurence Olivier: 'Can you hear the thunder?/Is the music too high or too soft?' Spoken over a rowdy jazz quartet, it's as if Ronald Firbank had become a beat poet" (quoted in *Incredibly Strange Music, Volume II*, ed. V. Vale and Andrea Juno [San Francisco: Re/ Search Publications, 1994], 66).

Roussel, Raymond. [works]

This French contemporary of RF's was a Firbankian character in his own right and composed fantastical poems and novels that have reminded some readers of RF's work.

Rudnick, Paul. *Social Disease*. New York: Knopf, 1986.

Thomas Reed Whissen discusses RF's influence on this novel (corroborated by Rudnick) concerning the late-1970s club scene in New York City in his *Devil's Advocates: Decadence in Modern Literature* (13-14, 32).

Sansom, William. *A Bed of Roses*. London: Hogarth, 1954.

Numbering Sansom among RF's imitators, critic John McCormick notes (with disapproval) that "Firbank's contortions to invent unusual situations— two women struggle to reach their confessor, and push over the confessional— are duplicated at the beginning of William Sansom's *A Bed of Roses*, which opens with the heroine locked in an armoire by her lover" (*Catastrophe and Imagination*, 299).

Sitwell, Osbert. *Before the Bombardment*. London: Duckworth, 1926.

Evelyn Waugh believed this novel owed a little to *Valmouth*, but Humphrey Carpenter believes it owes much more to Jane Austen and Mrs. Gaskell (*The Brideshead Generation*, 153).

Slavitt, David. *Anagrams*. Garden City, NY: Doubleday, 1970; London: Hodder and Stoughton, 1970.

The protagonist of this novel has ghostwritten several theses for American doctoral candidates, including one on "the novels of Ronald Firbank" (22).

Sorrentino, Gilbert. *Mulligan Stew*. New York: Grove, 1979. 304-5.

One character mocks another by saying that he is, "if rumor is correct, off somewhere in Canada, where he purportedly teaches an honors seminar on Canadian influences in the novels of Ronald Firbank—surely hard and useful work, God knows."

Spackman, W. M. *An Armful of Warm Girl*. New York: Knopf, 1978.

A brief novel narrated, for the most part, in stylized dialogue reminiscent of RF's. Spackman's later novels—*A Presence with Secrets* (1980), *A Difference of*

Design (1983), *A Little Decorum, for Once* (1985)—also display some of RF's techniques.

Taylor, D. J. *A Vain Conceit*. London: Bloomsbury, 1989.

In this critical study of British fiction in the 1980s, there is an "interlude" in the form of "An imaginary conversation between Henry James, Anthony Trollope, Ronald Firbank, Kingsley Amis and Professor X of the University of Lyons, author of *Radiguet à Robbe-Grillet: l'artifice et l'audace*" (107-10). RF simpers and giggles throughout.

Tennant, Stephen. *Leaves from a Missionary's Notebook*. London: Secker & Warburg, 1937; London: Hamish Hamilton, 1986.

In his biography *Serious Pleasures: The Life of Stephen Tennant* (see part 3), Philip Hoare notes the unmistakable influence of RF's works on this novel, especially *Caprice* and *Prancing Nigger* (117, 133).

Theroux, Alexander. *Three Wogs*. Boston: Gambit, 1972; London: Chatto & Windus, 1973.

The last of the three novellas comprising this volume, "The Wife of God," is Firbankian in both style and subject matter. When I suggested this in "An Interview with Alexander Theroux" (*Review of Contemporary Fiction* 11.1 [Spring 1991]: 29-35), he replied, "Well, I had read Firbank by then. I've always admired stylists" (29).

―――. *Darconville's Cat*. Garden City, NY: Doubleday, 1981; London: Hamish Hamilton, 1983.

RF's "The Wavering Disciple" is among the works listed in the bibliographic chapter entitled "The Misogynist's Library" (445).

Updike, John. *Bech: A Book*. New York: Knopf, 1970.

The writer of a fictitious *Observer* review of *The Best of Bech* is "reminded, in the end, after the butterfly similes and overextended, substanceless themes of this self-anointed 'Best,' of (and the comparison may serve English readers as an index of present relevance) Ronald Firbank!" (168). After reading this review Bech thinks to himself: "Firbank dead at forty" (169).

Van Dyke, Henry. *Lunacy and Caprice*. New York: Ballantine/Available Press, 1987.

This blackly humorous novel is described on the back cover as "a story of pleasant madness in the tradition of Ronald Firbank and Henry Green." See also Van Dyke's earlier novels, *Ladies of the Rachmaninoff Eyes* (1965) and *Blood of Strawberries* (1968), which show the influence of his mentor Carl Van Vechten.

Van Vechten, Carl. *The Blind Bow-Boy*. New York: Knopf, 1923.

In his review of this novel in *Vanity Fair*, Edmund Wilson described it as "halfway between Ronald Firbank and Scott Fitzgerald." Firbank critic Robert Murray Davis believes that "Ronald, Duke of Middlebottom" is based on RF (letter to me, 26 April 1994).

―――. *Firecrackers*. New York: Knopf, 1925.

One of this novel's epigraphs is from RF's *Flower beneath the Foot*, and the novel itself is one of Van Vechten's most Firbankian efforts.

————. *Spider Boy*. New York: Knopf, 1928.
"Like the shimmering glissando-scenes of Ronald Firbank in which strange, stark notes are accented," Edward Lueders writes, "*Spider Boy* is Realism once-, twice-, three times-removed into fantasy and the hectic distillation of dream-consciousness" (*Carl Van Vechten* [New York: Twayne, 1965], 109).

Vidal, Gore. "Pages from an Abandoned Journal." In *A Thirsty Evil*. New York: Zero Press, 1956. Rpt. in *The City and the Pillar and Seven Early Stories*. New York: Random House, 1995.
    An American visiting cultured homosexual drug addicts in Paris learns that RF is an author he should read, and the story ends with a note to himself: "Return Steven's copy of 'Valmouth.'"

Waugh, Auberon. *The Foxglove Saga*. London: Chapman & Hall, 1960.
    In his *Butterfly's Speckled Wings*, John Anthony Kiechler quotes several passages from this novel that strike him as showing RF's influence (119-20).

Waugh, Evelyn. *Decline and Fall*. London: Chapman & Hall, 1928. Revised Uniform Edition: Chapman & Hall, 1962.
    Several readers have noted that the wounding, hospitalization, and death of Lord Tangent is clearly derived from the "fleas at the Ritz" motif in *The Flower beneath the Foot*.

————. *Vile Bodies*. London: Chapman & Hall, 1930. Revised Uniform Edition: Chapman & Hall, 1965.
    In his preface to the 1965 edition, Waugh admits, "I began under the brief influence of Ronald Firbank but struck out for myself" (7).

Willhoite, Michael. *Members of the Tribe: Caricatures of Gay Men and Lesbians*. Boston: Alyson, 1994.
    Contains a caricature of RF.

Wilson, Angus. *Hemlock and After*. London: Secker & Warburg, 1952.
    Critic John McCormick notes with disapproval that RF's "neuter . . . giggle turns into a snigger" in this novel about a novelist's attempt to establish a writers' center in a country house (*Catastrophe and Imagination*, 299).

Wilson, Sandy. *Valmouth*. 1958. London: Samuel French, 1985.
    A musical comedy adaption of RF's novel (with a few bits from *Prancing Nigger* and *Cardinal Pirelli*), produced in Liverpool (1958), London (1958-59), New York (1960), and Chichester (1982). A recording of the musical numbers was released on the Pye label. (See Benkovitz's *Bibliography* [2nd ed., pp. 17-18] for further details.) A cast recording of the Chichester revival was issued on compact disk by Ter Ltd. in 1995.

Woolf, Virginia. *Between the Acts*. London: Hogarth/New York: Harcourt, Brace, 1941.
    Critic Colette Daube sees RF's influence on Woolf's final novel. In a letter of 1929 Woolf mentions reading RF "with some unstinted pleasure" (see part 3).

Part 5

Dissertations
and Theses

Brennan, Neil Francis. "The Aesthetic Tradition in the English Comic Novel." Ph.D. diss., University of Illinois, 1959. *Dissertation Abstracts International* [*DAI*] 20 (1959): 1780-81.

Locates RF in the post-1890 British tradition of the aesthetic (as opposed to popular) comic novel, with special attention to *Caprice*.

Cantillon, Watt Joseph. "The Aesthete in the Novels of Ronald Firbank, Wyndham Lewis and James Joyce." Ph.D. diss., University of Illinois at Urbana-Champaign, 1973. *DAI* 34 (1974): 7222-23.

Identifies three kinds of aesthete in early 20th-century British fiction, with Firbank (and Beardsley) exemplifying the first: "the hedonistic aesthete, who attempts to cultivate a specialized sensibility by immersing himself unself-consciously in a world of unconventional or abnormal sensations. Experience for him is neither moral nor immoral; it is aesthetically or sexually interesting."

Carens, James Francis. "Evelyn Waugh: His Satire, His Ideas of Order, and His Relation to Other Modern English Satirical Novelists." Ph.D. diss., Columbia University, 1959. *DAI* 20 (1959): 1362.

Chap. 5 discusses the influence of "the oblique satirical techniques" of RF on Waugh.

Clark, William Lane. "Subversive Aesthetics: Literary Camp in the Novels of Ronald Firbank." Ph.D. diss., George Washington University, 1991. *DAI* 52 (1992): 2929.

Argues that an understanding of camp aesthetics are prerequisite to an appreciation of RF's achievement. Chap. 1 defines camp, setting it in the context of nineteenth- and twentieth-century sexual discourse, and discusses Wilde's role in establishing camp aesthetics. Chap. 2 discusses "the confluence of gender in the camp persona of male/female chimerism" and concentrates on the importance of clothing, fashion, and appearances in RF's work. Chap. 3 addresses RF's application of camp to "the conventions of respectability: restrictive sexuality, the concept of social progress and individual degeneracy, male dynamism, and the church as a feminine social component"; Clark also notes "the challenge to authority perceived by respectability in the private vice of masturbation" and "elaborates the pervasive masturbatory subtext in all of Firbank's camp novels," with special attention to *Valmouth*. Chap. 4 focuses on formal elements in RF's work ("disruption and opening of form, synaesthesia, inverted word order, simultaneity in multi-voiced conversation, and the suppression of direct speech"), and RF's use of jazz and cinematic techniques. The concluding chap. 5 discusses gay sensibilty and camp expression in general, and Firbank's influence on contemporary expressions of camp sensibility.

Cottrell, Beekman Waldron. "Conversation Piece: Four Twentieth-Century English Dialogue Novelists." Ph.D. diss., Columbia University, 1956. *DAI* 16 (1956): 2159.

In chap. 3, "Concerning the Eccentricities of Ronald Firbank" (61-76), Cottrell examines RF's impressionistic use of dialogue "to create shifting moods and mental climates and to present the reader with stimulating sensual experience." Cottrell believes RF's "best novels have the highest dialogue content, his failures, the least," and finds a forerunner of his technique in Swinburne's "exotic romance" *Lesbia Brandon*. RF "mastered the art of characterizing by dialogue," but is surpassed in this regard, Cottrell believes, by Ivy Compton-Burnett.

Davis, Robert Murray. "The Externalist Method in the Novels of Ronald Firbank, Carl Van Vechten, and Evelyn Waugh." Ph.D. diss., University of Wisconsin, 1964. *DAI* 25 (1964): 2509.

Notes that RF's novels began with an identifiable authorial presence that diminished until *Inclinations,* which presents "authorial summary and comments in a style little differentiated from that of the characters and giv[es] more information through a variety of momentary observers." Thereafter RF reversed the trend, making his authorial presence more and more apparent. RF's "novels lack tightly-knit plots and strong central characters on which to focus. Typically, they present the antics of a large number of characters whose actions form a series of unrelated and casually developed plot strands, the major mixed with and undifferentiated from the minor. The episodes are given coherence by significant relationships of comparison and contrast in terms of tone, pace, and texture. Thus rhythm and pattern replace or reinforce plot as the structural principle."

Dock, Leslie Ann. "Brigid Brophy: Artist in the Baroque." Ph.D. diss., University of Wisconsin, 1976. *DAI* 37 (1977): 5844-45.

Chap. 2 treats Brophy's work on RF and her own Firbankian novel *The Finishing Touch.*

Donohue, Agnes McNeil. "A Study of the Humor of Ronald Firbank as Revealed through Critical Analysis of His Novels." Ph.D. diss., Loyola University, 1954. (No *DAI* listing.)

Hollinghurst, Alan. "The Creative Uses of Homosexuality in the Novels of E. M. Forster, Ronald Firbank and L. P. Hartley." Oxford M.Litt. thesis, 1980.

Kiechler, John Anthony. "The Butterfly's Freckled Wings: A Study of Style in the Novels of Ronald Firbank." Ph.D. diss., University of Zurich, 1967.

See part 2.

Marini, Cristina. "The Broken Butterfly: The Life and Works of Ronald Firbank." *Tesi di laurea,* Università degli studi di Padova, 1987.

Pellegrini, Marina. "Ronald Firbank: His Life, His Works." *Tesi di laurea,* Università "L. Bocconi," 1970.

Potoker, Edward Martin. "Aesthetes' Yorick: A Critical Study of Ronald Firbank." Ph.D. diss., Columbia University, 1964.

Focuses on RF as a parodist and satirist, based on RF's own sense of the absurd (and which connects him, "however loosely, with Dadaism, Existentialism, and the 'Theatre of the Absurd'"). "The fictional world that Firbank painstakingly created out of his own daydreams and nightmares was essentially one of futility, frivolity, perversion, and decay. But Firbank's deeply sad, if heartless, world—which at once attracted and repelled him—was continually redeemed by gaiety and wit. The elaborate flippancy of his tone was always the flippancy of honest desperation." RF's fiction "is both poignant and richly comic. Firbank also created work that has the quality of timelessness. This quality, proceeding from the tough, brilliant fibers of wit which invigorate his prose, will continue to guarantee his reputation among a steadily increasing number of readers who appreciate the most insolent refinements of satire."

Robb, W. A. "The Dandy as Artist: An Examination of the Work of Ronald Firbank and an Attempt to Define His Influence on Some Later Writers." M.A. thesis, Manchester, 1972-73.

Robert-Nicould, E. L. "Evelyn Waugh and Conversion to Roman Catholicism among English Writers between 1890 and 1945." Ph.D. diss., Cambridge University, 1991. *Index to Theses* 40.4 (1991): 1614.

Shults, Terrance Glenn. "The Shadow of Reading Gaol: The Aesthetic-Ethic Motif in the Novels of Wilde, Firbank, Wain and Amis." Ph.D. diss., University of Louisville, 1979. *DAI* 40 (1980): 4062-A
    Discusses the influence of Wilde's *Dorian Gray* on RF, especially "Wilde's depiction of Aestheticism [as] cautionary rather than exemplary." RF "is a serious adapter of the Aesthetic motif. . . . In *Vainglory* and other novels, Firbank considers the interplay between women's Aesthetic views of themselves and Aesthetic religion." Shults later argues that Amis's *The Alteration* "intertwines religion and Aesthetics in the Firbank manner."

Sola, Orietta. "Ronald Firbank." *Tesi de laurea*, Università "L. Bocconi," 1959.

Sweeney, Daniel Christopher. "The New Rhythm: Camp in the Novels of Ronald Firbank." Ph.D. diss., Florida State University, 1975. *DAI* 36 (1975): 3738.
    A sociological study suggesting the camp sensibility is the most effective means for understanding RF's work and "that camp represents a central organizing principle which underlies almost the entire structure of the novels."

Part 6

Foreign-language Materials

Introduction

Ronald Firbank's status as a cult writer—a status he metanarratively articulated in his fiction, his contemporaries brought to actual existence, and later circulation of his works and persona have definitively established—is possibly even more strongly defined outside the English-speaking world, given the extreme difficulty a non-English native speaker finds in reading his somewhat esoteric writing and, more significantly, his marginal position in the canon, in literary histories, and in the academic agenda. Consequently, it is surprising to learn that in certain decades (the seventies and eighties, for example), Firbank has been more read in continental Europe than elsewhere—and often, what's more important, in sounder critical terms. Lacking, to a certain extent, the gay connotations the Firbank cult had, and the consequent clumsiness which has characterized, for instance, the criticism of Oscar Wilde's works in Great Britain and partly in the United States (Oscar Wilde's person and aesthetical theories, in fact, weren't relegated to embarrassed silence in continental Europe as they were in England), Firbank's writings were read in terms of narrative techniques, of structuring devices, and of literary experimentation, which gave him an extremely small place in literary history, but a fairly "safe" one. Moreover, the high appreciation of Firbank's fiction—it is hard to find in France, Italy, or Spain any reviews filled with the same kind of disgust or irritation his writings provoked when they appeared in England or the United States—is partly due to the fact that he was virtually unknown here until the 1960s, when "literature" as a practice and criticism as an institution had profoundly changed, making some textual strategies Firbank contributed to shaping more recognizable, understandable, and appreciable: in short, he was more "canonical" in the sixties—when the French *nouveau roman* and postmodern fiction and theories were imposing themselves as the new yardsticks of literary significance—than he was in the twenties.

In terms of academic research, what I have been noticing is especially true for Italy, which has produced an undisregardable number of acute analyses, and a conspicuous number of *tesi di laurea,* which is the necessary requirement for obtaining a degree (works averaging 100,000 words, similar to an M.A. or an M.Litt. thesis; those written in English are listed in part 5 rather than below). One reason why Italy is privileged in this bibliography is the frustrating inaccessibility, incompleteness, or complete absence of national and international indexes for non-English-speaking countries as far as reviews, unpublished dissertations, and many academic essays are concerned (these are sometimes listed in American works such as the *MLA Bibliography* or the *Arts and Humanities Citation Index*), and the still very limited use of computer-assisted bibliographical tools. This means that I had to seek out those who had shown an interest in Firbank, so that they could help me find dissertations, translations, or more essays; and this was, for obvious reasons, easier in Italy, where I could also plunge myself in often old-fashioned libraries looking for histories of English literature or other uncompiled materials, than elsewhere. What offsets the inevitable and frustrating incompleteness of the following bibliography (which has been restricted to Italy, France, Germany, Spain, Holland, and Argentina) was the great pleasure in compiling it, for I have been able to draw a sort of "map" of the Firbank cult I was alluding to, getting in touch with a large percentage of the Firbankians (just a few initiates, but surprisingly enthusiastic both in their appreciation and in their readiness to help me) that people Europe. My thanks to all of them for the extreme pleasure the letters and phone calls we have been exchanging in the last two years has given me: Mariacarla Ballarati, Benedetta Bini, Enrico Cozzolino, Luis Antonio de Villena, Colette Daube, Monica Giordano, Alan Hollinghurst, Trevor Joscelyne, Gérard Joulié, Carla Marengo Vaglio, Steven Moore, Viola Papetti, Francesca Pasquali, Umberto Pasti, Werner Peterich, Marco Pinnacoli, Sergio Pitol, Salvatore Romano, Luigi Sampietro, Rita Severi, Alberto Valtellina, and Sandy Wilson. And I would also like to express my gratitude to Giuliano Bernini, Fred Kannengiesser, and Liesbeth Schonkeren for their invaluable help in reading German and Dutch materials, and to the staff at publishing houses who kindly responded to my letters of inquiry and provided me with their review files (L'Age d'Homme, Anagrama, Apollo Maridoro, Galeati, Galerna, Gallimard, Garzanti, Hanser, Novecento, Rivages, Rizzoli) and at the libraries (British Library and Senate House Library, London; University of Bergamo; University of Genoa; University of Milan; British Council and Università Cattolica del Sacro Cuore, Milan) where my Firbank pursuit was conducted.

FABIO CLETO
Bergamo

1. Translations and their Reviews

"La Princesse artificielle" suivi de "Mon piaffeur noir"
Translated by Maurice Sachs (*The Artificial Princess*)
and Edouard Roditi (*Prancing Nigger*)
Paris: Gallimard, 1938. Reprinted in 1987,
with an afterword by Edouard Roditi

Anon. "Vient de paraître." *Nouvelle revue française*, 1 August 1938.
An announcement of the first French translation of RF.

Vanagloria
Translated with an introduction by Laura Lovisetti Fuà
Milan: Rizzoli, 1962

Anon. "Humour inglese." *Vita* [Rome]8.187 (15 November 1962): 50.
A brief notice about this "delightful novel," taking into account the Firbank revival and the appreciations by W. H. Auden, the Sitwells, Evelyn Waugh, Cyril Connolly, and Anthony Powell, and what had become by that time a kind of "Firbank case."

Anon. "Ronald Firbank: *Vanagloria*." *Oggi*, 31 January 1963.
An advertisment for RF's first Italian translation, "a sophisticated satire of Victorian high life," by a dandy writer whose defining traits are elegance and humor.

Anon. "*Vanagloria* di Ronald Firbank." *La Gazzetta di Reggio*, 16 November 1962. Also published in *La Gazzetta dell'Emilia* on the same day.
Finds RF's personal eccentricities to be the creative spring of his novels, which reproduce the madness of his own legendary life. The Italian publishers are excused for having waited so long to publish RF because his original texts are "monstruously difficult," and Lovisetti Fuà is thanked for undertaking such a task.

Anon. "*Vanagloria* di Ronald Firbank." *Giostra delle Muse*, 24 January 1963.
A hurried note on the first novel by "this complex and irregular writer," advancing in his work "the validity of moral duplicity and of an intentional curiosity for everything."

Bo, Carlo. "Firbank condannava la realtà ma ne salvava i riflessi." *L'Europeo*, 16 December 1962, 90.
RF's work is seen as a reaction to the war and to a distressing reality. Carlo Bo links RF with Denis Diderot and with the tradition of the conversation novel: while Diderot employed ideas and things, RF "wants to forget ideas and things, and prefers to play with their reflections." He condemned reality and denied the possibility of human agency: behind his mask an inert judge can be seen. RF thus belongs to the great number of "deniers, of those writers appearing at the turn of the century who refused reality."

B., O. "Le frivole donnine di Ronald Firbank." *Il Paese*, 21 November 1962.

RF's is "an artistic intelligence and a diseased *sensiblerie* that doesn't aspire to knowledge," and his "virtual masterpiece is thus reduced to a mere delicious little game." All he produces is "the perfect aestheticism or, at the utmost, a cruel analysis" of English intellectual high society, peopled by characters without souls and providing no substantial conversation: all that remains is "chit-chat."

Cam. "Stampe nuove: *Vanagloria* di Ronald Firbank." *Il Gazzettino* [Venice], 4 January 1963.
    RF can best be described as "a Proust reduced to mere ornaments and, so to speak, boned." His are "the most exceptional writings one can imagine," though this is precisely their drawback: he must be read in small quantities, for—given his mannerist style and his maniacal devotion to detail—he easily ends being "sickly." He is perfect as a "pure writer," that is, a writer disengaged from reality and uncommitted; he has an extraordinary talent for dialogue, taken from the Art Nouveau society he knew so well, which is aptly and patiently translated by Lovisetti Fuà.

del Buono, Oreste. "Lo snob che tira frecce." *Incom*, 28 December 1962, 66.
    Finds RF "a wonderful dilettante" and *Vainglory* "an authentically surprising book, an intelligent work," sparkling and never fatuous, nasty but never acid. RF despised women but he understood the nature of their conversations and rivalries much better than any other writer. Ends by tracing an Italian parallel to RF in Alberto Arbasino's witty journalism, announcing that the Italian writer is actually writing a conversation novel (it will be *Fratelli d'Italia*, in fact: see the "Creative Works" section) which the reviewer hopes will retain RF's secret: the rhythm, rather than the quantity or quality, of the exhilarating verbal exchanges. Thanks Lovisetti Fuà for her faithful translation.

Ferretti, Massimo. "Per Firbank la vita è un cicaleccio." *Il Giorno*, 14 November 1962, 5.
    RF portrays a meaningless life made up of "futile and immoderate chit-chatting." Anecdotes about RF are unsympathetically reported in order to claim that the "nothingness" of RF's conversations is the natural outcome of "a man who had given up self-knowledge."

G., R. "Due romanzi." *Carlino sera*, 16 January 1963. Also published in *Nazione sera* on the same day.
    A brief notice, summarizing *Vainglory*'s plot and discussing the main character. RF's novel, despite the nothingness of its plot, has an underlying seriousness arising from a refined humor and a paradoxical satire of characters and high society settings.

Golino, Enzo. "Uno squarcio ironico nell'ottimismo vittoriano." *La Voce repubblicana*, 1 January 1963.
    "Master of elegant metaphors linked together by a brilliant pictorial gift for carving images," RF has a dignified place in the literary history of his own country.

Gramigna, Giuliano. "Il lettore italiano nel dedalo di Firbank." *Settimo giorno* [Milan], 30 October 1962, 58.
    Tells of the Firbank revival in the U.K., with the publication of the Duckworth omnibus and the Penguin Modern Classics edition. RF is "one of those *petits-maîtres* who are not bothered by rules, poetics, cultural influences, and

whose work is so perfect and self-sufficient within its limits that it seems inimitable and imposes its own standards on the reader." The greatest and unsurpassed achievement of his "bizarre little masterpieces" is the "extraordinary and eccentric" conversation technique, which is absolutely devoid of any organizing and finalizing perspective: "RF's conversation exists on an ontological level, it lives in itself and for itself."

————. "Torna di moda Ronald Firbank." *Amica*, 11 November 1962, 69.

Behind RF's superficial, incoherent, and dandified facade lies "an unneglectable literary value and seriousness of intent." Story is not what matters in RF: a dialogue that doesn't convey any information, being only pleased of itself, succeeds in "giving the sense of human reality."

G[ramigna, Giuliano?]. "Letture: Firbank." *Il Corriere della sera*, 18 January 1963, 3.

The reviewer summarizes and partly reproduces Giuliano Gramigna's two previously published reviews (in *Settimo giorno* and *Amica*). RF's discovery in Italy, though taking place in an age of commitment that disregards witty games and literary futilities, is fully justified by the work's value.

I., M. "Vuol essere immortalata nella vetrata di una cattedrale." *La Notte*, 27-28 November 1962, 11.

Disregarding the appreciation RF has gained in some intellectual circles, the reviewer admits RF's sparkling and "technically perfect" dialogue to be the only substantial merit of the novel, spoilt by its snobbism and mere decoration.

Milano, Paolo. "La cenerentola di questa stagione." *L'Espresso*, 30 December 1962, 19.

This survey of recent publications announces the appearance of the Italian translation of *Vainglory*, by the "*petit-maître*" RF.

Porzio, Domenico. "Il primo romanzo dell'usignolo." *Oggi*, 22 November 1962. The same review appeared, with a few words added at the end, as "Vanagloria," *Progresso italo-americano* [New York], 5 December 1962.

Praises the "masterly translation" by Lovisetti Fuà, and relies on previous comments by Wilson, Auden, Forster, Connolly, and Powell to present a writer "gifted with uncommon observation and evaluation skills"—now become "a minor classic" for his dialogues and directionlessness—whose aesthetical posing reveals "a sociologist, transforming people into insects" underneath. *Vainglory* is a perfect example of RF's "Art Nouveau intaglio-like composition."

R., L. "Al pranzo in suo onore mangiò soltanto un pisello." *Il Giornale del mattino* [Florence], 22 November 1962.

Finds RF's biography "illuminating in order to approach his writings." His "cruel and calculated frivolity" and typically English irony eventually must be seen as a way of "passing a moral judgment on the world to which Firbank, with detached anxiety, gave himself up to."

Segre, Elena. "*Vanagloria* di Ronald Firbank." *La Voce adriatica* [Ancona], 12 February 1963.

A long review, summarizing Lovisetti Fuà's introduction and the novel's plot and main characters. RF's composition method anticipates many avant-garde contemporary authors, and this—along with his satirical vein—makes him "more an essayist than a novelist."

Siciliano, Enzo. "La cifra di Firbank." *Il Mondo*, 25 December 1962.
Draws a parallel with the Italian writer Guido Gozzano, for their subtle aestheticism, ironical sense of illusion, and their strong literary rigor lying behind an appearance of mundaneness and diseased madness. "It will never be possible to find a more rational tightrope walker" than RF, whose writing aims are precisely those of Mrs. Shamefoot in *Vainglory*, that is, becoming a filter of reality like a stained glass window in a cathedral.

Il Cardinal Pirelli
Contains *Concerning the Eccentricities of Cardinal Pirelli*, *The Artificial Princess* (translated by Diana Bonacossa), and *Prancing Nigger* (translated by Vittorio Sereni) Introduction by Giorgio Manganelli
Milan: Feltrinelli, 1964

B., F. "Il Cardinal Pirelli." *La Nazione*, 20 October 1964, 3.
This short review is simply a collection of uncredited phrases from Manganelli's introduction. All it adds is that the novels are "entertaining, showing us a man who could laugh at his own undisputed art."

Bisol, Gaetano. *Letture* 20.3 (March 1965): 208-10.
Highlights RF's grotesqueness and irony, and the puppetlike quality of his characters, whom he controls according to his childlike whims. RF's texts are "meant for collectors of stylistic refinements, documents for historians of language and of aesthetic theories, delightful material for those in search of eccentricities. They can't be read with the expectations arising from a normal novel" (209-10).

Debenedetti, Antonio. "Firbank elegante e cinico." *La Fiera letteraria* 46 (31 December 1964): 4. Reprinted as "La bacchetta magica di Firbank," *L'Avanti*, 5 August 1965, 3.
"Bold irony and ambitious imagination" are the most obvious characteristics of RF, who imposed himself on the art for art's sake scene when writers refused bourgeois creeds in favor of aestheticism. His novels have an outstanding musical quality achieved with strenuous care and effort, as if they were written in order to be set to music. In *Cardinal Pirelli* "ambiguity reaches a supreme and classical decorum," and the "negative presence" of character and story about which Giorgio Manganelli writes in his introduction makes RF a significant figure in the history of the contemporary novel.

Gigli, Lorenzo. "Satira e 'nonsense' dell'inglese Firbank." *La Stampa*, March 1965.
Praises the two translators for their philological rigor and spiritual community with the original texts. RF is fully contemporary, a precursor of experimentalism (Beckett is pointed out), even though one should not try and impose on his chit-chat a metaphysical dimension: he was above all a snob, amusing himself in telling tricky stories that endlessly invite the reader to discover their mechanism and solution.

Golino, Enzo. "I racconti di Firbank." *Il Mondo*, 2 March 1965, 8.
RF "reveals a distrust in the capacity of knowing through language" and belongs to the tradition of Compton-Burnett, Nathalie Sarraute, and Beckett. The reviewer refuses to regard the novels as comedies, preferring to call them

operettas: such a choice "justifies the musical sarabands of language, the settings and themes, the recovery of the most exhausted aestheticism to pastiche and to metaphysical irony." RF is therefore a dandy, hating bourgeois utilitarianism and dreaming a world in which things can be as precious as possible and "free from the slavery of usefulness."

Tagliaferri, Aldo. "I personaggi snob e tragici di Firbank." *Il Giorno*, 28 October 1964, 9.

The reviewer praises the unconventionality and ambiguities of RF's plots, his creation of "a frivolous and refined society," narrated in a way that makes reading completely "devoid of consolative purposes." RF is considered a literary descendant of the Wilde tradition, though he is far less aphoristic, and his characters are more Edenic and childish than Wilde's: that is, at once innocent and cruel.

Inclinazioni
Translated by Laura Lovisetti Fuà
Florence: Vallecchi, 1966

Gramigna, Giuliano. "Il gioco di Firbank." *La Fiera letteraria*, 15 September 1966, 15.

Emphasizes the essential role played by intermingling voices, apparently eluding meaning and the plot, which nonetheless can be extrapolated by the reader. RF doesn't belong to the aesthetic tradition, as he doesn't see a superior life in jewels and dresses: yet, "the representation of High Society doesn't have any polemical, critical, or reforming aim." The writer's relation to his age is not mimetic, nor expressed by contempt toward his characters, but rather through his use of stylistic devices, his "plot construction by means of empty spaces," representing the social dissolution of the twenties.

Las excentricidades del Cardenal Pirelli
Translated and with an introduction by Mario Trajtenberg
Buenos Aires: Galerna, 1968

No reviews could be found.

Die Exzentrizitäten des Kardinals Pirelli betreffend
Translated by Werner Peterich, with Arthur Waley's introduction
(translated by Gerd Wagner)
Munich: Carl Hanser, 1970

Anon. "Akt in Velours." *Der Spiegel* [Hamburg], 23, 1 June 1970, 160.

An account of the usual Firbankiana (single green pea, peaches and champagne diet, etc.), of critical interventions in favor of RF, and of *Cardinal Pirelli*'s plot and characters. RF is an impressionist and a late fin-de-siècle dandy: no more.

B., H. "Welke Schönheit." *Nürnberger Nachrichten*, 2 March 1971.

After noting RF's critical neglect during his lifetime ("he was considered a silly writer"), the reviewer regrets RF is not silly, but rather intolerably pretentious. The precious Carl Hanser edition, in fact, deceives the reader, promising pleasures the book won't fulfill. In its best moments *Cardinal Pirelli* reminds one of Sterne's *Tristram Shandy*, the masterpiece of eccentric literature, though only superficially: what is ironic sensibility in Sterne becomes snobbish pleasure in RF.

Blöcker, Günter. "Was ein rechter Geheimtip ist." *Frankfurter Allgemeine Zeitung*, 25 July 1970.

Tells of a RF cult in West Germany, promoted by Herbert Heckmann and Reinhard Lettau. In fact, RF was already a cult during his lifetime, not because he was ahead of his time but rather because he was behind his time, devoted as he was to Pater, Wilde, and Beardsley, who were simply epigones of a French tradition. An "epigone of epigones," RF is also a "committed decadent" (the reviewer plays on what seems an oxymoron or an opposition between commitment and decadence), making all efforts toward refusing reality, and responsible for an "Art Nouveau-like" textuality. RF's pointlessness, finally, is pointed out with some sarcasm as precisely that which makes him alluring to younger readers, who revolt against everything and are anti-bourgeois without being socialists.

Brinitzer, Carl. "Groteskes vom Kardinal." *Welt am Sonntag*, 21 June 1970.

Relates RF's fluctuation of popularity among critics, and says that this will always be so because it is typical of eccentric writers, among whom RF is a master. Laughs at Waley's definition of RF as an impressionist, claiming that his spiritual fathers are the romantics and fantastic literature: in fact, he was against all forms of realism in his life and works, and this is precisely the reason why *Cardinal Pirelli* is neither vulgar nor blasphemous, for it posits a fantastic realm with rules of its own, in which Pirelli gets nicer and nicer as the novel progresses.

Eichholz, Hildegard. "Geheimtip in rotem Velours." *Stern* [Hamburg], 16 April 1970.

RF's entertaining and "superb amateurism" combines in Pirelli all the vices of the Church and the decadence of aristocracy. Going back to the 1890s, RF proposes "a revolution backwards, an aesthetical regression, and a private amusement bringing confusion to all forms of progress."

Kramberg, K. H. "Austern in Kandis: Ein Fabelwesen in Gestalt eines Kirchenfürsten." *Süddeutsche Zeitung* [Munich], 2-3 May 1970.

Highly positive review of "a dish for literary snobs and for others as well," "open to endless interpretation." Finds RF's neglect surprising, for his silliness "is not an unintentional attitude, but rather the result of art and self-discipline." Pirelli, whose aestheticism receives most of the reviewer's attention, cannot be described in a few words: "one has to read the novel, absolutely."

Schuller, Renate. "Die heimliche Show." *Saarbrücker Zeitung*, 2-3 May 1970.

RF is closer to Wilde and Beardsley—he is "the advocate of their spiritual heritage"—than to his contemporaries. He is a literary conservative, building up a world made of nothing, of feathers and perfumes, in which aestheticism and the cult of the individual are dominated by the author's ironical superiority in directly taking part in his works.

Skasa-Weiss, Eugen. "Spät entdeckter Londoner Dandy in rotem Velours."
Münchner Merkur, 11-12 April 1970.
    Cardinal Pirelli is the "most precious jewel" among RF's "perfumed
satanisms," which—drawing on the most extreme versions of British fin-de-
siècle aestheticism—were intended for a small audience and not for the general
public. The reviewer finds the Carl Hanser edition appropriate in its choice of
a red velvet cover with gold stamping, but excessive in its use of italics in the
main text, for it makes RF's "pure foam novel" even more evanescent, that is,
unbearable for all its 105 pages.

Zimmer, Dieter E. "Andalusien ist natürlich weiss." *Die Zeit*, 10 April 1970.
    A long and insightful review. Notwithstanding those readers (probably refer-
ring to Waley's introduction) who have simply defined RF as a decadent or an
impressionist (which wouldn't justify the interest of an age and a place seeing
little value in impressionism and aesthetic decadence), he can be read as an
extremely contemporary writer, *Cardinal Pirelli* being a "historical pop novel."
Its pop-novel quality lies in its campiness (as defined by Susan Sontag), and in
its proposing a "secondary" form of textuality, entirely made of citations and
clichés. Pirelli's is "a Spain within quotation marks," represented as in a film,
distancing the reader from itself "by means of the ironical accumulation of
particularities" and by the systematic anachronism of materials which are juxta-
posed—that is, by the means which are used by contemporary writers such as
Christian Morgenstern and Alain Robbe-Grillet.

"Het Grillige leven van Kardinaal Pirelli" gevolgd door "Valmouth"
Translated and with an afterword by Gerrit Komrij
Amsterdam: Meulenhoff, 1975

No reviews could be found.

*La Flor pisoteada; o, la historia de la juventud de Santa Laura
de Nazianzi y de la época que la vió vivir*
Translated by Mariano Aguirre and Graciela Colombo
Madrid: Felmar, 1978

No reviews could be found.

Capriccio
Translated by Carlo Brera
Milan: Guanda, 1984

Almansi, Guido. "Capriccio inglese." *La Repubblica*, 8 August 1984, 19.
    RF delightfully offers "a series of acute comments on society and on morals
by means of interjections, adverbs, coughs, and wordplay." Almansi praises the
translator who managed to put into Italian a typically English conversation style
(taken from Wilde) hiding malignity and nastiness behind apparent courtesy.
Almansi then claims a better evaluation for RF than the one given by Mario
Praz in his literary history (see section 3 below), since he is a wholly "serious
writer" who believes in commitment although he escapes life by reducing it to

theater. If RF "consciously reduces the history of culture to the history of clothes," his theatrical fascination gives access to "a world of falseness that is better than actual life." Nonetheless, *Caprice* can also be seen as a satire on theatrical habits: although it is not a tragedy (as Brigid Brophy believes), it shouldn't be regarded merely as "a pure caprice, a literary joke to entertain the fashionable world."

En torno a las excentricidades del cardenal Pirelli
Translated with an introduction by Sergio Pitol
Barcelona: Anagrama, 1985

Acin, Ramon. "La lógica del sinsentido." 2 February 1986.
    The reviewer confesses to having been "disoriented" by the novel, whose "maximalist nonsense" is worthy of the best Edward Lear. The result is a reading experience that is hard, enjoyable, and unexpected; one has to work through an enormous mass of allusions and references filling up (along with one's own interventions) every single conversation or narrative fragment.

Anon. "*En torno a las excentricidades del cardenal Pirelli* de Ronald Firbank." *Laberinta.*
    Judges *Cardinal Pirelli* "bizarre . . . metaphorical, personal, nearly always unreal, faithful to its creator"; and a good novel, too.

Calleja, Pedro. "Ronald Firbank: *En torno a las excentricidades del cardenal Pirelli.*" *La Luna.*
    The reviewer finds RF's novel "the most modern" work he has reviewed lately, "one of the most exquisite dishes of English decadence of the beginning of this century," telling in a fragmentary fashion a story which is most of the time taking place off-stage, by "one of the most important innovators in all English literature."

Mañez, Julio A. "Pequeño gran libro." *Valencia.*
    RF's last novel is his best work, a work that "absolutely must be read." Loose, erotic, irreverent, homosexual, and original, it is pure "narrative honesty at the service of an extremely intelligent irony."

Martín Abril, José Luis. "Novela: *En torno a las excentricidades del cardenal Pirelli.*" *ABC*, 18 January 1986.
    Despite (or perhaps because of) discerning RF's influence on (or similarities with) Proust, Joyce, and Luis Cernuda, the reviewer doesn't appreciate *Cardinal Pirelli*, written by "a lucid madman" without any poetry and instead full of irreverence, stupidity, unconceivable fantasy, paranoia, and unacceptable scenes. It is "an abnormal book in form and content; a book of profanations and of evil influences."

Molina, Cesar Antonio. "Purpura pagana." *Cambio 16.*
    Cardinal Pirelli is a lovely work, "perfectly reflecting the decadent and transgressive world of both the end of the nineteenth and beginning of the twentieth century." Filmmaker Federico Fellini surely would have loved it.

Villena, Luis Antonio de. "Retrato de un delincuente." *Diario 16*, 20 October 1985, 2.

RF incarnates the time "when the ideals and manners of decadence—without renouncing themselves—are transformed into avant-garde, and when Art Nouveau lines become geometrical." He is "a precursor of the most classical *nouveau roman* techniques, a miniaturist and a mannerist painter," who—like Jules Laforgue and Raymond Roussel—turns disenchantment into parody, writing "deliberately artificial and frivolous texts in which language—full of neologisms and French locutions—tends to distort itself."

————. "Una cálida invitación a la extravagancia." *La Vanguardia*.

RF exemplifies what Edith Sitwell called "English eccentrics," writing novels that are "a river of images and metaphors" and which can be defined as "precious or mannerist rather than baroque": his perfect counterpart, in fact, is Aubrey Beardsley, whose images show "the same ingenious lightness and frivolity mingled with the dance of death." *Cardinal Pirelli* is the quintessence of his art, and "one of the oddest novels one can read nowadays."

La fleur foulée aux pieds
Translated and with an introduction by Jean Gattégno
Paris: Rivages, 1987

Les excentricités du cardinal Pirelli
Translated by Patrick Reumaux, and with an introduction by
François Dupuigrenet-Desroussilles
Paris: Rivages, 1987

(*Note:* These two volumes were published at the same time and often reviewed together, sometimes along with Gallimard's new edition of *"La Princesse artificielle"* suivi de *"Mon piaffer noir."*)

Bianciotti, Héctor. "Le revenant et l'inconnue." *Le Monde des livres*.
A review of new French translations of RF (whose comeback makes him a sort of *revenant*, a ghost) and of Sylvia Townsend Warner's *Lolly Willowes* (the *inconnue*, the unknown writer). RF is especially appreciated for his comic gift, relying on purely linguistic play, dominated by a keen and ferocious view of human follies: a view, still, "exprimé avec une légèreté sans faille, une frivolité élevée au rang du grand art." RF and Warner are thus judged "deux planètes invisibles, mais dont la force de gravitation est immense, et qu'il faut se hâter de découvrir."

Brison, Danièle. "Firbank, le maudit magnifique." *Dernières nouvelle d'Alsace*, 17 May 1987.
Calls RF's extravagance a benediction, a source of endless pleasure, and his work "un météore dans le monde cosmopolite des lettres . . . dont les retombées vont enflammer des dizaines d'écrivains." His novels are all masterpieces, and Anglo-Saxon writing owes him "une éternelle reconnaissance."

Cluny, Claude Michel. "Parfums des Années folles." *L'Express*, 31 July 1987.
The reviewer acknowledges his admiration for RF's sketching talent, which is all you can get from his novels: "De l'art du roman, Firbank ne retient rien, sinon la liberté, en tout cas pas l'épaisseur." RF's dialogue reminds him of Abel Herman's *Le Char de l'Etat*.

Desarzens, Corinne. "Firbank." *La Tribune de Genève*, 4 December 1987.

RF, more biting than Vita Sackville-West and a more extreme aesthete than Oscar Wilde, succeeds—after an initial irritating effect—in capturing the reader's heart.

Durand, Dominique. "Oh! tra-la-la, monsieur." *Le Canard enchaîné*, 13 May 1987.

Admires Reumaux's and Gattégno's translations, which aptly repropose RF's "étonnante prose nerveuse et languide," often reaching the sublime. Sees in Cardinal Pirelli a portait of both RF and Oscar Wilde, giving shape to the Edwardian aesthete's worldview.

Frank, Bernard. "Surprise: la littérature se cache!" *Le Monde*, 9 December 1987, 17.

In his column on the contemporary literary scene, Bernard Frank records the appearance of the two novels published by Rivages and the reprint of Gallimard's 1938 omnibus.

Jordis, Christine. "Une extraordinaire liberté." *La Quinzaine littéraire* 488 (16-30 June 1987): 7-8.

Sees both a satirical intention and an absence of message: RF's books "sont parcours de cette veine de non sens, de cette fantaisie sans faille qui recouvrent en général le plus complet pessimisme et la certitude de n'avoir rien à demontrer" (8). RF is a great innovator, a satirist, and a master of the technique of pastiche, "si poussée qu'on a pu les comparer aux collages de Max Ernst" (7).

Lindon, Mathieu. "L'extravagant monsieur Firbank." *Libération*, 14 May 1987, 47-48.

A long review welcoming the new French translations. RF's world is highly transgressive of conventional morality and original in itself, based as it is "sur l'heureuse rencontre du catholicisme et de la sexualité (n'importe quelle sexualité, homme ou femme, l'Eglise ne s'appesantit pas sur ces distinctions bien terre à terre), sans oublier l'argent dont chacun sait l'influence sur la religion et le plaisir" (47). RF was more concerned, in fact, with literature than with the *image* of literature: "c'est à dire de ce qu'elle devrait être aux yeux d'une certaine catégorie de lecteurs peu aventureux" (48).

Montremy, J.-M. de. "L'excentrique Mr. Firbank." *La Croix*, 16 May 1987.

Prefers *The Flower beneath the Foot* (a magical work, Lewis Carroll meets Paul-Jean Toulet) to *Cardinal Pirelli* ("plutôt raté, en dépit de son iconoclaste propos"). RF's final work shows its author at the end of his narrative powers, offering nothing more than a caricature of his own style.

Fiori calpestati
Translated and with an introduction by Salvatore Romano
Palermo: Novecento, 1990

Anon. "In bozze." *La Repubblica*.

Announces the appearance of this Italian translation of *The Flower beneath the Foot*: "It was high time that we got something from the subtle and raving RF, the priest of eccentricity, the extraordinary architect of kitsch, world traveler, replete with drink, intelligence, and malice." In RF's Kairoulla one is always expecting one of the Marx Brothers to pop up.

Caradonna, Antonella. "La società artefatta." *Il Giornale di Sicilia*, 25 June 1990, 13.
    Welcomes Romano's highly praised translation of this "entertaining, different, and enjoyable" book, unflattering as it is to women, men, and the author himself.

Panzeri, Fulvio. "Collana Narciso di Novecento." *L'Esagono*, 3 September 1990.
    In this survey of recent publications published by Novecento, RF's *Flower* is singled out as exemplary of the whole series, characterized by "an Art Nouveau taste, somewhat snobbish and dandified." RF has a scenographic talent that reminds the reviewer of the great Italian film director Luchino Visconti (but Firbank is deemed much funnier and lighter), devoted to playful futilities.

Pasti, Umberto. "L'universo fatto di 'tic'." *Il Giornale*, 6 July 1990, 3.
    Enthusiastically positive review. Considers RF "a genius often fragmentary to the point of obscurity, elusive to the point of nothingness." Pasti discusses RF in relation to camp, both as a refusal of reality and as a taste for transvestism and kitsch "expressing itself in the very structure of his short novels." RF's world is "a sort of poetical *summa* of twentieth-century culture. Firbank's reverie is one of the last unified visions of our century: it is made up solely of tics, idiosyncrasies, exasperated and childish snobbisms." It is fully modernist, "located between Beardsley's Arcadia and Raymond Roussel's symbolism."

Picchi, Mario. "Mal di dandy." *L'Espresso*, 36.36 (9 September 1990): 100.
    A general article on RF, with little reference to *The Flower*. Underlines RF's "fantastic and perverse humor" as taking form through "a self-mocking use of precious language and of a sense of the absurd, in order to describe a world marked by uselessness and vacuity." RF is described as the master of the conversation school (Compton-Burnett, Waugh, Spark), using dialogue with no message: "all emptiness, and yet full of embroidered irony."

P[icchi], M[ario]. "Ronald Firbank: *Fiori calpestati*." *Libri e riviste d'Italia* 42.487-90 (September-December 1990): 328-29.
    Essentially the same review that appeared in *L'Espresso*, with some of the same mistakes—Picchi says he is describing *Inclinations* when actually summarizing *Valmouth*, and *The Flower* is said to be RF's third novel—and the same lack of reference to the book being reviewed.

Oeuvres romanesques
Translated by Gérard Joulié, with an afterword by Sylvoisal
Lausanne: L'Âge d'Homme, 1991. 2 vols.

Anon. *Esprit et vie*, November 1991, 601.
    In RF "l'irréalisme vient d'une fantaisie vive, spirituelle, débridée, qui rebondit comme un plaisant feu d'artifice." This makes his outrageousness and lack of respect for religion excusable: he must not be taken seriously.

Bianciotti, Héctor. "Il aurait tant voulu être Oscar Wilde." *Le Monde*, 3 May 1991, 15.

Praises translator Gérard Joulié and publisher L'Age d'Homme for their "heroic" enterprise. RF's cult for Oscar Wilde is underlined, even though this doesn't make him a mere epigone, thanks to his unique characters and atmosphere. In fact, RF is considered the creator and main representative of the *style "folle"*—*la "folle"* referring to something like a camp queen (homosexual, outrageously effeminate, and master of parodic nonsense), the only (*sic*) literary example apart from RF being Divine in Jean Genet's *Our Lady of the Flowers*.

Bredstroem, Christian Samuel. "Ronald Firbank, un Wilde au carré." *Ergo: Le magazine des étudiants suisses*, February 1992, 11.
   The reviewer devotes his attention not to the novels but to the outstanding quality of the translation—"meilleure que l'original même"—by Gérard Joulié, "esthète et homme d'esprit, qui n'est pas simplement le traducteur mais aussi le co-auteur de ces *aquarelles* de romans." The L'Age d'Homme edition must be welcomed by anybody interested in literature and beauty.

Carcassonne, Manuel. "Les excentricités de Ronald Firbank." *Le Figaro*, 31 July 1991, 11.
   RF is "le plus singulier des écrivains," and not "une simple curiosité édouardienne": on the contrary, "sur le chapitre de l'extravagance, de l'artificiel, de la vie devenue douloureuse oeuvre d'art, Ronald Firbank est un maître."

Cressole, Michel. "Homo britannicus." *Libération*, 30 May 1991.
   Reviewing together the L'Age d'Homme edition and the French translation of Alan Hollinghurst's *The Swimming-Pool Library* (claiming the latter to be the perfect introduction to the former), Cressole calls RF "a human orchid," a key character in Hollinghurst's novel, and a sort of secret badge of recognition for all closeted British homosexual writers.

Gattégno, Jean. "Ronald Firbank redécouvert." *La Quinzaine littéraire* 577 (1-15 May 1991): 11-12.
   Traces RF's typicality in the 1920s rediscovery of decadent aestheticism, which had been repressed after Wilde's trials. RF is the necessary means for tracing a (somehow lost) tradition of British comedy going from the experiments of Fielding and Sterne to Huxley, Waugh, and Compton-Burnett, a tradition "où l'écume l'emporte sur l'épaisseur, l'allusion sur la thèse, le divertissement sur l'engagement" (11). Gattégno—who had translated *The Flower beneath the Foot* in 1987—devotes half of his review to a biting critique of Joulié's translation.

L., J. "Ronald Firbank: un romancier singulier." *Ouest-France*, 8 July 1991.
   Highlights RF's uniqueness and the high quality of Joulié's translation. RF "anime tout un théâtre onirique et caricatural dont les personnages pourtant sont étrangement vrais et profonds derrière leur masque."

2. Books about Firbank

(and their reviews)

Luigi Sampietro, *La narrativa di Ronald Firbank*
Imola: Galeati, 1979

The only book-length study to appear outside the U.K. and U.S. so far is this useful—and enjoyable, though somewhat unanalytical—introduction to RF's fiction, chronologically following its evolution from an "English Phase" to an "Exotic Phase": that is, from "the tendency toward nonsignification" (chap. 2) in *The Artificial Princess* to "the decorative nature and the slanting architecture" (chap. 3) of *Vainglory*, from "the verbal virtuosity and the symbolist heritage" (chap. 4) of *Inclinations* to "the music-hall exoticism" (chap. 5) of *Valmouth* and later novels with foreign settings. Besides disentangling RF's complex plots, Sampietro offers a critical analysis of RF's mimetic method and narrative structures in the chapter devoted to *Caprice*, "the masterpiece of RF's English phase" (chap. 1). Challenging previous claims for the originality of RF's technique and his theoretical fecundity—he wanted only "to produce a beautiful text, and not to substantiate some abstractly and deliberately elaborated literary theories" (8)—Sampietro traces RF's values in dandyism and fashion, categories devoid of philosophical articulation, thus justifying the absence in his work of a satirical depth that would necessarily imply "some serious values" (16) on RF's part. On the other hand, RF's fragmentary and inconsequent writing must be seen as a simple and excellent mimetic tool, much more realistic than literary realism itself, taking into account the actual modes of perception of reality. In fact, the significant elements—what Sampietro calls "the decree of destiny," exemplifying it with the various references to mice preceeding Sarah Sinquier's "death by mouse-trap"—lay buried beneath a mass of irrelevant elements: it is in the process of decoding such scattered elements that we try and understand reality. This is what links RF to the symbolist tradition, in which reality is a forest of hieroglyphs to be interpreted, and plot (or fiction) a secret that can be decoded.

*

Anon. "Bibliografia." *Tuttolibri*, 12 January 1980, 21.
   A brief notice announcing Sampietro's book.

Praz, Mario. "Strutturalismo per una farfalla." *Il Tempo*, 11 May 1980, 3. Reprinted as "Analisi strutturale di una farfalla" in his *Studi e svaghi inglesi*. Milan: Garzanti, 1983. 2:300-304.
   Praises Sampietro for his analysis, adding that RF must be seen as a final disciple of Jules Laforgue and of his satire (in *Moralités légendaires*) of those who want to live in the realm of fictionality and not more simply and naturally, "à la bonne franquette." The second part of the review is devoted to a polemical acknowledgment of Rita Severi's 1977 and 1978 structuralist articles (see section 3 below), whose technical jargon and achievements are satirized on Forster's assumption that a butterfly should not be broken upon a wheel.

3. Essays, Parts of Books, and Other Commentary

Agosti, Giovanni. "La condizione del dolore." *La Rivista dei libri* 4.1 (November 1994): 40-42.

Calls RF "one of the manes" (42) of the Alberto Arbasino's *Fratelli d'Italia* (see section 4 below).

Anon. [Editorial staff of the *Dictionnaire des Oeuvres Laffont*]. "Caprice." In *Kindlers Literatur Lexikon*. Zürich: Kindler, 1965. 1:2130-31.

In his works, RF creates characters in his own image and reveals a great sense of the absurd and of the fantastic. He is most interesting as a stylist, for he—with little effort—manages to re-create a world resembling the eighteenth-century worldly *fasti*.

Anon. [Editorial staff of the *Dictionnaire des Oeuvres Laffont* and that of the *Kindlers Literatur Lexikon*]. "Concerning the Eccentricities of Cardinal Pirelli." In *Kindlers Literatur Lexikon*. Zürich: Kindler, 1966. 2:123.

Says *Cardinal Pirelli* is "a study in character," different from RF's other writings in its nostalgic and melancholic tone. RF's language is open to many interpretations, and it is used deliberately to obscure events rather than clarify them.

Arbasino, Alberto. *Parigi o cara*. Milan: Feltrinelli, 1960. 458, 483, 610-14.

In addition to references to some "Ronald Firbank-like sophisticated and entertaining" bars and clubs (458), and to RF among minor but important writers like Beerbohm, Saki, the Sitwells, Rolfe, and Douglas (483), Arbasino declares his enthusiasm for the "sublime" RF in relation to Sandy Wilson's "incomparable" 1958 production of *Valmouth*. Arbasino devotes three pages to an overview of RF's wanderings, friendships, and eccentricities, and of the most entertaining characters in his novels, the reading of which is "one of those 'joys for ever'" (612).

———. *Certi romanzi*. Milan: Feltrinelli, 1964. 20, 40, 89, 109.

Contains various passing references to RF, in which he is placed alongside such writers as Céline and Joyce for their common "awe-inspiring" and "labyrinthine" writing, at once rigorous and perverse. RF is also identified as a significant influence on Arbasino's *Fratelli d'Italia* (see section 4), whose conversation technique is deliberalely indebted to RF, Henry Green, and Compton-Burnett.

———. *Off-off*. Milan: Feltrinelli, 1968. 73.

Notes RF's vogue with young Italian intellectuals of the fifties.

———. *Sessanta posizioni*. Milan: Feltrinelli, 1971.

This volume of short pieces has some rather laconic references to RF (Arbasino, a camp writer himself, often deliberately lists writers and critics without comment, presupposing a reader who already knows what he is talking about). He traces in Djuna Barnes some Firbankian touches (47) and identifies RF as the ultimate literary camper, "organizing postdecadent artifacts and theatricality with outstanding critical lucidity" (221).

Bacigalupo, Massimo. "Introduzione: l'importanza di essere Joe." In Joe Orton. *Farse quotidiane*. Genoa: Costa & Nolan, 1983. 5-46.

This introduction to an Italian translation of Orton's plays refers to RF's conspicuous influence on Orton, and in particular on the still unpublished novels—*The Silver Bucket, The Mechanical Womb, The Last Days of Sodom,* and *The Boy Hairdresser*—which Orton and Kenneth Halliwell wrote during the fifties and sixties.

Bini, Benedetta. "Ronald Firbank: il comico e l'artificiale." Paper presented at the Eighth National Congress of the Associazione Italiana Anglistica (Italian Association of English Studies), Turin, 28-30 October 1985, devoted to "The Forms of the Comic." Subsequently published in the Proceedings of the Congress: Carla Marengo Vaglio, Paolo Bertinetti and Giuseppina Cortese, eds. *Le forme del comico*. Alessandria: Dell'Orso, 1990. 81-89.

Analyzes RF's artificiality at the level of language—his parody of previous forms of writing, of narrative archetypes, and of decadent themes and phrases; the defamiliarizing sentence structures and words—in order to show that it is precisely this artificiality that is the actual raison d'être of his humor. RF thus offers "the first metaphysical model of nineteenth-century comic dimension" (81), arousing in the reader "the consciousness of language and its crisis" (87). Such consciousness tells us that RF "doesn't belong to the margins of a culture of decadence, along with those 'late violets from the nineties,' but rather somewhere between Beardsley's *débris* and T. S. Eliot's fragments shored against his ruins" (88).

Cecchin, Giovanni. *Waugh controcorrente. Avventure e problemi di un enfant terrible*. Turin: Imabooks, 1970. 42, 54 n18, 135 n.

Notes Waugh's debt to RF's conversation technique and finds Firbankian echoes in *Decline and Fall* and *Brideshead Revisited*.

Cernuda, Luis. "La novela arabesco de Ronald Firbank" (1958); in his *Poesía y literatura*. Barcelona: Seix Barral, 1960. 181-90. Rpt. in *Poesía y Literatura I y II*. Barcelona: Seix Barral, 1971. 142-48 (cited below), in *Prosa completa*. Ed. Derek Harris and Luis Maristany. Barcelona: Seix Barral, 1975, and in his *Obra completa*, vol. 2: *Prosa I*. Ed. Derek Harris and the heirs of Luis Maristany. Madrid: Siruela, 1994. 592-97.

In introducing RF to a literary scene (the Spanish scene in particular) that would consider him a minor writer, Cernuda prefers to call him "eccentric," for he went along different paths, choosing something like a literary *divertissement*—made of caprices, exotica, and extravagancies—while at the same time taking part in the experimentation of the early century. In RF, whose best novels are *The Flower beneath the Foot* and *Cardinal Pirelli*, Catholicism and scenery are nothing more than a spectacular stage set, represented through cinemagraphic techniques (RF uses, for instance, something like film "fadings") and with "coldness," denying the reader's identification with characters and suspension of disbelief (that is, any sentimentalism in the writing and reading processes). His are not novels in a strict sense, but rather "arabesque novels" (147), in which the manner of telling is more important than what is actually told.

Cianci, Giovanni. "Ronald Firbank." In Giuseppe Sertoli and Giovanni Cianci, eds. *Letteratura inglese e americana*. Milan: Garzanti, 1989. 258.

A checklist of major biographical and critical writings on RF.

Cleto, Fabio. "Biografia, ideologia, autor-ità interpretativa (con un caso esemplare)." *Textus: English Studies in Italy* 6 (1993): 179-220.

Uses RF as an exemplary case in discussing the return of biographical evidence in contemporary literary theory (that is, the reaction by conservative critics and by some recent post-structuralist theorists to death-of-the-author claims). It points out three main phases in RF's Anglo-American critical reception, corresponding to the three paradigms of the authorial image represented by the major biographies by Fletcher, Benkovitz, and Brophy. It thereafter claims that different ideologies work in both biographical accounts and linked interpretations in order to manage the semantic elusiveness of the text, although they hide themselves behind an appeal to authorial intention.

––––––. " 'Camp': l'estetismo nella cultura di massa." In Franco Marenco, ed. *Storia della civiltà letteraria della Gran Bretagna*, vol. 3. Turin: UTET, 1996. 529-69.

This essay in literary history opens with a long quotation from *Cardinal Pirelli* exemplifying what camp has been as a style, as a reading practice, as a homosexual code, and as a way in which intellectuals coped with the emergence of mass culture. Then RF's revival during the fifties and sixties, along with his influence on Brophy's novels, is proposed within the process of explosion of camp as a mass phenomenon. Later RF's novels are discussed at some length, being considered the most extreme example of camp during the first part of the century, exemplary of camp both as a gay code and as clandestine ritual after the Wilde trials. Attention is given to their exclusiveness, their privilege of surfaces and trivia, and to their overlapping of religion, fashion, and culture in what seems to be among the very first instances of artistic self-consciousness of the "religious" status of stardom (i.e., its political function and its demystification through a camp approach).

Curtis, Jean-Louis. "L'orchidée Firbank." *Cahiers des saisons* 26 (Summer 1961): 101-3.

Tells of a small Parisian "Société des Amis de Ronald Firbank," and explains RF's elitist appeal in terms of his unique frivolity and irresponsibility, far beyond Wilde's and Norman Douglas's. The publication of Duckworth's *Complete Ronald Firbank* is announced with pleasure, though Curtis hopes it won't widen RF's circulation to the general public—that is, out of his traditional and elitist clique of admirers.

Dupuigrenet-Desroussilles, François. "Portrait de l'artiste en archevêque." Introduction to RF's *Les Excentricités du Cardinal Pirelli*, 9-13.

Argues that *Cardinal Pirelli* has an emblematic value in RF's oeuvre, being his only novel centered on a single character. It is in fact a sort of hagiography of himself and of Wilde, that is, of the Wilde cult in which RF took part: "en se peignant sous les traits de Pirelli, c'est Wilde dont Firbank nous donne le portrait" (11). RF must be seen as one of the strangest and most refined flowers of Edwardian decadence.

Fortunati, Vita. "Homosexualité et maladie dans la littérature anglaise de 1890 à 1930." In Max Milner, ed. *Littérature et pathologie*. Saint-Denis: Presses Universitaires de Vincennes, 1989. 213-25.

Refers to RF's flower symbolism as one of the coded strategies gay writers adopted at the beginning of the century in order to signify their homosexuality.

Gattégno, Jean. "'Le presque rien' ou 'Le je ne sais quoi'?" Introduction to RF's *La fleur foulée aux pieds*, 7-14.

Criticizes Forster's and Waugh's views of RF's superficiality and unseriousness, contrasting them with Wilson's appreciation of RF's complexity. Still, RF's are not novels but *soties* (9), farces belonging to the tradition of British comedy going back to the sixteenth century and relying on sexual innuendo, satire, and witty dialogue: "Tout se passe en effet comme si, pour Firbank, l'espace du langage parlé (même s'il est retranscrit par l'auteur, simple porteplume) suffisait à circonscrire la réalité romanesque" (11). Thus RF "a maintenu ouverte une piste en voie de disparition et en a défriché d'autres" (14).

Ha[semann], G[ertraud F.]. "Sorrow in Sunlight." In *Kindlers Literatur Lexikon*. Zürich: Kindler, 1971. 6:1754-55.

Summarizes *Prancing Nigger* and its author's narrative techniques, relying on Waley's introduction to the German translation published the year before.

Hill, Roland. "Firbank, (Arthur Annesley) Ronald." In *Lexikon der Weltliteratur im 20. Jahrhundert*. Freiburg-Basel-Vienna: Herder, 1960. 1:650.

A short biobibliographical note. RF uses the impressionistic musical method of Debussy, his *Inclinations* is pure dadaism, whereas *Sorrow in Sunlight* is more realistic, due to the fact that it is a result of RF's voyages to the West Indies.

Izzo, Carlo. *Storia della letteratura inglese*. Milan: Sansoni/Accademia, 1968. 1318-19.

Dismissive presentation of RF's literary achievement. Quotes a paragraph from *Vainglory* as exemplifying his artificiality and inconsequential dialogue, which "dissolves—rather than gives form to—narration." RF is valuable only as "embryonically representing the negative world which Samuel Beckett would later interpret" (1318). While Beckett's is an hyperactive and decentered mind, RF is characterized merely by "an emptiness of mind" (1319).

Jannattoni, Livio. "La tomba di Arthur Annesley Ronald Firbank." *English Miscellany* 3 (1952): 281-83.

Concerns RF's first burial at the Protestant cemetery at the Testaccio, in Rome, and his later removal (on 6 June 1927) to the Catholic cemetery of the Campo Verano in Rome.

Jullian, Philippe. *Oscar Wilde*. Paris: Librairie Académique Perrin, 1967. English translation by Violet Wyndham. London: Constable, 1969.

Has a passing reference to *Cardinal Pirelli* and to RF's conversion to the Catholic religion, which was adopted for aesthetic reasons and because of his fascination with the sumptuous Roman ritual.

Komrij, Gerrit. "Nawoord." Afterword to RF's *"Het Grillige leven van Kardinaal Pirelli" gevolgd door "Valmouth,"* 171-75.

RF is absolutely unique and one of the greatest innovators—greater than Joyce and Proust, actually—of the twentieth-century novel. He is little known not because his writings have less importance, but rather because he avoided the usual means for achieving literary popularity, which explains why it has taken some fifty years to make a classic of him. In RF's works and person one discovers a "savage humor" (172), a *fou rire* built with careful attention and profound artistic commitment so that what seems meaningless becomes, eventually, highly significant. The afterword is followed by a bibliography (176) of RF's works and major criticism.

Lovisetti Fuà, Laura. "Introduzione." In RF's *Vanagloria*, 5-13.

In the introduction to her translation, Lovisetti Fuà retells all the major anecdotes of the Firbank legend, and points out the many analogies between RF's lifestyle and his narrative eccentricities. His novels cannot be seen as novels per se, but rather as "precious embroideries" (10) made up of chosen decorative images, devoid of narrative function. Yet they show a "profound artistic seriousness, an extreme intellectual attention, and reveal a highly balanced mixture of culture and frivolity" (11). Their value is entirely in "the extraordinary conversation technique" and in "the bitingly moralistic representation of a fundamentally amoral society, reduced to dry rationalism and unable to produce anything" (12). RF is therefore set alongside Waugh and Huxley for their satirical achievements. His touch is lighter than Waugh's, but his harsh critique is less optimistic than Huxley's, as he doesn't show a way out through intuition and feeling as Huxley does.

Manganelli, Giorgio. "Prefazione." In RF's *Il Cardinal Pirelli* (1964), 7-18. Reprinted as "Ronald Firbank" in his *La letteratura come menzogna*. Milan: Feltrinelli, 1967. 9-17.

A brilliantly written preface to the Italian translation of *Cardinal Pirelli, The Artificial Princess,* and *Prancing Nigger.* RF is "an ironic writer, whose irony is metaphysical and never social, direct, or didactical" (1964: 9). He didn't destroy or invent literary languages but rather narrative structures, for his "delicate and schizoid snobbism" (14) is translated into writing as a "tangential structure," that is, the choice of ornamentation not so much for its aesthetic beauty as for its value as a means by which RF refuses to narrate a story or develop a character: what we find in RF is "more than the absence of a story, a negative presence of it, and a negative presence of the character as well" (10). In these tales of pure sounds, of italicized words, of childlike speech and exquisite nonsense, language and form are directed toward an absolute and explicit artificiality, redeeming their communicative sterility through style and elegance, and assuming "a condition implicitly bent toward death" (11).

Marengo Vaglio, Carla. *Frederick Rolfe "Baron Corvo."* Milan: Mursia, 1969. 35, 161, 167 n25, 195.

RF is identified as a follower of Rolfe in his use of italics, fragmentary narration (though RF carries it to an unprecedented extreme), and fascination for Egypt.

Mauriès, Patrick. *Second manifeste camp: essai.* Paris: Seuil, 1979. 17-18, 106.

In this analysis of camp sensibility, Mauriès uses RF as an exemple of the camp tendency toward "la voie qui ne mène à rien": Harold Nicolson's account, in which the young RF is depicted as always talking of writing, but never actually writing, is quoted to support Mauriès's thesis that camp writers privilege "la dépense" (expenditure) over productive activity. A remark from *Caprice* is used as an epigraph (106).

Maymone Sinischalchi, Marina. *Aubrey Beardsley: Contributo ad uno studio della personalità e dell'opera attraverso l'epistolario.* Rome: Edizioni di Storia e Letteratura, 1977. 60-64.

Analyzes the "delicious metamorphoses" of *Under the Hill*'s themes, images, style, and "divagating graphical comments" (61) into RF's "refined inconsistency and kaleidocopic flashes" (60), with particular reference to *Cardinal Pirelli, The Artificial Princess,* and *The Flower beneath the Foot.* "RF's humor is not merely thoughtless frivolity, and the inconsistency of his microscopical heroes is a delightful and wise madness. They live their season of infantility and maturity, and the perception of the transitoriness of things veils with sadness and boredom the inconsistency in which they seem to take shelter" (62). The similarities betwen Beardsley and RF reach an end when Beardsley's illustrations for *Salomé* are taken into account, for these have a sharp, scratchy quality that is missing in RF's female characters, whose essence is constituted by their quintessential "artificiality and transience" (63), lightness and evanescence.

Papetti, Viola. "Il romanzo 'diminuito' di Firbank." Paper presented on 28 April 1978 at the First National Congress of the Associazione Italiana Anglistica, Rome, 27-29 April 1978, devoted to "Experimentalism and Innovation in Contemporary English Literature." Subsequently published in *Annali dell'Istituto Universitario Orientale: Anglistica* 21.1-2 (1978), 35-44.
  Views the category of anthropological and linguistic "subtraction" or "reduction"—the means by which "the offended, the diminished, the different, paradoxically reveals itself as creative" (35)—as central in RF's oeuvre, explaining both the individual novels and their relation to the literary experimentation of the twenties. Fragmentation of phrases, reduction/prolification of the narrator figure, reduction of syntactical and logical connections, and emptiness of the syntagmatic axis in favor of the paradigmatic axis are then traced in an analysis of the linguistic strategies in *Inclinations*.

————. "Ronald Firbank." In Vito Amoruso and Francesco Binni, eds. *I contemporanei: Letteratura inglese*. Rome: Lucarini, 1977. 1:459-66.
  A biobibliographical introduction, surveying RF's life and works and previous Firbank criticism. RF is linked both to fin-de-siècle decadence and modernist experimentation. Acknowledges that "there is still much to be learned from a re-reading of his work, should we avoid a moralistic or content-oriented approach" (465).

Pétillon, Pierre-Yves. "William Gaddis et le babil des ténèbres." *Critique: Revue générale des publications françaises et étrangères*, 45.502 (1989): 133-53. Rpt. (in different form) in his *Histoire de la littérature américaine: notre demi-siècle 1939-1989*. Paris: Fayard, 1990.
  In this essay-review of the French translation of William Gaddis's *Carpenter's Gothic*, Pétillon notes Gaddis's affinity with RF and debt to *Cardinal Pirelli* along with other writings of the twenties.

Pitol, Sergio. "Prólogo." Introduction to RF' *En torno a las excentricidades del cardenal Pirelli*, 7-21.
  This introduction by the Mexican translator Sergio Pitol (a highly regarded novelist himself) offers a general survey of RF's novels, emphasizing his skillful and bizarre use of language, described as reticent, "allusive, constantly fragmented, and incorporating fashion-talk" (8). Attention is given to RF's mingling of sacred and mundane and to "the ambition of the soul to attain divinity" (13-14), with special reference to the many saints or would-be saints peopling his novels, and to the bullfight symbolism in *Cardinal Pirelli*, whose Clemenza is a literary transposition of Sevilla even though "RF's novels are all set in an imaginary geography" (7). Claims that, among the English avant-garde, RF avoided the means employed by Woolf and Joyce (interior monologue, stream of consciousness, etc.) in favor of super-objectivity (*supraobjetividad*), which influenced Waugh, Compton-Burnett, and Wyndham Lewis: "Today it is impossible not to see him as one of the most original, strange, and entertaining writers of our century" (17).

Praz, Mario. *Storia della letteratura inglese.* Florence: Sansoni, 1960. 607, 705, 707, 709. Rpt. as *La letteratura inglese, vol. 2: Dai Romantici al Novecento.* Florence: Sansoni, 1967. 192, 275, 278, 280.

Along with some scattered references, Praz devotes a paragraph of his literary history to defining RF as an extremely refined epigone of Decadence, turning it into a capricious ballet. Describes the characters and the plots as elegant and bizarre, witty, and absurd, taking part in "a fictitious and maniacal world" (192). Jean Lorrain, Beardsley, and Laforgue, more than Wilde, are cited as the main influences on RF.

Roditi, Edouard. "Postface". In RF's *"La Princesse artificielle" suivi de "Mon Piaffeur Noir,"* 221-26.

This afterword to the later edition of his translation concerns the meeting with Carl Van Vechten in New York—who suggested the translation of RF— and with Maurice Sachs, the co-translator, which led to the original publication (1938) of this French omnibus.

Romano, Salvatore. "Introduzione." In RF's *Fiori calpestati,* 7-21.

Provides some historical and biographical information about RF and the literary England of the time. The novel is seen as a portrayal of an extinct world, the outcome of "a dandy who mocks his fellow-countrymen's moralism, and indulges in imagining sumptuous scenarios and operetta-like sovereigns" (18). The incompleteness of RF's dialogue reminds Romano of Henry James, and of Wittgenstein's account of reality, in which "there are no interior feelings: only what is enunciated exists" (14). Though derived from Wilde and Pater, RF's narrative lacks their totalizing aesthetics and ideological engagement; its coherence and its unique quality are due to "an extraordinarily sympathetic perception of silliness" (14) and to a hypnotic fascination for the vortex of the absence of thought. The novel can also be read as a guide to the stupidity of our present-day literary high society.

Saint-Phalle, Nathalie de. *Hôtels littéraires: Voyages autour de la terre.* Paris: Quai Voltaire, 1991. 400-401.

Tells of RF's staying at the Hotel Quirinale in Rome (Via Nazionale 7) until his death, with the usual anecdotes concerning his eccentricities.

Sampietro, Luigi. "'Don't, dear, forget a mouse-trap!' Ovvero l'apoteosi teatrale di Miss Sarah Sinquier." *Spicilegio moderno: Saggi e ricerche di letterature e lingue straniere* 10 (1978): 153-66.

The first chapter of his book (re-titled "La parodia di un'apoteosi: la crudele musa di *Caprice,* capolavoro del periodo inglese"), published the following year (see section 2 above).

Sandoz, Maurice. "Ronald Firbank." In his *La salière de cristal.* Paris: Editions de la Table Ronde, 1952. 131-149. English translation: London: Guilford Press, 1954, 78-88. Reprinted in his *Diaghilev, Nijinski and Other Vignettes.* New York: Kamin, 104-15, and as "A Fantastic Young Englishman" in Horder's *Memoirs and Critiques,* 138-144.

Memoirs of RF in Italy shortly before his death. Sandoz admired RF's novels: "They are fluid, subtle, elusive creations, sweet, or bitter, always with a flavour of their own, but carefully worked out, woven as one might say round certain recognized landmarks which are sufficiently stable to give definite shape to the whole work."

Severi, Rita. "Tecnica narrativa e tradizione letteraria in *The Artificial Princess* di Ronald Firbank." *Spicilegio moderno: Saggi e ricerche di letterature e lingue straniere* 8 (1977): 143-53.

Analyzes *The Artificial Princess* deploying Greimas's structural semantics tools (narrative structure, organization and roles, linguistic codes, figures of speech), with special reference to the literary allusiveness of the text. RF offers a pointed parody of the decadent literary tradition, and establishes a surprising relationship of *contaminatio* with Proust's *Remembrance of Things Past*, parts of which are traced directly in RF's novel. This would indicate RF's "active participation in his own cultural scene, and show him not so much as a remote eccentric but rather as a refined craftsman of the word" (153).

―――. "Comunicazione e meta-comunicazione in *Caprice* di Ronald Firbank." *Paragone letteratura* 29.336 (February 1978): 57-71.

A behavioristic analysis of *Caprice* focusing on its metacommunicative traits. By drawing on decadent artificality, RF's novel "analyzes in a mock-heroic mode (in Fielding's sense) the philosophy of the *vie factice*" (62), deflating it through the failure of the protagonist Sarah Sinquier. In the consciousness and frustration of Sarah's narcissism one can find the value and contemporaneity of the novel: "By stating that reality is what we make it, Firbank belongs to the twentieth-century novelistic tradition of Virginia Woolf, Joyce, Proust, describing the fragmentation of everyday life in many relatively experienced realities" (67).

―――. "Un autografo firbankiano nella Biblioteca 'A. Panizzi' di Reggio Emilia." *Contributi. Rivista semestrale della Biblioteca "A Panizzi," Reggio Emilia,* 5.10 (July-December 1981): 151-58.

Concerning a copy of the first edition of *Sorrow in Sunlight*, inscribed to Lord Berners: "For Lord Berners, from Ronald Firbank, in Gaiety and Joy. 1924." Laments RF's lack of fame in Italy—notwithstanding his remarkable influence on contemporary Italian writers such as Niccolò Tucci, Giorgio Manganelli, and Alberto Arbasino—and the impossibility of his novels' translation into Italian. Severi then summarizes and offers some criticism of the novel, with reference to its jazzlike quality, its portayal of Firbank as Negro, and its linguistic eccentricities (proving "the substantial identity of signifier and signified" [157], making his language absolutely new and similar to poetic diction).

―――. "Ronald Firbank (1886-1926)." *Bollettino del C.I.R.V.I.* 10.19 (January-June 1989): 133-35.

An account of RF's stay in Bordighera (Italy) between 1922 and 1923, where he completed *The Flower beneath the Foot* and wrote *Prancing Nigger*, which is said to reproduce the atmosphere of Bordighera (and of L'Avana, where RF also worked on the novel) in the creation of Cuna-Cuna.

Sylvoisal [Gérard Joulié, comte de Sylvoisal]. "'A Fellow of infinite jest.'" In RF's *Oeuvres romanesques*, 1:363-67; 2:306-10.

RF—"ecrivain original qui n'emprunte à personne ni les modèles de ses personnages ni le tour de ses dialogue (1:363)—belongs more to the seventeenth century (Congreve especially) than to our century. He is an excellent moralist, devoted to the analysis of the human heart even though he is only offering an art "de l'insaissable, de l'instant, de l'instantané, de l'éphémère, de la sensation" (1:364). He combines irony, wit, and insolence with a talent superior to Wilde's.

Tosser, Yvon. *Le sens de l'absurde dans l'oeuvre d'Evelyn Waugh*. Paris: Champion, 1977. 377.

Cites RF as an influence on Waugh's fascination for futility, insignificance, and nothingness.

Trajtenberg, Mario. "Prólogo." Introduction to RF's *Las excentricidades del Cardenal Pirelli*, 7-20.

Largely devoted to RF's life, which "could have been created by Marcel Schwob" (7). His dialogue—"insinuating, precious, complex and perverse and full of humor" (13)—also receives attention, being the main bases of the novels: even though as RF grew as a writer the narrative voice and its descriptions had more and more importance. The novels are "funny, enigmatic, a little exasperating" (17), built on a literary *micrometría* of structural allusiveness, and their author is both an eccentric of the literary scene of his time and an impossible task for those who would like to fully understand him.

4. Creative Works

Arbasino, Alberto. [novels]

Arbasino, a well-known Italian novelist, journalist, and essayist, explicitly acknowledged in his essays (see above) RF's remarkable influence on his most popular novel, the mastodontic *Fratelli d'Italia* (Milan: Feltrinelli, 1963; revised and enlarged edition, Milan: Adelphi, 1993). Arbasino mentions RF a few times, and tells of a visit or tribute the narrator makes with some friends to RF's tomb at the Campo Verano in Rome (4: 10), during which RF's and Cardinal Pirelli's eccentricities are self-satisfiedly reported. The influence can be easily traced in Arbasino's dialogues (constituting the bulk of the novel) and erratic narration, but also—as I have argued in my *tesi di laurea* (see below)—at the metafictional level, which is present in both *Fratelli d'Italia* and in RF's texts; or, in short, in the high camp narrative style of which Arbasino has become an outstanding example by drawing on the lessons of Firbank, Compton-Burnett, and the early Huxley. In fact, RF's influence can be traced in many other novels by Arbasino, and in other cases—*L'Anonimo Lombardo* (1954) is an example—Firbank is also referred to within the narration.

Cernuda, Luis. [poems]

RF's influence on the great Spanish poet Luis Cernuda, who also wrote an article on RF in 1958 (see above), has been noted by Spanish reviewer José Luis Martín Abril.

Jullian, Philippe. [drawings]

Jullian, a highly regarded French artist and scholar of Decadence, and a member of the Parisian Societé des Amis de Ronald Firbank, illustrated—as Benkovitz notes in her *A Bibliography of Ronald Firbank* (30)—the Duckworth 1956 edition of *Valmouth* with seven illustrations, line cuts in colour on text paper facing pp. 14, 32, 40, 46, 62, 80, and 126. Jullian also made black and white illustrations (line cuts on text paper) for the limited edition of 200 numbered copies of RF's *La Princesse aux Soleils & Harmonie* (London: Enitharmon Press, 1974), on p. ix and between pp. xiv-xv and 6-7.

Manganelli, Giorgio. [novels and short stories]

According to Italian critic Rita Severi ("Un autografo firbankiano nella Biblioteca 'A. Panizzi' di Reggio Emilia") Giorgio Manganelli's writings—which were an important part of the Italian literary scene of the sixties and seventies—show, as a whole, a complex Firbankian quality.

Scimitarra, Attanasio, and Alberto Valtellina, directors. *Numerosi cubetti di porfido*. Italy, 1992. 9 mins., color, 16 mm. Screenplay by Scimitarra and Valtellina, text by Maria Luisa Satriani. Produced by Produzioni Apollo Maridoro. Short film presented at the 22nd International Film Festival "Figueira da Foz" in Portugal, 9-19 September 1993.

Though this independent film doesn't particularly show the influence of RF's works, the two actors playing leading roles have pseudonyms (Lallah Miranda, Vittorio Virtù—Italian for "Victor Virtue") taken from RF's fiction. Lallah Miranda also appears in Valtellina and Scimitarra's later film *El Extraño del pelo largo* (1995). Produzioni Apollo Maridoro confirmed that a film version of *Caprice* had been planned by Valtellina in 1993; money was lacking, the film hasn't been produced, and Valtellina is still awaiting financing.

Tucci, Niccolò. [novels]

Both Giorgio Manganelli and Rita Severi ("Un autografo firbankiano") identify Niccolò Tucci as an example of an Italian writer influenced by RF. In a personal communication, Severi specified Tucci's *Gli atlantici. Dei e semidei* (Milan: Serra e Riva, 1987) as a particularly Firbankian work.

Villena, Louis Antonio de. "'Capriccio.'" In his *El tártaro de las estrellas*. Valencia: Pre-Textos, 1994. 7-22.

This short story, written in 1985, has as its framework the meeting of RF and Antonio de Hoyos y Vinent, son of the Spanish ambassador Marqués de Hoyos, Grande de España and a writer himself, in Madrid, during RF's stay in 1905 (cf. Benkovitz's *Biography*, p. 63, where Antonio's surname is erroneously given as "de Hoyos y Vincent"). Their conversation, carried on under the aegis of Oscar Wilde, "saint and patriarch of all perversions" (7), touching Huysmans, Villiers, Lorrain, and Petronius, leads them to dine together, during which de Hoyos asks RF if he has ever taken up vampirism or explored "the theme of blood-and-beauty" (11). They eventually go to de Hoyos's luxuriously furnished house with a beautiful local youth named Serafín, where the three of them have a homosexual "night bullfight."

Wilcock, J. Rodolfo. *Lo stereoscopio dei solitari*. Milan: Adelphi, 1972.

On the rear flap of the 1989 reprint of this novel Wilcock is quoted as saying RF is among his favorite authors. It has not been possible to trace the source of the quotation.

5. Dissertations and Theses

Ballarati, Mariacarla. "Il sentimento religioso nella vita e nella narrativa di Ronald Firbank." *Tesi di laurea*, Università degli Studi di Milano, Milan, 1994.

Reads RF's portrayal of the Church in his novels autobiographically, with particular attention to the shift from the clear dichotomy of good vs. evil in his early writings to a later blurring of categories. RF's novels thus reveal the discrepancy between the prescriptions of Christianity and their actual (perverse and mundane) practice within the Church, which is therefore revealed as occupying the same moral plane as the local opera house.

Barina, Antonella. "Ronald Firbank." *Tesi di laurea*, Università "La Sapienza" di Roma, Rome, 1978.

Part 1 of this well-written thesis gives an account of the critical work on RF, lamenting the lack of a reading suitable for a non-mimetic narrative, and regards his achievements in terms of literary history, that is, emphasizing RF's novels' novelty on the intellectual scene of the early century and their relation to the avant-garde rather than to the fin de siècle. Part 2 proposes a recognition of RF's narrative techniques on such terms, avoiding the study of the content or themes of the texts in favor of an analysis of the means by which the texts construct themselves.

Castelli, Elisabetta. "Evelyn Waugh e il romanzo dei 'Bright Young People.' " *Tesi di laurea*, Universita degli Studi di Bergamo, Bergamo, 1996.

Discusses RF's influence on Waugh's *Vile Bodies,* specifically narrative viewpoint, the use of counterpoint, and conversation techniques.

Cleto, Fabio. "Lo specchio ilare. La poetica dell'apparenza in Ronald Firbank." *Tesi di laurea*, Università degli Studi di Bergamo, Bergamo, 1992.

The basis of a forthcoming book. Among the excluded parts, it has an opening chapter devoted to the evolution of RF's biographical accounts, from Sewell Stokes's 1924 chapter down to *Firbankiana*. The fourth chapter is a Barthesian reading of RF's "erotics of the text" as an invitation both to interpretive freedom on the reader's part and to a perpetually unfulfilled hermeneutical desire. Perversion and childish behavior are thus seen as metaphors of the interpretation the text asks the reader to pursue. This chapter has been greatly reduced in the book version, along with an appendix discussing at length RF's critical reception in the United Kingdom, North America, and Italy.

Colombo, Barbara. "Ronald Firbank e *Concerning the Eccentricities of Cardinal Pirelli* (1926)." *Tesi di laurea*, Università degli Studi di Milano, Milan, 1991.

This thesis could not be annotated because Ms. Colombo refused the required authorization for a reading. In response to my insistent requests, Ms. Colombo's husband, a policeman, threatened legal and/or physical retaliation. The whole episode had strong Firbankian nuances.

Cozzolino, Enrico. "Il romanzo di Ronald Firbank." *Tesi di laurea*, Istituto Universitario Orientale di Napoli, Naples, 1980.

A survey of RF's eight novels, explicitly neglecting their entertaining and absurd aspects in order to recover "the personal and social meanings to be found in RF's narratives" (28). With topics such as homosexuality, intellectuality, and religiousness as a focus, the author examines the relation between fiction and context, author and reader, finding in RF an effort toward redefining the role of the intellectual after the First World War which had spoiled the expressive possibilities suggested by the aestheticism of Wilde. Fiction was to RF a means toward intellectual growth, definition of his own existence, and at the same time a space devoted to analyses of conditions of creativity.

Daube, Colette. "Ronald Firbank 1886-1926. L'homme et l'oeuvre." Thèse de Doctorat es-Lettres, Université de Paris-Sorbonne, Paris IV, 1982.
    RF's oeuvre takes on new significance in light of postwar critical theory and literary practices (viz, the French *nouveau roman*), which make RF's method more understandable as a way of dealing with representation and as an artistic achievement. The first part of this substantial dissertation is an introductory analysis of RF's works, framed by biographical accounts of their composition, claiming the relevance of a psychological approach, and emphasizing the importance of literary influences such as D'Annunzio, Maeterlinck, Baudelaire, Mallarmé, Huysmans, Flaubert, Samain, Verlaine, Montesquiou, Régnier, Symons, Dowson, Beerbohm, Beardsley, Wilde, and many others. The second part is devoted to an analysis of RF's narrative method, to its exceptional synthesis and exclusions, to settings and characters, to the presence of a magical dimension, and to his influence on literary practices from Huxley and Waugh in the twenties to Orton and Brophy in the sixties. What emerges from the general crisis of values is RF's defense of the value of art and aesthetic principles.

Giordano, Monica. "La narrativa di Ronald Firbank" *Tesi di laurea*, Istituto Universitario di Lingue Moderne, Milan, 1992.
    A critical introduction, basically summarizing previous scholarship in a survey of RF's narrative technique, composition, figures of speech, themes, imagery, meaninglessness, and humor.

Maes-Jelivek, Jena. Paris, 1970.

Oppertshäuser, Otto. Berlin, 1968.

Severi, Rita. "I racconti di Ronald Firbank (con particolare riferimento a *The Artificial Princess*)." *Tesi di laurea*, Università degli Studi di Bologna, Bologna, 1975.
    A study, mainly focused on *The Artificial Princess*, employing structuralist and semiotic tools (and the basis for her 1977 essay). The first chapter is devoted to an analysis of the literary parodies in the novel, and to the presence of rhetorical tropes. Chap. 2 analyzes some highly used linguistic functions, such as French expressions, typographical oddities, and iterations that are typical of children's and fairy-tale language. Chap. 3 studies from a Greimasian perspective the split between reality and artificiality, and the irony that emerges when a character projects—in her/his desire—a caricature of him/herself.

————. "*Salomé* di Oscar Wilde. Dal Mito alla Moda." *Tesi di laurea*, Università degli Studi di Bologna, Bologna , 1979.
    Contains some scattered references to RF's *The Artificial Princess* as a rewriting of Wilde's play.

Index

RF's books and plays are set in boldface. All references to his stories and magazine contributions have been indexed under *Complete Short Stories*; references that predate that publication are placed in parentheses. Translations of RF's works are indexed under their English titles.

ABC, 124
Acin, Ramon, 124
Acton, Harold, 48, 53, 54, 61, 70, 86, 92, 97
Adams, Bernard, 38
Adams, Phoebe, 39
Aercke, Kristiaan P., 53
Agosti, Giovanni, 130
Aguirre, Mariano, 123
Alastair (Hans Henning Voight), 89
Albert, Edward, 53
Alford, Norman W., 53
Allen, Trevor, 39
Allen, Walter, 53
Almansi, Guido, 123-24
Alvarez, A., 24
American Book Review, 19
American Institute of Discussion, 5
American Mercury, 22
Amica, 118, 119
Amis, Kingsley, 54, 97, 105, 111
Anderson, David, 28
Annali dell'Istituto Universitario Orientale: Anglistica, 135
Annali: Sezione Germanica, 65
Ansen, Alan, 55
Apffel, Edmund, 97
Arbasino, Alberto, 118, 130, 137, 139
Aretino, Pietro, 89
Arizona Quarterly, 40, 69
Arlen, Michael, 41, 75, 77
Armstrong, Martin, 16
Arrow, Simon, 39, 41
Artificial Princess, The, 16-17, 20, 25, 44, 59, 69, 73, 74, 92, 117, 120, 129, 134, 137, 142
Ash, John, 22, 55, 101
Athenæum, 6, 77
Atkin, Gabriel, 87
Atlantic, 39
Aubrey, Bryan, 78
Auden, W. H., 18, 29, 55, 97, 117, 119
Austen, Jane, 28, 71, 73, 104
Avanti, 120

B., F., 120
B., H., 121-22
B., O., 117-18
Bacigalupo, Massimo, 131
Baker, Ernest A., 55-56
Balfour, Patrick, 92
Ballarati, Mariacarla, 141
Barber, Michael, 24
Barina, Antonella, 141
Barnes, Djuna, 67, 130
Barnhill, Sarah, 28-29, 56
Barone, Dennis, 101
Barthes, Roland, 141
Bartlett, Neil, 56
Baudelaire, Charles, 61, 66, 142

Beardsley, Aubrey, 6, 11, 12, 14, 16, 19, 37, 40, 43, 53, 55, 59, 62, 63, 67, 69, 75, 79, 80, 81, 83, 84, 88, 89, 91, 92, 93, 109, 122, 127, 131, 134-35, 136, 142
Beaton, Cecil, 70
Beaumont, Cyril, 87
Beckett, Samuel, 97, 120, 133
Beckford, William, 53, 59, 66, 75, 82, 93
Beerbohm, Max, 13, 15, 27, 40, 65, 97, 130, 142
Belfast Whig, 3
Benét, William Rose, 17
Benkovitz, Miriam J., 38-43, 45, 46, 56-57, 66, 67, 71, 77, 88, 93, 97, 106, 132, 139
Bennett, Alan, 54
Bennett, Arnold, 13-14
Benson, E. F., 30
Benson, Robert Hugh, 46, 75, 88, 97
Berkson, Bill, 103
Bermal, Albert, 57
Berners, Gerald Tyrwhitt, Lord, 35, 47, 73, 137
Betjeman, John, 38, 68, 97
Bezel, Julian, 57
Bianciotti, Héctor, 125, 127-28
Bigland, Eileen, 58
Binding, Paul, 104
Bini, Benedetta, 131
Birmingham Gazette, 11
Birmingham Post, 11
Bisol, Gaetano, 120
Blackmer, Corinne E., 58
Blamires, Harry, 58
Blöcker, Günther, 122
Bloom, Harold, 58
Bloomfield, Paul, 18
Bloxham, John Francis, 63
Bo, Carlo, 117
Bollettino del C.I.R.V.I., 137
Bonacossa, Diana, 120
Book Collector, 38
Booklist, 29, 32, 39
Bookman, 10, 11, 12, 14, 36, 62
Bookman's Journal, 79
Books, 24
Books Abroad, 38
Books and Bookmen, 39, 46, 49
Bookseller, 18, 31
Booth, Mark, 58
Boston Evening Transcript, 11, 17
Boutell, H. S., 58
Bowles, Paul, 58, 78
Bradford, Sarah, 58
Braine, John, 54-55
Brautigan, Richard, 101
Braybrooke, Neville, 21, 58-59, 82
Brazil, Angela, 20

Breakwell, Ian, 30, 98
Bredstroem, Christian Samuel, 128
Brennan, Neil, 59, 109
Brera, Carlo, 123
Brickell, Herschel, 11
Brinitzer, Carl, 122
Brison, Danièle, 125
Bristow, Joseph, 59
British Book News, 6, 38
Broadwater, Bowden, 22
Bronski, Michael, 59
Brooke, Jocelyn, 25, 37-38, 59, 75, 103
Brooke, Rupert, 35
Brooklyn Eagle, 11
Brooks, E. H. J., 35-36
Brophy, Brigid, 26, 39, 43, 45-48, 54, 59-60, 65, 98, 110, 124, 132, 142
Brosnahan, John, 29
Brossard, Chandler, 22
Brummell, Beau, 69
Bryfonski, Dedria, 60
Buechner, Frederick, 78
Bulletin of Bibliography, 64
Bulletin of the New York Public Library, 56, 57
Burkhart, Charles, 60
Burns, Edward, 60
Burroughs, William S., 30
Butler, Samuel, 16
Byng, Douglas, 20

Cabell, James Branch, 17
Cahiers des saisons, 132
Calder-Marshall, Arthur, 45-46, 97
Calleja, Pedro, 124
Cam, 118
Cambio 16, 124
Cambrian Leader, 11
Campbell, Mrs. Patrick, 87
Canard enchaîné, 126
Cantillon, Watt Joseph, 109
Capote, Truman, 61, 71, 78, 98
Caprice, 3, 5, 10, 14, 22-23, 37, 47, 54, 56, 60, 64, 65, 68, 69, 70, 76, 80, 81, 82, 86, 92, 100, 104, 105, 109, 123-24, 129, 130, 134, 136, 137, 139
Caradonna, Antonella, 127
Carcassonne, Manuel, 128
Carens, James F., 60, 109
Carleton Miscellany, 42
Carlino sera, 118
Carpenter, Humphrey, 60-61, 104
Carroll, Lewis, 11, 17, 18, 27, 89, 97, 126
Caserio, Robert L., 98
Castelli, Elisabetta, 141
Castlemaine, Countess of, 3
Cecchin, Giovanni, 131
Céline, Louis-Ferdinand, 130
Cernuda, Luis, 124, 131, 139

Cézanne, Paul, 90
Chambers, Ross, 100
Chameleon, 63
Charney, Maurice, 61
Charques, R. D., 18
Cherwell, 53
Chicago Evening Post, 54
Chicago Tribune, 29, 40
Choice, 46
Chronicles, 30
Cianci, Giovanni, 131
Cithara, 41
Clark, Laurence, 98
Clark, William Lane, 61, 109
Clarke, A., 13
Clarke, Gerald, 61
Cleto, Fabio, 61, 132, 141
Cloud, Maurice B., 98
Cluny, Claude Michel, 125
Cocteau, Jean, 89
Colette, 65
College English, 76
Colombo, Barbara, 141
Colombo, Graciela, 123
Columbia Library Columns, 57
Commonweal, 9
Comparatistica: Annuario italiano, 85
Complete Plays, 31-32, 79
Complete Ronald Firbank, The, 24-26, 64, 66, 81, 82, 83, 119, 127-28, 132
Complete Short Stories, (27), 28-30, (44), (56), (57), 71, 79, (82), (105), (139)
Compton-Burnett, Ivy, 8, 24, 29, 43, 78, 87, 109, 120, 127, 128, 130, 135, 139
Concerning the Eccentricies of Cardinal Pirelli, 13, 15, 17, 20, 21, 22, 37, 39, 40, 41, 43, 44, 49, 53, 55, 59, 60, 63, 64, 65, 67, 69, 73, 74, 81, 82, 84, 86, 87, 90, 91, 92, 93, 97, 99, 103, 106, 120-23, 124-26, 130, 131, 132, 133, 134, 135-36, 141
Conder, Charles, 20, 73
Congreve, William, 20, 27, 35, 59, 137
Conjunctions, 103
Connolly, Cyril, 24, 43, 61-62, 78, 83, 98, 117, 119
Conrad, Joseph, 62
Contemporary Literature, 65
Contemporary Review, 39
Contributi, 137
Convivium, 68
Cooper, Frederic Taber, 62
Core, Philip, 62
Corelli, Marie, 37, 87
Corriere della sera, 119
Corvo, Baron. *See* Frederick Rolfe
Cottrell, Beekman Waldron, 109
Coward, Noël, 29, 32

Cozzolino, Enrico, 141-42
Cressole, Michel, 128
Crisp, Quentin, 63, 98
Critical Quarterly, 77
Cummings, E. E., 53
Cunard, Nancy, 41, 45, 48, 57
Curtis, Anthony, 30, 92
Curtis, Jean-Louis, 132
Cushman, Keith, 39

Daiches, David, 62
Daily Express, 7
Daily Graphic, 69
Daily Herald, 11, 97
Daily News, 6, 11
Daily Telegraph, 30, 42
Dalhousie Review, 58
Dalton, F. T., 7, 8
D'Annunzio, Gabriele, 142
d'Arcangelo, Angelo, 63
d'Arch Smith, Timothy, 49, 63
Dash, Robert Warren, 8
Daube, Colette, 101, 103, 106, 142
Davenport-Hines, Richard, 63
Davey, Norman, 10
Davies, Paul, 63
Davis, Robert Murray, 29, 31, 38, 39-40,
    46, 63-65, 105, 110
Day, Wesley, 99
Debenedetti, Antonio, 120
Debussy, Claude, 37, 133
Deghy, Guy, 65, 77
del Buono, Oreste, 118
Denver Quarterly, 41
Dernières nouvelle d'Alsace, 125
Derrida, Jacques, 79
Desarzens, Corinne, 126
Dial, 3, 11
Diario 16, 124
Dickinson, Patric, 65
Diderot, Denis, 117
Dinnage, Paul, 18, 22
Dirda, Michael, 5, 6, 18, 29, 31, 65
Disciple from the Country, A, 27, 31-32
Disraeli, Benjamin, 55
Dock, Leslie, 65, 110
Dold, Bernard E., 65
Donohue, Agnes McNeil, 110
Double Dealer, 12, 89
Dougill, David, 15, 46, 49, 97
Douglas, Lord Alfred, 41, 56
Douglas, Norman, 16, 68, 75, 76, 80,
    83, 87, 90, 103, 130, 132
Dowell, Coleman, 104
Dowson, Ernest, 75, 89, 142
Drabble, Margaret, 66
Du Barry, Comtesse, 3
Dublin Magazine, 19, 23
Duck, David, 66
Duckworth, Gerald, and Co., 66

Ducornet, Rikki, 99
Duncan, Isadora, 87
Dupuigrenet-Desroussilles, François,
    125, 132
Durand, Dominique, 126
Durrell, Lawrence, 24, 68, 92
Duse, Eleonora, 87

Early Firbank, The, 30-31, 71, 79
Eichholz, Hildegard, 122
Eliot, T. S., 24, 27, 37, 62, 78, 92, 131
Elle, 57
Elliman, Michael, 66
Ellis, G. U., 66
Ellis, Havelock, 80
Encounter, 40, 48, 58
Enemy, 75
English Literature in Transition, 28, 31,
    56
English Miscellany, 133
English Studies in Africa, 93
Ergo, 128
Ernst, Max, 126
Esagono, 127
Espresso, 119, 127
Esprit et vie, 127
Eton Candle, 61
Europeo, 117
Evans, Montgomery, 60
Evening Standard, 13, 40
Ewart, Gavin, 40, 54
Express, 125
Extravaganzas, 17

Fairbanks, Lauren, 99
Fallowell, Duncan, 63, 66-67
Farrelly, John, 19
Fausset, Hugh l'Anson, 12, 14
Fellini, Federico, 124
Ferretti, Massimo, 118
Fiedler, Leslie A., 22-23, 67
Field, Andrew, 67
Fielding, Henry, 128, 137
Fiera letteraria, 120, 121
Figaro, 128
Financial Times, 30
Firbank, Heather, 49, 80
Firbank, Lady Harriette, 30, 45, 49, 71
Firbank, Thomas J., 48-49, 80
Firbankiana, 50, 141
Fitzgerald, F. Scott, 23, 70, 105
Five Novels, 18-21, 40, 41, 83
Flaubert, Gustave, 81, 142
Fletcher, Ian, 67
Fletcher, Ifan Kyrle, 21, 25, 35-36, 37,
    42, 45, 48-49, 57, 65, 67, 132
Flower beneath the Foot, The, 3, 9-11,
    15, 19, 25, 37, 53, 55, 56, 57, 59, 60,
    61, 65, 67, 68, 69, 71, 73, 76, 79, 81,
    84, 86, 89, 90, 91, 92, 92, 94, 98,

Flower beneath the Foot, The (cont.)
103, 105, 106, 123, 125-27, 128,
131, 134, 137
Fontaine, Robert, 67
Ford, Ford Madox, 83
Forster, E. M., 14, 49, 86, 91, 119, 129,
133
Fortnightly Review, 16
Fortunati, Vita, 132
Foster, Jeanette H., 67
Francis, John, 67-68
Frank, Bernard, 126
Frankfurter Allgemeine Zeitung, 122
Franklin, John, 12
Fraser, G. S., 68
Frayn, Michael, 54
Freedman, Richard, 40
Freeman's Journal, 4
Furbank, P. N., 46-47

G., R., 118
Gaddis, William, 79, 99, 135
Gale, Patrick, 30-31
Gallup, Donald, 68
Galsworthy, John, 62
Gardner, Philip, 97
Gaskell, Elizabeth Cleghorn, 104
Gattégno, Jean, 125-26, 128, 133
Gay News, 49
Gazzetta dell'Emilia, 117
Gazzetta di Reggio, 117
Gazzettino, 118
Genet, Jean, 128
Gerhardi, William, 76, 92
Gershwin, George, 11, 89
Gide, André, 74
Gigli, Lorenzo, 120
Gilbert, Sir William Schwenk, 21
Gilmore, Louis, 12
Ginsberg, Allen, 104
Giordano, Monica, 142
Giornale, 127
Giornale del mattino, 119
Giornale di Sicilia, 127
Giorno, 118, 121
Giostra delle Muse, 117
Gish, Robert F., 47
Glasgow Evening News, 8
Glasgow Herald, 4
Glendinning, Victoria, 68
Goldring, Douglas, 68
Goldschmidt, Ernst, 48-49
Golino, Enzo, 118, 120-21
Gordon, Karen Elizabeth, 99
Gorey, Edward, 27, 99
Gould, Gerald, 4, 5, 68
Gozzano, Guido, 120
Gramigna, Giuliano, 118-19, 121
Granta, 57
Graver, Lawrence, 47

Green, Henry, 20, 22, 78, 92, 99, 105,
130
Green, Martin, 68, 97
Greene, Graham, 69, 88
Greif, Martin, 68-69
Greimas, Algirdas Julien, 137, 142
Griffin, Jasper, 69
Gross, John, 69
Guadalupi, Gianni, 77
Guevara, Alvaro, 60, 89
Guinness, Bryan, 55, 103

Haddow, G. C., 69
Hafley, James, 40, 69
Halliwell, Kenneth, 103, 131
Hamnett, Nina, 49, 69, 71
Harcourt-Smith, Simon, 40
Hardy, Thomas, 82, 90
Harris, Alan, 26, 70
Harris, Bertha, 99-100
Harrison, William H., 5
Harrogate Herald, 4
Hartley, L. P., 78
Harvard Library Bulletin, 64
Harwood, H. C., 10
Hasemann, Gertraud F., 133
Hastings, Selina, 70
Haycroft, Howard, 74
Heath, Jeffrey, 70
Heckmann, Herbert, 122
Hemingway, Ernest, 24, 25, 70, 83, 92
Heppenstall, Rayner, 40, 100
Hergesheimer, Joseph, 12
Herman, Abel, 125
Hewitt, Douglas, 70
Heycock, David, 80
Higgins, Patrick, 70
Hill, Roland, 133
Hoare, Philip, 55, 70, 105
Hobson, Anthony, 38, 70
Hodgart, Matthew, 40-41
Holland, Vyvyan, 35, 36, 70
Hollinghurst, Alan, 10, 30-31, 65, 71,
100, 110, 128
Hogan, William, 24
Hooker, Denise, 71
Horace, 62
Horder, Lord Mervyn, 35, 38-39, 48-50,
56, 71
Hortus, 67
Howard, Brian, 61, 63, 103
Hoyos y Vinent, Antonio de, 140
Humphries, Barry, 30, 41, 74
Huxley, Aldous, 6, 13, 19, 20, 21, 24,
25, 27, 29, 35, 37, 45, 59, 62, 75, 76,
78, 92, 100, 128, 134, 139, 142
Huysmans, Joris Karl, 6, 53, 82, 89, 140,
142

I., M., 119
Inclinations, 4, 22-23, 25, 37, 43, 68, 69, 81, 86, 91, 100, 101, 110, 121, 127, 129, 133, 135
Incom, 118
Inge, M. Thomas, 71
Irish Life, 6
Irish Times, 4
Irwin, W. R., 71
Isherwood, Christopher, 103
Izzo, Carlo, 133

James, Elizabeth, 39
James, Henry, 24, 26, 78, 82, 91, 92, 105, 136
James, Jamie, 19
Jannattoni, Livio, 133
Jebb, Julian, 71
Jenkins, Nicholas, 55
John, Augustus, 35, 36, 54, 72
Jones, Alun R., 24-25, 81
Jones, Ernest, 19, 22-23, 49, 72
Jones, Iva G., 76
Jonson, Ben, 21
Jordis, Christine, 126
Joulié, Gérard, 127-28, 137
Journal of Modern Literature, 39, 44, 46
Joyce, James, 24, 44, 62, 66, 76, 90, 101, 124, 130, 133, 135, 137
Jullian, Philippe, 133, 139

Kantra, Robert A., 44
Karl, Frederick R., 72
Keenan, Joe, 100-101
Kellner, Bruce, 72, 90
Kennard, Sir Coleridge, 16, 49, 73
Kennelly, Louise, 31
Kiechler, John Anthony, 43, 106
Kiernan, Robert F., 73
King, Francis, 54
King, Viva, 48-49, 73
Kipling, Rudyard, 62, 82, 93
Kirkup, James, 73, 101
Kirkus Reviews, 8, 19, 29, 41
Knight, Grant C., 73-74
Knoll, Robert E., 74
Kopelson, Kevin, 74
Kramberg, K. H., 122
Kromek von Kunst un Kultur, 58
Kromrij, Gerrit, 123, 133
Kronenburger, Louis, 17
Krutch, Joseph Wood, 12
Kunitz, Stanley, 74

L., J., 128
Laberinta, 124
Laforgue, Jules, 22, 125, 129, 136
Lahr, John, 74, 80, 103
Lambda Book Report, 5, 28, 31
Lancaster, Marie-Jacqueline, 103

Land and Water, 6
Landsberg, A. C., 48-49
Lane, Christopher, 74
Langrishe, Caroline, 63
Lawrence, D. H., 21, 89, 91
Leamon, Warren, 102
Lear, Edward, 97, 124
Lee, Patricia, 75
Lees-Milne, James, 75
Leslie, Shane, 48-49, 75, 88, 97
Lesserday, Lynton, 10
Lessing, Doris, 101
Lettau, Reinhard, 122
Letture, 120
Leverson, Ada, 23, 35, 86, 94
Lewis, Wyndham, 45, 48, 75-76, 79, 101, 135
Libération, 126, 128
Library, 39
Library Chronicle of the University of Texas, 53
Library Journal, 5, 20, 28, 32, 39, 47
Libri e riviste d'Italia, 127
Life and Letters, 14, 15, 91
Lindon, Mathieu, 126
Listener, 25, 26, 28, 37, 42, 46, 49, 55, 80
Literature Interpretation Theory, 74
Literary Digest International Book Review, 12
Liverpool Post, 6, 9
Locher, Francis C., 76
Lodge, David, 76
London Magazine, 26, 40, 66
London Mercury, 6
London Times, 8, 37
London Times Saturday Review, 8
Long, Chris, 104
Long, Richard A., 76
Lorrain, Jean, 136, 140
Loti, Pierre, 8, 9
Lovelace, George, 69
Lovisetti Fuà, Laura, 117-19, 121, 134
Luckett, Richard, 47
Lueders, Edward, 76, 106
Luna, 124

M., W. P., 19, 23
MacCarthy, Sir Desmond, 37
MacInnes, Colin, 76
Mackaye, Milton, 54, 77
Mackenzie, Compton, 101, 103
MacKiernan, Elizabeth, 101
MacNeice, Louis, 97
MacQuilland, Louis, 7
Madden, David, 77
Maes-Jelivek, Jena, 142
Maeterlinck, Maurice, 27, 35, 37, 70, 82, 102, 142
Mais, S. P. B., 77

Mallarmé, Stéphane, 88, 142
Manchester Guardian, 11, 18, 41, 47, 98
Mañez, Julio A., 124
Manganelli, Giorgio, 120, 134, 137, 139, 140
Manguel, Alberto, 77
Mann, Thomas, 67
Mannin, Ethel, 77
Mansfield, Katherine, 77
Marengo Vaglio, Carla, 134
Marini, Cristina, 110
Marsh, Edward, 83, 87
Martín Abril, José Luis, 124, 139
Martinetti, Ronald, 19, 41
Marvin, John R., 47
Marx, Groucho, 26, 127
Marx Brothers, 127
Maschwitz, Eric, 77
Massenet, Jules, 58
Massie, Allan, 101
Mathews, Harry, 101-2
Matisse, Henri, 90
Maupin, Armistead, 102
Mauriès, Patrick, 134
Mauve Tower, The, 31-32
May, James Boyer, 27
Maymone Sinischalchi, Marina, 134-35
Mayne, Richard, 27
McAlmon, Robert, 74, 77
McCarthy, Shaun, 77-78
McCartney, George, 78
McCormick, John, 78, 98, 102, 104, 106
McCourt, James, 102
McDonnell, Jacqueline, 78
Melchiori, Girogio, 78
Mendelson, Phyllis Carmel, 60
Merritt, James Douglas, 44
Meyers, Jeffrey, 79
Michel, Walter, 79
Milano, Paolo, 119
Miller, Clyde, 41
Miller, Howard E., 32
Mills, Florence, 87
Milton, John, 69
Miró, Joan, 22
Mitchell, Julian, 27, 41
Modern Fiction Studies, 47
Molina, Cesar Antonio, 124
Monde, 126, 127
Monde des livres, 125
Mondo, 120
Monk, Leland, 79
Montesquiou, Robert de, 142
Montremy, J.-M. de, 126
Moore, Steven, 5, 6, 9, 10, 28, 30, 31, 50, 79, 98, 102, 105
Moorsom, Raisley, 48-49
Morgan, Evan, 45, 57, 72, 84
Morgenstern, Christian, 123
Morning Post, 12

Morris, Lloyd, 17
Morrissette, Bruce, 58
Mortimer, John, 10, 79
Mosley, Nicholas, 49-50
Mozart, Wofgang Amadeus, 55
Muir, Frank, 99
Muir, Percy H., 79
Münchner Merkur, 123
Murdoch, Iris, 78, 102
Murray, Robert Middleton, 77

Nabokov, Vladimir, 47
Natale, A. Stephen, 41
Nation, 12, 22, 36
Nation and Athenæum, 15
Nazione, 120
Nazione sera, 118
Neill, S. Diana, 79
Neohelicon, 53
Nevinson, C. R. W., 49, 65, 80, 87
New England Review, 19
New Mexico Quarterly, 8
New Republic, 13, 19, 47, 93
New Rythum, The, 26-28, 43, 44, 54, 69, 70, 71, 92,
New Statesman, 4, 5, 9-10, 12, 15, 24, 27, 36, 41, 47-48, 50, 68, 103
New Statesman and Nation, 16, 19
New Witness, 3, 4
New York Herald Tribune, 10, 14, 17, 25
New York Post, 3, 10, 11, 36, 54, 77
New York Review of Books, 40
New York Times, 54, 55
New York Times Book Review, 3, 10, 12, 17, 18, 22, 24-25, 28, 38, 43, 48, 81, 102
New Yorker, 20, 23, 27, 42, 80
Newsweek, 9, 42
Nichols, Beverly, 80
Nicolson, Harold, 16, 42, 49, 75, 80, 94, 102, 134
Notes and Queries, 39
Notte, 119
Nouvelle revue française, 117
Nürnberger Nachrichten, 121
Nye, Robert, 99

Oates, Quentin, 31
O'Brien, Edna, 80
O'Brien, Flann, 101
Observer, 3, 9, 11, 25, 42, 47, 87, 88, 104, 105
Odette: A Fairy Tale for Weary People, 4, 15, 25, 58-59, 86, 89
Odette d'Antrevernes and *A Study in Temperament*, 3, 44, 89
Oggi, 117, 119
O'Hara, Frank, 103
O'Hara, J. D., 19
Oke, Richard, 103

Olivier, Laurence, 104
Olson, Ray, 32
Oppertshäuser, Otto, 142
Orrick, James, 36
Orton, Joe, 30, 61, 74, 80, 85, 103, 131,
    142
Osborne, Charles, 80
Ouest-France, 128
Ouida, 37, 58, 69, 83, 87
Ousley, Ian, 80
Outlook, 10
Oxford, Countess of, 3

Packman, James, 55-56
Paese, 117
Pall Mall Gazette, 3
Panter-Downes, Mollie, 80-81
Panzeri, Fulvio, 127
*Papers of the Bibliographical Society of
    America,* 56, 64
Papers on Language and Literature, 64
Papetti, Viola, 135
Paragone letteratura, 137
Paris Review, 71, 106
Park, Bertram, 54
Parker, Peter, 31, 67, 81, 99, 101
Partisan Review, 81
Pasti, Umberto, 127
Pater, Walter, 75, 85, 102, 122, 136
Paul, David, 25-26, 27-28, 81
Peacock, Thomas Love, 21, 23
Pearson, John, 81
Pekar, Harvey, 29, 32
Pellegrini, Marina, 110
People, The, 87
Perloff, Marjorie, 103
Peterich, Werner, 121
Pétillon, Pierre-Yves, 135
Petronius, Gaius, 140
Phelps, Donald, 29-30
Philip, Neil, 6
Picchi, Mario, 127
Pilcer, Harry, 80
Pinter, Harold, 30
Pinto, Vivian de Sola, 48, 81
Pitol, Sergio, 124, 135
Plomer, William, 26, 28, 81
Porter, Cole, 61
Portfolio, 54
Porzio, Domenico, 119
Potoker, Edward Martin, 25, 28, 42, 44-
    45, 81-82, 110
Potter, Beatrix, 97
Pound, Ezra, 27
Powell, Anthony, 7, 10, 24-25, 26, 29,
    37, 42, 47, 59, 65, 72, 82, 83, 87,
    100, 103, 119
Powell, Dawn, 103
Prancing Nigger, 3, 11-13, 14, 15, 18,
    37, 43, 44, 49, 53, 56, 59, 60, 61, 65,

69, 72, 73, 74, 77, 78, 81, 84, 85, 86,
    89, 90, 91, 93, 98, 101, 102, 105,
    106, 117, 120, 133, 134, 137
Praz, Mario, 82, 123, 129, 136
Prescott, Orville, 55
Princess Zoubaroff, The, 7-8, 9, 21, 25,
    31-32, 37, 43, 49, 57, 61, 63, 69, 74,
    75, 84, 88, 90, 91
Pritchett, V. S., 19-20, 69, 83, 86
Progresso italo-americano, 119
Prokosch, Frederic, 83
Proust, Marcel, 24, 26, 37, 41, 69, 76,
    93, 118, 124, 133, 137
Pryce-Jones, Alan, 68, 103
Publishers Weekly, 3, 5, 12, 17, 20, 23,
    30, 32, 42, 58
Puig, Manuel, 28
Pumphrey, Arthur. *See* Alan Pryce-Jones
Punch, 7, 10, 83
Purdy, James, 103-4
Putnam, Samuel, 83

*Quaderni del Dipartimento di Linguistica
    e Letterature Comparate,* 61
Quennell, Peter, 16, 83
Quilp, Jocelyn, 41
Quinton, Anthony, 47-48
Quinzaine littéraire, 126, 128

R., L., 119
Ramparts, 58, 82
Raven, Simon, 26, 104
Redman, Ben Ray, 12-13, 20-21, 23
Régnier, Henri de, 142
Reid, Forrest, 48, 83
Rendezvous, 64
Renoir, Pierre, 90
Repubblica, 123, 126
Resnais, Alain, 78
Reumaux, Patrick, 125-26
Review of Contemporary Fiction, 5, 6, 9,
    10, 81, 101, 102, 105
Reviewer, 13, 60, 89
Reynolds, Stanley, 83
Rice, Thomas Jackson, 83
Richmond, B., 10
Richards, Grant, 16, 39, 48, 84
Richardson, Dorothy, 6
Richardson, Maurice, 20
Richardson, Sallyann, 84
Ricketts, Charles, 69
Rickword, Edgell, 14-15, 57
Riggs, Thomas, Jr., 84
Rilke, Rainer Maria, 82
Rivista dei libri, 130
Robb, W. A., 111
Robbe-Grillet, Alain, 78, 105, 123
Robert-Nicould, E. L., 111
Robinson, Herbert Spencer, 84
Robson, Jeremy, 104

Robson, W. W., 84
Roditi, Edouard, 117, 136
Rogers, Michael, 5
Rolfe, Frederick, 37, 46, 57, 66, 88, 91, 130, 134
Roll, Frederick, 66
Romano, Salvatore, 126-27, 136
Rosenthal, Michael, 48
Rousseau, Henri, 22
Roussel, Raymond, 104, 125, 127
Rudnick, Paul, 92, 104

Saarbrücker Zeitung, 122
Sacher-Masoch, Leopold von, 89
Sachs, Maurice, 117, 136
Sackville-West, Vita, 68, 94, 126
Sage, Lorna, 50
Saint-Phalle, Nathalie de, 136
Saki (H. H. Munro), 27, 30, 40, 65, 82, 83, 130
Samain, Albert Victor, 142
Sampietro, Luigi, 129, 136
San Diego Tribune, 29
San Francisco Bay Guardian, 32
San Francisco Chronicle, 24
Sandoz, Maurice, 48, 84, 136
Sansom, William, 78, 104
Santal, 8-9, 15, 21, 24, 25, 37, 43, 55, 72, 74, 86, 91
Sappho, 63, 102
Sarraute, Nathalie, 120
Sassoon, Siegfried, 48, 70, 81, 84-85, 87
Saturday Review (London), 16, 36
Saturday Review (U.S.), 42
Saturday Review of Literature, 17, 20, 23
Schuller, Renate, 122
Schwarzenegger, Arnold, 63
Schwob, Marcel, 138
Scimitarra, Attanasio, 139
Scotsman, 4, 7
Secker, Martin, 48-49
Segre, Elena, 119
Sereni, Vittorio, 120
Settimo giorno, 118, 119
Severi, Rita, 85, 129, 137, 139, 140, 142
Seymour-Smith, Martin, 85
Shakespeare, William, 82
Shaw, George Bernard, 41, 59, 90
Shelley, Percy Bysshe, 6
Shepherd, Simon, 85
Sheridan, Philip, 42
Sherrin, Ned, 55
Shults, Terrance Glenn, 97, 111
Siciliano, Enzo, 120
Sitwell, Edith, 37, 53, 78, 81, 84, 93, 117, 125, 130
Sitwell, Osbert, 21, 35, 36, 40, 49, 58, 78, 81, 82, 84, 85, 91, 92, 93, 104, 117, 130
Sitwell, Sacheverell, 58, 78, 81, 84, 130

Skasa-Weiss, Eugen, 123
Slater, Ann Pasternak, 85
Slavitt, David, 104
Snow, C. P., 23
Sokolov, Raymond A., 42
Sola, Orietta, 111
Sontag, Susan, 61, 85, 123
Sorrentino, Gilbert, 103, 104
Sorrow in Sunlight. See Prancing Nigger
Soskin, William, 36
South Wales Argus, 67
South Wales News, 67
Southport Guardian, 9
Spackman, W. M., 65, 104-5
Spark, Muriel, 29, 50, 127
Spectator, 7, 18, 23, 26, 27, 31, 41, 47, 97
Speedie, Julie, 86
Spicilegio moderno, 136, 137
Spiegel, 121
Spurling, John, 48
Stace, H. W., 13
Stagg, Hunter, 13, 60
Stampa, 120
Stannard, Martin, 86
Stapleton, Michael, 86
Steegman, John, 49
Stein, Gertrude, 58, 60-61, 68, 70, 85, 90
Stephens, James, 12
Stern, 122
Sterne, Laurence, 15, 45, 74, 81, 83, 100, 122, 128
Sterne, Mabel Dodge, 90
Stevens, Wallace, 86
Stevenson, Lionel, 86-87
Stevenson, Randall, 87
Stokes, Sewell, 48, 87, 141
Studies in Short Fiction, 5
Style, 63
Süddeutsche Zeitung, 122
Sullivan, John F., 9
Sunday Referee, 14
Sunday Telegraph, 92
Swaffer, Hannen, 87-88
Swann Galleries, 88
Sweeney, Daniel Christopher, 111
Swift, Jonathan, 18, 81
Swinburne, Algernon, 109
Sykes, Christopher, 42
Sylvoisal. See Gérard Joulié
Symons, A. J. A., 88
Symons, Arthur, 142

Tablet, 75
Tagliaferri, Aldo, 121
Tatler, 8, 54
Taylor, D. J., 31, 103, 105
Taylor, John Russell, 43
Tempest, Marie, 87

Tempo, 129
Tennant, Stephen, 55, 70, 105
Textus, 132
Theroux, Alexander, 99, 102, 105
Three Novels, 22-23, 72
Tibullus, Albius, 62
Time, 19, 25
Times Literary Supplement, 3, 4, 5, 7, 8, 10, 13, 15, 16, 18, 22, 25, 27, 31, 35, 37, 38, 43, 45, 56, 66, 71, 76, 98, 100, 103
Tindall, William York, 88
Tosser, Yvon, 138
Toulet, Paul-Jean, 126
Toulouse-Lautrec, Henri, 61
Town Topics, 5
Toynbee, Philip, 26, 88
Trace, 27
Trajtenberg, Mario, 121, 138
Tribune de Genève, 126
Trollope, Anthony, 79, 105
Troubridge, Una, 73
Tucci, Niccolò, 137, 140
Turner, Reginald, 53
Tuttolibri, 129
Twentieth Century, 58
Tyler, Parker, 88

University of Toronto Quarterly, 69
Updike, John, 105

Vainglory, 3-4, 14, 17, 22-23, 25, 37, 43, 44, 54, 55, 56, 57, 58, 59, 60, 64, 69, 81, 84, 86, 91, 102, 111, 103, 117-20, 129, 133
Valencia, 124
Valmouth, 3, 6-7, 9, 17, 18, 24, 25, 26, 37, 43, 49, 53, 54, 59, 61, 63, 64, 69, 71, 72, 74, 77, 81, 83, 86, 89, 90, 91, 92, 94, 100, 104, 106, 109, 127, 129, 130, 139
Valtellina, Alberto, 139
Van Dyke, Henry, 105
Van Leer, David, 88
Van Vechten, Carl, 10, 11, 13, 17, 36, 41, 45, 49, 56, 60, 61, 68, 69, 72, 75, 76, 84, 85, 88, 89-90, 92, 104, 105-6, 110, 136
Vanguardia, 125
Vanity Fair, 105
Verlaine, Paul, 66, 142
Vidal, Gore, 106
Villena, Luis Antonio de, 124-25, 140
Villers de L'Isle-Adam, Comte de, 140
Vines, Sherard, 90
Visconti, Luchino, 127
Vita, 117
Voce adriatica, 119
Voce repubblicana, 118
Voice Literary Supplement, 22

Wagner, Gerd, 121
Waley, Arthur, 14, 15, 49, 90, 91, 121-23, 133
Wall Street Journal, 19, 41
Walpole, Horace, 3, 21
Ward, A. C., 91
Wardle, Irving, 8
Warner, Sylvia Townsend, 125
Washington Post Book World, 5, 18, 29, 40, 48, 55, 65, 102
Wason, Sandys, 68
Waterhouse, Ellis, 49, 91
Waterhouse, Keith, 65, 77
Waters, John, 91
Watson, Frederick, 10-11
Watson, John Gillard, 39
Waugh, Auberon, 43, 106
Waugh, Evelyn, 24, 25, 27, 29, 30, 40, 45, 47, 49, 50, 54, 60, 61, 63, 64-65, 68, 70, 71-72, 75, 76, 78, 79, 81, 83, 85, 86, 87, 91-92, 98, 103, 104, 106, 109, 110, 117, 127, 128, 131, 133, 134, 135, 138, 141, 142
Webster, Harvey Curtis, 38
Weintraub, Stanley, 43, 92
Welt am Sonntag, 122
West, Geoffrey, 15, 16-17
West, Paul, 92
Westminster Gazette, 11
Whissen, Thomas Reed, 92, 104
White, Edmund, 92-93
Wilcock, J. Rodolfo, 140
Wilde, Oscar, 3, 16, 22, 27, 29-30, 31, 32, 36, 37, 40, 41, 46, 47, 54, 55, 59, 61, 63, 66, 70, 71, 74, 75, 77, 79, 83, 85, 87, 90, 92, 109, 111, 121, 122, 123, 126, 127-28, 132, 133, 136, 137, 140, 142
Wiley, Paul L., 93
Willes, Peter, 80
Willhoite, Michael, 106
Williams, Tennessee, 78
Williamson, Chilton, Jr., 30
Willis, Katherine Tappert, 20, 28
Windmill, 65, 81
Wilson, A. N., 24, 54
Wilson, Angus, 54, 78, 93, 106
Wilson, Edmund, 11, 20-21, 48, 49, 50, 93, 105, 119, 133
Wilson, Sandy, 54, 71, 106, 130
Wind and the Rain, 21
Wittgenstein, Ludwig, 136
Wodehouse, P. G., 65, 79, 83, 101
Woodcock, George, 100
Woodward, A. G., 93
Woolf, Leonard, 15
Woolf, Virginia, 15, 94, 106, 135, 137
Works of Ronald Firbank, The, 13-15, 90, 94
World Literature Today, 29, 31

Wright, Cuthbert, 36
Writer, 67
Wyndham, Violet, 94, 133

Yeats, William Butler, 40, 41, 54
Yellow Book, 11, 14, 15, 20, 21, 24
Yohalem, John, 102

Young, Ian, 94

Z, 103
Zeit, 123
Zimmer, Dieter E., 123
Zola, Émile, 90